A HISTORY

OF THE

COMMANDMENTS OF THE CHURCH

BY THE

REV. A. VILLIEN

Professor at the Catholic University
of Paris

ST. LOUIS, MO., 1915
PUBLISHED BY B. HERDER
17 SOUTH BROADWAY

FREIBURG (BADEN) GERMANY | LONDON, W. C.
68, GREAT RUSSELL STR.

NIHIL OBSTAT

Sti. Ludovici, die 12. Dec., 1914

F. G. Holweck,
Censor Librorum.

IMPRIMATUR

Sti. Ludovici, die 12. Dec., 1914

✠*Joannes J. Glennon,*
Archiepiscopus,
Sti. Ludovici.

Copyright, 1915
by
Joseph Gummersbach

All rights reserved

Made in U. S. A.

TABLE OF CONTENTS

CHAPTER		PAGE
I	Number and List of the Commandments	1
II	The First Commandment	23
III	The First Commandment (Concluded)	63
IV	The Second Commandment	110
V	The Third Commandment	151
VI	The Fourth Commandment	189
VII	The Fifth Commandment	224
VIII	The Sixth Commandment	277
IX	The Precept of Contributing to the Support of Church and Pastor	320

HISTORY of the Commandments of the Church

CHAPTER I

NUMBER AND LIST OF THE COMMANDMENTS

All French catechisms insert in the morning prayer, after the Commandments of God, the text of six precepts, designated by the name: "The Commandments of the Church," and they devote a series of chapters to those six precepts immediately following the explanation of the Decalogue. The traditional formula is as follows:

> Les dimanches messe ouïras,
> Et fêtes de commandement.
> Les fêtes tu sanctifieras,
> Qui te sont de commandement.
> Tous tes péchés confesseras
> A tout le moins une fois l'an.
>
> Ton Créateur tu recevras
> Au moins à Pâques humblement.
> Quatre-Temps, Vigiles jeûneras,
> Et le Carême entièrement.

> Vendredi, chair ne mangeras,
> Ni le Samedi mêmement.

> On Sundays mass shalt thou hear
> And on feasts commanded.
> Feast days shalt thou sanctify,
> Which are for thee appointed.
> All thy sins thou shalt confess
> Once at least each year.

> Thy Creator, at least at Easter,
> Humbly shalt thou receive.
> On Ember days shalt thou fast,
> On Vigils and throughout Lent.
> On Friday from flesh shalt thou abstain,
> And on Saturday likewise.

A tendency, that has become a real principle for many, renders us prone instinctively to attribute great antiquity to all that exists in the Church. Hence many would undoubtedly be tempted to assign an Apostolic origin, not indeed to these rather poor rhymes, but to the precepts they embody, and even to their catalogue. Such a conclusion however would not be warranted. For on the very contrary, this collection of the Commandments of the Church is of a rather late date. The well known catechism of the Council of Trent, while containing a copious summary of Christian doctrine, composed in collaboration by eminent theologians and learned bishops, submitted to many revisions in order to insure its orthodoxy and integrity of doctrine, and finally addressed "ad parochos" by Pope St. Pius V, hence surely a model catechism, does not contain the catalogue of the Commandments of the Church—nor even alludes to them.

The treatise on prayer which occupies the whole of the fourth and last part, comes right after the explanation of the Decalogue, to which the third part is entirely devoted. Would not this omission lead us to the conclusion that, in 1566, the year in which this catechism appeared, a catalogue of the Commandments of the Church was yet unknown, or that, if a collection of this kind existed, its value was at most but that of a private work?

Nevertheless, that the Church had imposed precepts which bound all Christians, precepts often recalled in the synods and ancient councils according to circumstances or need, was certainly not unknown. Nay more, collections of these precepts had already been compiled.

Three years before the appearance of the catechism *ad parochos*, the Jesuit Edmund Auger published at Lyons a "Catechism and Summary of the Christian Religion" (*Catéchisme et Sommaire de la Religion Chrestienne*), in which, after an explanation of the ten commandments of God, the following questions were asked:

TEACHER. Are there any other precepts we must observe?

ANS. Yes, some very ancient ones: they are the commandments of the holy Catholic Church.

TEACHER. What are they?

ANS. They are: (1) To celebrate feast-days; (2) To assist at Mass on Sundays and feast-days; (3) To observe the prescribed fasts, Lent, Ember-days and Vigils; (4) To confess to the priest at least once a year; (5) To receive the Blessed Eucharist at least at Easter.

Edmund Auger had not invented this list. It was already to be found in the same order in the Small Catechism of Canisius, which appeared in Germany in 1556. Here is the text according to the French translation (edition of 1610). The question is asked:

"How many commandments of the Church are there?" and it is answered thus: "There are five chief commandments: (1) Observe the feast-days appointed by the Church; (2) Listen reverently to the holy office of mass on the feast-days; (3) Observe the fast appointed for certain days and abstinence from proscribed meats; (4) Confess thy sins every year to thine own pastor, or to one approved by him; (5) Receive the Blessed Sacrament of the altar at least once a year, and that near the feast of Easter."

But not only in Germany was there extant a

NUMBER AND LIST OF THE COMMANDMENTS

collection of the precepts of the Church. In France they formed part of the catechetical instruction, as the following prescription of the Council of Narbonne testifies: "Pastors shall preach every Sunday, shall read and explain the Gospel to their people and shall teach them the *Pater Noster*, the *Ave Maria*, the *Credo*, the *Confiteor*, the Commandments of God and the *five commandments of the Church*." [1] That they formed a part of that teaching is so undoubtedly a fact that, in order to render them easier to memorize, they were put into rhyme.

Let us open, *e. g.*, a large book made of 195 folios, "composed by the lately deceased William Parvi, of pious memory, doctor of theology, bishop of Senlis, and confessor to the king," and entitled "The Training of Man" (*La formation de l'homme*). The second part of this work is designated thus: "The Way of Salvation; containing the exposition of the Creed, of the ten commandments of the Law, of the Pater Noster, and of the Ave Maria; composed by the said Reverend Father in God." A long exposition of the symbol in rhymes, in quatrains, commences at folio 70, and at folio 110, we read the five distichs of the commandments of the Church. The volume is dated 1538—almost thirty years anterior to the catechism of Pius V.

[1] *Concil. Narbonnen.* (1551), c. xxxv. MANSI, t. xxxiii, 1264.

But we should not be misguided by the title. William Parvi was not the author of the list nor of the rhymes, for both are found about fifty years earlier in the "Book of Jesus" (*Livre de Jhésus*), which forms the second part of the "Calendar of Shepherds" (*Compost ou Kalendrier des bergers*), the first dated editions of which appeared in the years 1491 and 1492.[2] Here is the text with all the commentaries which accompany it:

> *V Quomandemens saincte eglise*
> Les dimenches messe orras (ouïras),
> Et les festes de commandement.
> Tous tes peches confesseras,
> A tout le moins une foys lan.
> Et ton createur recepvras,
> Au moins a Pasques humblement.
> Les festes sainctifireas,
> Qui te sont de commandement.
> Quatre temps vigiles jeuneras,
> Et le Caresme entierement.

The Five Commandments of Holy Church
On Sundays mass shalt thou hear,
So also on feasts of obligation
All thy sins shalt thou confess
Once at least a year.
And thy Creator, at least at Easter,
Humbly shalt thou receive.
Feasts thou shalt sanctify,
Which are for thee appointed.

[2] *Dictionnaire de Théologie Catholique* (VACANT-MANGENOT), t. III, 390.

> On Ember days thou shalt fast,
> On vigils and throughout Lent.

(Commentary.) "Fifthly in the book of Jesus are the five commandments of Holy Church which must be observed as far as possible by all who have attained the use of reason. It is said 'as far as possible,' so that the man or woman who could not confess, or hear Mass, or receive Our Lord at Easter, or observe the prescribed feast-days or the fasts of obligation, even when willing to obey, but legitimately prevented, would not sin at all. But let the man or woman beware, whom avarice, sloth or desire to witness worldly frolics, such as dances, games or charlatans, or anything else that casts contempt on Holy Church, would cause to infringe or transgress the commandments, so that they would incur damnation, from which may the mercy of Jesus preserve us.

"Here it is to be noted that the transgression of the Commandments of Holy Church obliges under pain of mortal sin, and consequently of damnation, just the same as the commandments of the Law about which we have spoken before. For those who hear the priest recalling the commandments in the church at the parochial mass on Sundays and keep those commandments, hear God and do His will. But those who show contempt for His priests in such circumstances, and do not observe what they command according to the ordinance of the Church, despise God and sin mortally."

This commentary plainly indicates that the collection of the commandments of the Church was not altogether new, since the priests used to read them in church during the parochial mass. But the volume containing this commentary antedates any other work in which I found this list in French rhyme, or even in ordinary French prose. At an earlier period we find the Decalogue in French rhyme, ordinarily in quatrains: the numerous *Sommes le Roi* of the National Library contain countless editions of it. But practically no mention of the commandments of the Church is to be found in these manuscripts. Manuscript 952, f. fr., dated 1478, contains the earliest reference, and this is more than a summary, as can be seen from the following quatrain, the only one of its kind, under the title: "The Way of Paradise" (fol. 190, *Le chemin du paradis*):

> Frequenter le doux sacrement
> Du saint aultier (autel) devotement,
> Ne trespasser en quelque guise
> Les commandemens de l'église.

> To frequent devoutly the sweet sacrament
> Of the holy altar,
> Not to transgress in any wise
> The commandments of the Church.[3]

[3] I have consulted a certain number of other manuscripts

However, though no early collection is to be found in French, we have several in Latin.

In 1486 appeared in Venice the *Summa casuum conscientiae* of Angelo Carletti, known as Angelo de Clavasio. This collection contains two separate and slightly different lists of the commandments of the Church.

The first list occurs at the heading "Praeceptum no. 18." After having enumerated the sixteen evangelical precepts, the author adds: "There are other precepts imposed by the Church which oblige everyone. They are: (1) The celebration of

containing summaries of the Christian doctrine with or without quatrains, viz. The A, B, C's of Simple Folks (*l'A. B. C. des simples gens*); The Introduction to the Faith (*Introduction a la foy*); The XII Articles of the Faith (*les XII articles de foy*); The VII Sacraments of the Church (*les VII Sacraments de l'église*); The Commandments of God (*les commandments de Dieu*); The VIII Beatitudes (*les VIII Béatitudes*); The Spiritual and Corporal Works of Mercy (*les oeuvres de miséricorde spirituelle et corporelle*); also models of examination of conscience by means of the five senses and the seven mortal (capital) sins; but no indication of the Commandments of the Church is to be found. Once I thought that at last I had found an older attestation, in the MS. f. fr. 19,362. The catalogue announced (fol. xxvii): The great commandments of our Holy Mother the Church, and (fol. xxxiii) the brief commandments of Holy Church. But alas! I was to be disappointed. The mansuscript indeed bears on the folios indicated the titles: "The great commandments . . . the brief commandments;" but nothing of the kind appears in the text; there are only allocutions of the pastor to his flock, expressing requests for prayers; the rites of betrothal, prayers for the dead, formulas for the publication of the bans; announcements of vigils and even a formula for a will; but not a word concerning the commandments of the Church.

feasts; (2) the obligation of hearing mass; (3) that of fasting during Lent and on vigils; (4) that of confessing; (5) that of communicating; (6) that of paying tithes; (7) that of avoiding excommunicated persons. There are many others which affect special categories of persons. They are spoken of in the various chapters of this summary."[4]

This is the longest and most complete list we have met with so far. But the same book furnishes us another, more detailed and none the less interesting. Under the heading *Interrogationes*, in dealing with the questions which the confessor must put to his penitents, the author gives a most minute examination of conscience in eighty numbers. At no. 4 he commences thus: "Order of the questions on the sins that must be [made] known." At no. 14, apropos of the capital sins, he adds, concerning the second daughter of vainglory, disobedience, under the title: On disobedience concerning the precepts of the Church make the following inquiries:

[4] "Sunt et alia precepta ab ecclesia indita generaliter omnes ligantia quae sunt: primum de celebratione festorum, secundum de auditione misse, tertium de ieiunio in quadragesima et aliis vigiliis, quartum de confessione, quintum de communione, sextum de decimis, septimum de visitandis (*sic*) excommunicatis. Multa sunt alia quae tangunt speciales personas: de quibus habetur in diversis capitulis huius summe." (*Summa angelica de casibus conscientie*, Lyon, 1495.)

NUMBER AND LIST OF THE COMMANDMENTS 11

"Has he [the penitent] observed the feasts appointed by the Church?

Has he fasted on the appointed vigils?

Has he confessed once a year?

Has he received the Eucharist at least once a year?

Has he heard mass on the appointed feast-days?

Has he partaken in or permitted tournaments?

Has he contracted a clandestine marriage?

Has he committed any action forbidden under pain of excommunication?

Has he been excommunicated by anyone?

Has he associated with excommunicated persons?

As to acts of disobedience committed by certain categories of persons see further on."[5]

[5] Here is the text of the same edition, with references of the author to the other parts of his work: "De inobedientia circa precepta ecclesiae sic interroga.

Si observavit festa precepta ab ecclesia, et que sint. habes Ferie § 3.

Si jejunavit in vigiliis preceptis: vide Jejunium § 7 que sunt precepta.

Si confessus est semel in anno. vide Confessio. 2. § 2 et 3.

Si suscepit sacramentum corporis Christi semel in anno, vide Eucharistia 3 in principio et per totum.

Si audivit missam in festis preceptis. Vide Ferie § 42.

Si fecit torneamenta seu consensit ut fierent. Vide Torneamentum per totum.

Si contraxit matrimonium clandestine. Vide clandestinum per totum.

Si fecit aliquod eorum quod prohibetur sub poena excommunica-

These ten questions bore on the obligations that the Church imposed on all her faithful, and to omit one of them was a fault to be made known to the confessor,—in short, these precepts were really commandments imposed by the Church.

Furthermore, even before Angelo de Clavasio, these precepts were known and catalogued by Saint Antoninus. He also gives a list of ten "precepts of the Church which oblige under pain of mortal sin." This list differs slightly from the preceding one on two or three points. It is the oldest I have found and runs as follows:

(1) To observe feast-days;

(2) To observe the fasts on the days appointed by the Church, such as throughout Lent;

(3) To abstain from eating flesh-meat every Friday of the year;

(4) To hear Mass on Sundays and feast-days;

(5) To confess at least once a year;

(6) To communicate once a year on Easter Sunday and to do so fasting;

(7) To pay the tithes;

(8) To abstain from all acts prohibited under pain of excommunication, especially those incurring excommunication *latae sententiae;*

tionis late sententie, ad quod vide Excommunicatio, 5, 6 et 7.

Si fuit excommunicatus ab aliquo.

Si participavit cum excommunicato. Vide Excommunicatio, 8, per totum.

De inobedienta certarum personarum, habes infra circa status."

(9) To avoid excommunicated persons during the divine office, and even at other times, as in conversation, at table, when such association could be construed as contempt of the Church;

(10) Not to assist at mass and offices celebrated by clerics who publicly live in concubinage.[6]

Consequently one would not be greatly mistaken in dating the collection or catalogue of the commandments of the Church as far back as the second third of the fifteenth century, and this catalogue was exactly the same as the one that is still widely in use. Since the beginning of the sixteenth century our catechisms have not always adhered to the list given by the "Book of Jesus;" later on, even as late as the second half of the seventeenth century, some of them, for example that of Clermont, 1674, do not contain the commandments of God, nor consequently, those of the Church; but such cases are exceptional. In France, in Germany, in Spain, and in the distant New World, theologians and catechists everywhere give in a few precise numbers a summary of the obligations imposed by the Church on every Christian.

For a long time the division into five commandments was maintained[7] and it is still in use to-day,

[6] *Summa theologica*, pars 1a, tit. xvii, de lege canonica, par. 13.
[7] Cf. Catechism of Lima, 1585; FAGUNDEZ, *In quinque Ecclesiae*

for instance in the Catechism recently approved by Pius X for the Province of Rome.

Some few catechisms have only the first four, for example "The Instruction of the Christian" (*l'Instruction du chrétien*) of Richelieu:

> Les festes tu sanctifieras
> Qui te sont de commandement.
> Gardes religieusement
> Les jeusnes de commandement.
> Tous tes pechez confesseras
> A tout le moins une fois l'an.
> Ton Créateur receuvras
> Au moins à Pasques humblement.

> Feasts shalt thou sanctify
> Which are for thee appointed.
> Religiously observe
> The fasts commanded.
> All thy sins shalt thou confess
> Once a year at least.
> Thy Creator, at least at Easter,
> Humbly shalt thou receive.

But the author remarks that there are other precepts already dealt with in the chapter on the Decalogue.

In France most catechisms have adhered to the

praecepta; BINSFELD, *Enchiridion theologiae moralis;* AZOR, *Institutiones Morales,* l. VII, *de quinque Ecclesiae praeceptis;* DIANA, *Summa;* Praecepta Ecclesiae quinque sunt; DE MOURS, *Examen de la Théologie morale;* BONACINA, *de Praeceptis Ecclesiae;* TAMBURINI, *Tractatus quinque in quinque Ecclesiae praecepta,* etc., etc.

number six. One of the oldest to use that number is the "Catechism or Brief Instruction in the Catholic Christian Religion" (*Catéchisme ou briefve instruction de la Religion chrestienne catholique*, Paris, 1612). The list is in prose and more complete than most others. It contains the following enumeration:

"COMMANDMENTS OF THE CHURCH

(1) To observe the appointed feast-days;

(2) To hear Mass on Sundays and appointed feast-days;

(3) To fast during Lent, on the vigils and ember-days; to eat no flesh-meat either on Fridays, Saturdays, on the day of St. Mark or on the Rogation days;

(4) To confess one's sins at least once a year;

(5) To receive the Blessed Sacrament of the Altar at least at Easter;

(6) Not to celebrate marriage in the forbidden times, that is, from the first Sunday of Advent to the day of the Epiphany, or the feast of the Kings; and from the first day of Lent to the octave of Easter."

But this enumeration in prose was too lengthy and cumbersome to be memorized and well grasped by children. Verses were preferable—even though they were only rhymes—for musical assonances and scanned syllables were a help not to be despised. A return was therefore made to the list of the "Book of Jesus," to which was added a distich on Friday and Saturday abstinence:

> Vendredy chair ne mangeras
> Ny le samedy mesmement.
>
> On Friday and on Saturday likewise,
> Flesh thou shalt not eat,[8]

as a Paris catechism of 1667 expresses it.

Yet in spite of the happy symbolism of the number six, it was feared in certain dioceses that the faithful might forget the obligations which were not frequently recalled, and accordingly the bishops tried to complete the list as much as possible. They reached a total of nine by adding the three distichs:

> Hors le temps nopces ne feras,
> Payant les dîmes justement.
> Les excommuniez tu fuïras,
> Et dénoncés expressément.
> Quand excommunié tu seras,
> Fais toy absoudre promptement.
>
> Out of season weddings thou shalt not hold,
> Justly paying the tithes.
> Excommunicated persons shalt thou fly from,
> And expressly denounce.
> When thou art excommunicated
> Promptly have thyself absolved.[9]

[8] Cfr. the Catéchisme pour le Diocèse de Sens, 1670, the Catéchisme d'Angers, La Rochelle et Luçon, 1676, and the *Institution Chrestienne* by Louis Abelly, bishop of Rodez, 1692.

[9] Cf. Catéchisme de Besançon, 1687.

For more than a century this list was commonly received. It is still found in certain catechisms at the end of the eighteenth century,[10] and the *Catéchisme de l'Empire français,* which stuck to the ordinary list of six, adds in a note, undoubtedly in the spirit of the ancient texts: "There are still other commandments of the Church, such as not to marry within forbidden seasons, to avoid excommunicated persons, etc." (We note that there is no mention of the tithe.)

In the nineteenth century we find a list of seven commandments, v.g. in Gousset and Berardi, although the lists are not absolutely identical throughout.

However, scruples were entertained not only concerning the list of the commandments but also in regard to their form. In the seventeenth century, it was realized that those rhymes were very poor and a more harmonious classification was attempted. Whoever may have taken the initiative of recasting the rhyme, the result shows considerably more good will than ability. The new verses are dull and diffuse, and in very bad taste. Still they were printed and inserted in the Catechism of Angers, La Rochelle and Luçon for 1676. They form a counterpart to the ancient rhymes, enclosing between them a prose commentary, which oc-

[10] Cfr. the Catéchisme de Mgr l'évêque de Chambéry, Michael Conseil, about 1780–1790.

cupies the middle of the page. We give them here as they stand in that collection, pages 357 and 358:

(1) Entend la sainte Messe aux jours saints au Seigneur,
     En luy rendant honneur.
(2) Au moins une fois l'an va confesser ton crime
     Au Pasteur légitime.
(3) Et pour le moins à Pâque avec amour reçoy
     Ton Sauveur et ton Roy.
(4) Employe à servir Dieu chaque fête en l'année
     Par l'Église ordonnée.
(5) Jeûne au temps commandé et tout le saint Carême,
     Où jeûna Jésus même.
(6) Deux jours de la semaine observe en ton manger
     L'abstinence de chair.

(1) Hear holy Mass on days sacred to the Lord,
     And thus pay Him honor.
(2) Once at least each year confess thy sins
     To thy legitimate pastor.
(3) And at least at Easter receive with love
     Thy Saviour and thy King.
(4) Each feast of the year, by the Church ordained,
     Employ in serving God.
(5) Fast at the appointed times and all through Lent,
     When Jesus Himself fasted.
(6) In thy meals, two days of the week,
     Abstain from flesh-meat.

That these verses obtained but little success can be easily explained. Far from eclipsing the ancient distichs, they caused them to be more appreciated, and I have found them in no other catechism.

The reader has probably observed from the few citations made thus far, that, like the list of the commandments, the contents also varied. The usual list of five or six is not found equally complete everywhere. Some of them appear regularly in each enumeration; *viz.:* the sanctification of feasts; the Lenten fast and that of vigils and Ember days; the annual confession and the paschal communion; others in nearly all the lists; *viz.:* the sanctification of Sundays (sometimes contained in the commentary on the third commandment of God); and abstinence on Fridays and Saturdays; some appear very frequently, at least they so appeared formerly (and even now in certain countries), *viz.:* the obligation of paying the tithes, to which were added the first-fruits, and a little less frequently the prohibition of celebrating marriage within the forbidden seasons; rarely (especially since the radical changes made under this heading in the nineteenth century) do we see the precept of avoiding excommunicated persons and securing prompt absolution from excommunication; lastly, the commandment which mentions abstinence from flesh on the festival of St. Mark and the Rogation Days has long since fallen into desuetude.

Moreover, the lists containing the most numbers

are not always the most comprehensive. That of Diana, for instance: (1) To hear mass on Sundays and feast-days; (2) To abstain from flesh meat on Fridays and Saturdays, and to fast during Lent, on vigils, and Ember Days; (3) To confess once a year; (4) To communicate at Easter; (5) To pay the tithes,—is more complete than our list of six precepts, where the second looks somewhat like a repetition of the first. But the most comprehensive and at the same time most condensed list is certainly that of the new catechism of Pius X, which runs as follows:

Q. "How many commandments of the Church are there, and what are they?"

A. "The Commandments of the Church are five in number:

(1) To hear mass on Sundays and all other feast-days of obligation.

(2) To fast during Lent, on Ember Days and appointed vigils; not to eat meat on forbidden days.

(3) To confess at least once a year and to communicate at Easter, each one in his own parish.

(4) To pay tithes to the Church, according to usage.

(5) Not to celebrate weddings in prohibited seasons, that is, from the first Sunday of Advent to the feast of the Epiphany, and from the first day of Lent to the octave of Easter."

These are the precepts imposed and quoted everywhere. The bishops never believed that these lists were exclusive. As circumstances required, they added one or more obligations imposed by the Church, though not contained in the usual lists. Such is the case with the English-German catechism of Fr. Deharbe, edited for the United States, which contains under number six the following prescriptions: not to contract marriage without the presence of a priest and witnesses; not to solemnize weddings in forbidden times; not to espouse non-Catholics or those related within a prohibited degree, and to contract no marriage forbidden in any way by the Church. The catechism of Fr. Färber, which is also widely used in America, gives under No. 4 the prohibition of affiliation with condemned societies. The bishop is the one to decide what teaching is most necessary for the faithful of each diocese or region. It would not be surprising, some day, to see inserted in our French catechisms, not the precept of tithes, such as it is enforced in French Canada:

> Droits et dîme tu paieras
> A l'Église fidèlement;

but the less blunt injunction of certain American catechisms: "Thou shalt contribute to the support of the Church and of the pastor according to thy means."

Little remains to be said on the order in which the commandments are arranged,—a matter of small importance. We merely note that the precept of keeping holy the Sabbath and feast-days is always placed first. Second, outside of France, comes the precept of fasting and abstinence; in France, on the contrary, this precept follows after the ones that enforce the annual confession and the paschal communion. This order is characteristic of French catechisms as far back as the latter part of the fifteenth century. The precept not to contract marriage in forbidden times, that of paying tithes, and that of avoiding excommunicated persons, regularly follow one another in the same order in all French catechisms; outside of France that of paying the tithe generally is enumerated first. Besides the peculiar order of the commandments observed in the French catechisms, they alone employ terms of childlike simplicity in stating them, and rhymed distichs easy to memorize.

When one has studied the more scientific formulas used by theologians, or other Christian nations, he is apt to return with genuine pleasure to the old French *"Compost ou Kalendrier des bergers"*:

> Les dimanches messe ouïras
> Et fêtes de commandement.

CHAPTER II

THE FIRST COMMANDMENT

In the old French version this commandment reads:

> Les dimanches messe ouïras
> Et fêtes de commandement.

The catechism of the Third Plenary Council of Baltimore states it as follows: "To hear Mass on Sundays and holydays of obligation."

According to the common teaching of theologians this commandment imposes a twofold obligation: To assist at Mass and to refrain from servile labor. We will see what the councils, the ancient records and theologians teach us about each of these obligations.

A. ASSISTANCE AT MASS

In the Time of the Apostles. The sanctification of Sunday is of Apostolic origin, but it would be an error to attribute it to a definite decision of the Apostles. There is no such decision mentioned in the Apostolic documents. This law was evolved by the force of circumstances. After the death of our Lord the Apostles continued to attend the Jewish liturgical gatherings. The Acts show that they frequented the Temple,[1] and visited the synagogues. On arriving in a city, they put themselves in contact with the Jewish colony, faithfully assisted at the gatherings of the synagogue, and partook in its worship. Paul and Barnabas, entering the synagogue at Antioch of Pisidia on the day of the Sabbath, take their place among the other Jews. After the reading of the Law and the Prophets, the elders of the synagogue send one of their assistants to tell them: "Brethren, if you have any exhortation to give the people, speak." Paul stands up and addresses the assembly, preaching Christ, His coming, His death, and His resurrection. His discourse stirs up some emotion and he is asked to come again on the following Sabbath.[2] The same thing occurs at Iconium,[3] at Thessalonica,[4] where St. Paul, "according to his custom," enters the synagogue on three successive Sabbaths and preaches the Gospel; thus also at Athens[5] and at Corinth.[6] The Apostles and their first disciples therefore continued to frequent the Temple and the synagogues and to take part in the sabbatic gatherings.

[1] Cf. *Acts*, ii, 46; iii, sqq.; v, 12, 20; xxi, 26; xxii, 17.
[2] *Acts* xiii, 14, 42.
[3] Ibidem, xiv, 1.
[4] Ibidem, xvii, 1 and ff.
[5] Ibidem, xvii, 17.
[6] Ibidem, xviii, 4.

However this common worship could not suffice them; as disciples of Jesus they felt the need of adoring among themselves alone that Messiah whom the majority of their compatriots refused to recognize. For that worship they needed private gatherings, which became more and more necessary when the first Gentiles, absolute strangers to Judaism, were added to the number of the faithful. Sunday, already mentioned once in the Acts [7] and once in the first Epistle to the Corinthians,[8] was soon joined to the Sabbath. This addition probably occurred as follows: After having assisted at the services in the synagogue, the Apostles and their disciples came together apart from the Jews to partake of the Eucharistic meal "in memory" of Christ. Their gathering began towards evening and lasted till day-break. This must have been the usual order, especially at the time when the Christians were scattered in small communities, each of which could not have an Apostle or priest, and were consequently obliged to travel a longer distance than was allowed on the Sabbath if they wished to partake of the Last Supper in common.[9] Thus the first day of the week was added to the Sabbath. "From a very early period," says Msgr. Duchesne, "the Chris-

[7] *Acts*, xx, 7.

[8] *I Cor.*, xvi, 2.

[9] The day of the Sabbath started on Friday night and ended on Saturday at the same hour. Cf. *Levit.* xxiii, 32.

tians adopted the Sunday. It is possible that, at the outset, the choice of this day was not suggested by any hostility towards Jewish customs, but that they observed it merely in order to have side by side with the ancient Sabbath, which they celebrated with their Israelite brethren, a day set apart for exclusively Christian assemblies. . . . The observance of the Sunday was at first supplemental to that of the Sabbath, but in proportion as the gulf between the Church and the synagogue widened, the Sabbath became less and less important, and ended in being entirely neglected." [10] In being substituted for the Sabbath, as a more perfect form of worship, Sunday assumed those of its obligations that were reconcilable with the law of the Gospel.

The principal object of the Sunday assemblies was the liturgical office of the New Law—the celebration of the Mass. It was now as obligatory to assist at Mass as it had previously been to assist at the service held in the synagogue. Assistance at Mass became the discriminating badge of faithful Christians.

From the Time of the Apostles to the Fourth Century.—Henceforth testimonies become more and more numerous concerning the liturgical assemblies on Sunday, now called the Day of the Lord. "On the day of the Lord unite your-

[10] *Christian Worship*, London, 1903, p. 47.

selves," says the *Didache*, "break the bread and give thanks after having confessed your sins, so that your sacrifice may be pure."[11]

The Epistle of Barnabas, after having shown that the Lord rejects the feasts of the New Moon and the Sabbaths, adds: "We celebrate with joy the eighth day, on which Jesus rose from the dead."[12]

It is on Sunday, according to St. Justin, that the faithful of the city or of the country gather together in one place to hear the reading of the "commentaries of the Apostles" and the writings of the prophets, and to assist at the celebration of Mass.[13]

Sunday has taken the place of the Sabbath, says St. Ignatius, among those who have transferred to the New Testament the faith before given to the Old.[14]

On the observation of Sunday (περὶ κυριακῆς) Melito of Sardis composed a whole treatise, which unfortunately was lost.

Dionysius of Corinth, writing to the Church of Rome, mentions Sunday as a day of gathering. "To-day," he says, "we have celebrated Sunday and we have read your letter and also that which was addressed to our church by Clement."[15] The

---
[11] *Didache*, xiv, 1.   [12] *Epistle of Barnabas*, xv, 9.
[13] *Apolog.*, i, 67.
[14] *Epist. Magnes.*, ix. Migne, P. G., t. v, 768.
[15] Eusebius, *Hist. Eccles.*, iv, 23.

Ebionites, in order to pass for Christians in spite of their Jewish observances, were wont to celebrate Sunday exactly like the faithful.[16]

Sunday is the festal day, says St. Irenæus, the day on which, since the time of the Apostles, we need not bend the knee to pray. To assist at the Sunday gathering is to perform a Christian act, it is to assist at the Eucharistic sacrifice.

Such is the form under which the obligation of assisting at the Sunday Mass is presented during the first three centuries. It is an unwritten law, imposed by tradition, which could not be neglected without somehow abandoning Christianity, and consequently exposing one to the divine threat contained in the Gospel: "But he that shall deny me before men, I will also deny him before my Father who is in heaven" (Matth. x, 33).

After the Fourth Century.—From the fourth century on, the Church, living in broad daylight, saw the number of her children rapidly increase. But the quality of their faith was not always proportionate to their number, and the councils had to multiply admonitions and prescriptions. The first of these bore on the assistance at Sunday Mass. Even before the Edict of Milan, the Council of Elvira, undoubtedly sanctioning an already ancient discipline, made the following decision: "If anyone remains three Sundays in a city with-

[16] *Ibid.*, iii, 27.

THE FIRST COMMANDMENT

out going to church, he shall be deprived of communion for a time."[17] This sanction was tantamount to temporary excommunication. Although the law itself was not altogether attributable to past neglect on the part of the faithful, the penalty was none the less grave and testifies to the importance attached to the Sunday precept.

The prescription of Elvira did not remain a dead letter. At the Council of Sardica, almost half a century later, Bishop Osius spoke of it as a well known text,[18] and he used it as an argument against some other bishops.

Another proof of its importance is afforded by the *Apostolic Constitutions* (end of the fourth century). This document bears on our point in the following manner. Not to unknown disciples, nor even to mere Apostles does it attribute the law which prescribes the sanctification of the Sunday; but to the two principal members of the Apostolic College. "We, Peter and Paul, decide that during five days of the week slaves shall work, but that they shall pass Saturday and Sunday in church."[19]

---

[17] "Si quis in civitate positus, tres dominicas ad ecclesiam non accesserit, pauco tempore abstineatur, ut correptus esse videatur." *Conc. Eliberitan.* (about 300), c. xxi. BRUNS, *Canones Apostolorum et Conciliorum*, t. ii, 5. Henceforth we shall cite this collection thus: BRUNS, t. I or t. II.

[18] *Conc. Sardicense*, c. xi (Greek text) and xiv (Latin version). BRUNS t. 1, 100 and 101.

[19] "Ego Petrus et ego Paulus constituimus ut servi quinque diebus opus faciant, sabbato autem et dominico die vacent in

In a previous passage is found this even more explicit testimony: "On Sunday gather together to give thanks to God and to acknowledge the gifts He has given us through Christ, . . . so that your sacrifice be also without reproach. . . ."[20]

In the meantime the practice of the Christian populace and the teaching of the bishops had inspired Constantine to take measures which were destined to exercise a wholesome influence. Eusebius in his Life of Constantine tells us that the first Christian Emperor desired that one day be consecrated to prayer, and chose Sunday. He not only encouraged the observance of this practice by his example but also made use of various means to enable others to do likewise. All Christian soldiers were free to obey the precept of the Church on that day and gathered together in an appointed place to address to God a prayer which the Emperor himself had composed.[21]

ecclesia propter doctrinam religionis (διὰ τὴν διδασκαλίαν τῆς εὐσεβείας)." (*Constit. Apostol.*, l. VIII, c. xxxiii. *P. G.*, t. I, 1133.)

[20] "Die resurrectionis Domini, quem dominicum dicimus, convenite sine ulla intermissione ad agendum gratias Deo, et profitendum beneficia, quibus nos Deus per Christum affecit, . . . ut sic sacrificium vestrum reprehensione careat; sitque Deo acceptum et gratum." (*Ibid.*, l. VII, c. xxxi, col. 1022.)—Cf. *Didascalia* in Syriac, c. xiii.

[21] *Vita Constantini*, l. IV, c. xviii, xix, xx, et sq. Migne, *P. G.*, t. xx, 1166 ff. Cf. *De Solemnit. Pascali*, c. vii and ix: "Omni die dominica per corpus sanctificatum ipsius salutaris Paschatis vivificamur, et pretioso sanguine ipsius in anima obsignamur." *P. G.*, t. xxiv, 706.

It therefore seems that the principle of obligatory assistance at Sunday Mass in cities provided with the necessary clergy was admitted as early as the fourth century. But obedience was not always complete.

The decrees of certain councils held in the fifth century, for example that of Africa, to be cited further on, which demanded the closing of theatres and other spectacles on Sunday,[22] and that Council called the first of St. Patrick,[23] show that the obligation of attending church on Sunday was known and that lukewarm Christians made use of all kinds of pretexts to secure exemption. However, there is reason to believe that during the fifth century obedience was more complete than later. Sunday was chosen for the election and ordination of clerics,—those of whom St. Leo the Great said: "Let him who is to command, be elected by all";[24] an unmistakable sign that, on that day, all the faithful attended church.

In the sixth century, if we are to interpret literally the remonstrances of St. Caesarius, fervor had notably diminished. The Bishop of Arles often insists on the obligation of sanctifying Sunday. His sermons, whilst they bear witness to the negligence of many Christians, show the current

[22] *Codex canonum Ecclesiae africanae*, c. LXI, BRUNS, t. 1, 170.
[23] C. xviii, BRUNS, t. II, 303.
[24] Cf. Epist. X, *ad episcopos per provinciam Viennensem constitutos*, c. vii. *P. L.*, t. LIV, 630.

teaching of the Church on our subject. "Come to church every Sunday," says Caesarius; "on Sunday Christians must occupy themselves only with God and must gather in church for the salvation of their souls."[25] He affirms that Sunday is reserved to Divine worship by Divine institution: "The Apostles and Apostolic men have decided that Sunday should be consecrated to acts of religion, and on that day Divine worship only should be attended to. To that day they transferred the glory of the Jewish Sabbath. Let us therefore observe the Sunday, my dear brethren, and let us sanctify it as the Divine Legislator commanded the ancients to observe the Sabbath. From Saturday night to Sunday night let us give ourselves up entirely to divine worship."[26] Going further so as to insure the observance of what he considered essential in the precept, the Bishop urgently invites his flock to follow every service on

[25] "Omni die dominico ad ecclesiam convenite . . . Christiani in die dominico soli Deo vacare, et pro animae suae salute debent ad ecclesiam convenire." *Sermo* 265 inter opera S. Augustini, t. V; Migne, *P. L.*, t. XXXIX, 2238.

[26] "Dominicum diem apostoli et apostolici viri . . . religiosa solemnitate habendum sanxerunt . . . ut in eo tantum divinis cultibus serviamus . . . Ac ideo sancti doctores ecclesiae decreverunt omnem gloriam judaici sabbatismi in illum transferre . . . observemus ergo diem dominicam, fratres, et sanctificemus illam, sicut antiquis praeceptum est de sabbato, dicente Legislatore: *a vespere usque ad vesperam celebrabitis sabbata vestra* (*Levit.*, xxiii, 32). . . . A vespera diei sabbati usque ad vesperam diei Dominici . . . soli divino cultui vacemus." (*Sermo* 280, *ibid.*, 2274.)

Sunday without exception: "All who can should come to the evening and night office and pray to God together; the others will pray each in his own house; but on Sunday let no one omit assistance at mass and lazily remain at home." [27]

In another sermon he adds that it is a mortal sin, not precisely to miss Mass on Sunday—he does not consider the omission of mass alone as so serious —but to fail to sanctify the day of the Lord.[28]

Assistance at the Entire Mass.—An obligation which had to be insisted on more at length was that of assisting at the whole of mass, that it did not suffice to be present merely at the beginning and to leave at the sermon. The Bishop of Arles with all his colleagues had signed the following prescription at the Council of Agde: "We ordain, by a very special prescription, that lay people assist at the entire Sunday mass and that no one presume to leave before the priest's benediction. Those who dare to do so, shall be publicly reprimanded by the Bishop." [29] He saw to its observ-

[27] "Veniat ergo cuicumque possibile sit, ad vespertinam atque nocturnam celebrationem, et oret ibi in conventu Ecclesiae pro peccatis suis Deum. Qui vero hoc non possit, saltem in domo sua oret, et non negligat Deo solvere votum, ac reddere pensum servitutis: *in die vero* [dominico] *nullus se a sacra missarum celebratione separet*, neque otiosus quis domi remaneat." (*Ib.*)

[28] "Si toto die dominico lectioni insistere et Deo supplicare negligimus, non leviter in Deum peccamus." (*Serm.* 281, *ib.* 2278.)

[29] "Missas die dominico a saecularibus totas teneri speciali ordinatione praecipimus; ita ut ante benedictionem sacerdotis egredi populus non praesumat. Qui si fecerint, ab episcopo

ance; sometimes he had the doors of the church closed immediately after the Gospel, thereby forcing all to remain until the end of the service.[30] At other times he had recourse to prayer, supplication, and doctrinal arguments. One of his arguments is particularly interesting, as it shows that, if the direct object of the precept was the sanctification of the Sunday, its principal injunction was assistance at mass, *i. e.* the Eucharistic Sacrifice: "With a moment's reflection you will realize that mass is celebrated not exactly at the time of the reading of the lessons, but when the offering and the consecration of the Body and Blood of the Lord are made. You can read the books of the prophets, the writings of the Apostles, and even the Gospel at home, but the consecration you can only hear and see in the house of God. . . . Those of you who will persist in their remissness will be condemned by the just judgment of God. Notify them, therefore, and tell them most explicitly that it is useless for them to listen to the readings if they leave before the end of mass."[31]

publice confundantur." (*Conc. Agathen*, c. XLVII, Bruns, t. II, 155.)

[30] *Vita Caesarii*, l. I, c. ii. Migne, *P. L.*, t. LXVII, 1010.

[31] "Si diligenter attenderitis, cognoscetis quia non tunc fiunt missae quando divinae lectiones in ecclesia recitantur, sed quando munera offeruntur, et corpus et sanguis Domini consecratur. Nam lectiones, sive propheticas, sive apostolicas, sive evangelicas etiam in domibus vestris aut ipsi legere, aut alios legentes audire po-

THE FIRST COMMANDMENT

The whole of Caesarius' sermon is worth reading, for its very prolixity shows how urgently the Church insisted that the faithful hear the whole mass and that she admitted no excuse as legitimate except necessity or sickness.[32]

It proved very difficult to secure this assistance at the entire mass. During the whole sixth century the synods were obliged to renew the prescription of the Council of Agde. Thus the Council of Orleans, A. D. 511, said: "When the people gather to assist at mass, let them not leave before the end of the office and the benediction,[33] or if there is no bishop present, before the Lord's Prayer has been said."[34]

testis: consecrationem vero corporis et sanguinis Domini non alibi, nisi in domo Dei, audire vel videre poteritis. Eos qui negligentes sunt, [Deus] justo judicio damnabit. Et ideo, fratres, monete eos ... dicentes et definitissime comminantes, quia nihil eis prodest quod divinas lectiones audiunt, si antequam divina mysteria compleantur abscedunt." (*Serm.* 281.)

[32] "Nullus de ecclesia discedat, nisi forte quos aut gravis infirmitas aut publica necessitas stare diutius non permittit." *Ib.*

[33] "Cum ad celebrandas missas in Dei nomine convenitur, populus non ante discedat, quam missae sollemnitas compleatur, et ubi episcopus defuerit, benedictionem accipiat sacerdotis." *Conc. Aurel.*, c. xxvi. *Monum. Germ., Concilia*, t. I (MAASSEN), p. 8.

[34] "De missis nullus laicorum ante discedat, quam dominica dicatur oratio, et, si episcopus praesens fuerit, ejus benedictio exspectitur." *Conc. Aurelian.* (538), c. xxxii, *ib.* p. 82.—Compare with the decisions of the Western Church, those of the Greek Didascalia, which perhaps date back to the seventh century. I give the version of Fr. Nau in the *Revue de l'Orient Chrétien*, 1907, p. 248: "Woe to those who do not hear the holy liturgy in the church, because I will deliver them to the Tartar.

However, the precept of hearing mass ordinarily obliges only those who live near a church. This has been observed above in the statutes of the Council of Elvira, which were made for those dwelling in the episcopal "city." It can also be deduced from this prescription of the Council of Mâcon: "Be entirely occupied with praising God on Sunday, and if some of you live near church, let them go there, shed tears and pray. And know well that if you do not do this, but scorn our exhortation, you will be first of all punished by God and expose yourselves to the wrath of the priest."[35] Another decree of the same council specifies more particularly the duties of those who live close enough to church to be obliged to hear mass: they are commanded, under threat of excommunication, to bring to the altar during the Sunday sacrifice an offering of bread and wine, in conformity with a custom which had unfortunately fallen into desuetude.[36]

... Woe to those who receive the Holy Mysteries and leave before the end"; (chap. xiv); and the quotation of the "Ὅρος κανονικός that Fr. Nau adds in a footnote: "If anyone shall leave the church before the priest finishes, let him be accursed."

[35] "Custodite diem dominicam ... Estote omnes in himnis et laudibus Dei animo corporeque intenti. Si quis vestrum proximam habet ecclesiam, properet ad eandem et ibi dominico die semetipsum precibus lacrymisque afficiat ... si quis vestrum hanc salubrem exhortationem parvi penderit aut contemtui tradiderit, sciat se pro qualitatis merito principaliter a Deo punire et deinceps sacerdotali quoque irae implacabiliter subjacere." *Conc. Matiscon.* (585), c. i. MAASSEN, p. 165.

[36] "Cognovimus quosdam christianos a mandato Dei aliquibus

Assistance of Bondmen at Mass.—There was an unfortunate class of persons, condemned to perpetual labor, bondmen of the lowest condition, whose masters, believing them incapable of leading a Christian life, kept them employed the whole year round in forests or remote farming districts. The obligation of assisting at Sunday mass existed also for them. Redeemed by Christ they had both the right and the duty of presenting their homage to Him. A Council of Rouen commended these bondmen to the special solicitude of the clergy. The pastors were exhorted to notify their parishioners to send the drovers, swineherds, shepherds, and ploughmen in the interior of the country, who lived as if they were not human beings, to mass on Sundays and holydays, or at least to allow them to attend.[37] To insure the help of a good example for all, the same Council pointed out the practical means to be employed by pastors in obtaining the

locis deviasse . . . Propterea decernimus, ut omnibus dominicis diebus aris oblatio ab omnibus viris vel mulieribus offeratur tam panis quam vini . . . omnes autem, qui definitiones nostras per inobedientiam evacuare contendit, anathema percellatur." *Ib.*, c. iv, p. 166.

[37] "Admonere debent sacerdotes plebes subditas sibi, ut bubulcos atque porcarios, vel alios pastores, vel aratores, qui in agris assidue commorantur, vel in sylvis, et ideo velut more pecudum vivunt, in dominicis et in aliis festis diebus saltem vel ad missam faciant vel permittant venire: nam et hos Christus pretioso suo sanguine redemit: quod si neglexerint, pro animabus eorum absque dubio rationem se reddituros sciant." *Conc. Rothomagen.* (650), c. xiv. BRUNS, t. II, 271.

attendance of their negligent parishioners at the Sunday services: in each city and town loyal and God-fearing men were to be chosen to urge the careless and negligent and to denounce to the priests all who were neglectful of their duty.[38]

Mass and Religious Instruction.—These conciliar prescriptions undoubtedly obtained the desired result, to some extent at least, for during the seventh and eighth centuries the bishops directed their efforts towards another point involved in the prescriptions concerning assistance at mass, *viz.* the religious instruction of the faithful. During the fifth and sixth centuries, lukewarm Catholics who came to mass, often got tired and went out immediately after the Gospel. We have seen the means used by St. Caesarius to prevent this exodus. The decision of the Council of Agde, which recommended the bishop publicly to shame those who did not remain until the end of mass, undoubtedly obtained some results, and all thenceforth waited for the benediction of the celebrant. But carelessness always regains its

[38] "Ut populus admoneatur, ut in dominicis et festis diebus omnes ad vesperas et nocturnas vigilias et ad missam omnimodis occurrant: et ut decani in civitatibus et vicis publicis viri veraces et Deum timentes constituantur, qui desides et negligentes commoneant, ut ad Dei servitium absque dilatione properent: et ut ipsi decani sacramento adstringantur, ut nulla interveniente causa, scilicet aut amoris, aut propinquitatis, muneris negligentes et transgressores reticeant, quin propriis sacerdotibus proprias eorum culpas manifestent." *Ibid.*, c. xv.

ground sooner or later; in this case it satisfied itself by retarding beyond reason the arrival at church, and now it became necessary to insist on the obligation of hearing the word of God. This is clearly shown by a canon of the English Council of Cloveshow: "Sunday must be piously observed by all; the priest must invite the people to come to church, hear the word of God, and assist at mass and instruction."[39] The following passage of a Saxon capitulary bears the same testimony: "On Sunday let all the parishioners gather in church to hear the word of God."[40]

Excepting a council of Paris, which, while congratulating the masters on the care with which they sanctified the Sunday, reproached them for not allowing their servants time or means of observing this precept,[41] the other synodal assemblies of that age, it seems, merely recalled from time to time the general precept of assisting at Mass.

[39] "Ut dominicus dies legitima veneratione a cunctis celebretur . . . eo die . . . populus per sacerdotes Dei ad ecclesiam saepius invitatus, ad audiendum verbum Dei conveniat: missarumque sacramentis, ac doctrinae sermonibus frequentius adsit." *Conc. Cloveshov.* II (747), c. xiv. MANSI, t. xii, 399.

[40] "Ut in dominicis diebus . . . omnes ad ecclesiam recurrant ad audiendum verbum Dei." *Capitulatio de partibus Saxoniae*, c. xviii, BORETIUS, t. I, 69.

[41] "Utcumque enim a quibusdam dominis venerando custodiri videtur, sed a conservis servitio eorum pressis perraro debito honore coli invenitur." *Conc. Parisien.* VI (829), lib. I, c. L. MANSI, t. XIV, 568.

Pope Nicholas, writing to the Bulgarians, tells them that they must honor the Lord's day and observe it with prayer.[42] Rodulf of Bourges reminds his flock that assistance at mass and prayer is a well-known obligation, and like Theodulf, bishop of Orleans, he seems to place on the same footing two works of piety which subtle minds would to-day distinguish as being respectively precept and counsel: assisting at mass and assisting at the vigil and night office.[43] Herard, archbishop of Tours, also insisted on this same rule: "On Sunday the entire mass and sermon must be heard."[44] Occasionally, too, abuses were condemned, such as infallibly creep in among men who are ardent in defending their temporal interests and carry the heat of their discussion into church, instead of recollecting themselves to hear the word of God.[45]

In a word, while the precept is substantially

[42] *Ad consulta Bulgaror.*, c. x. MANSI, t. XV, 407.

[43] "Conveniendum est sabbato die cum luminaribus ad ecclesiam, conveniendum est ad vigilias sive ad matutinum officium, concurrendum est etiam cum oblationibus ad missarum solemnia." *Ib.* col. 956. Cf. *Theodulfi Aurelian. capitula*, c. xxiv, Migne, *P. L.*, t. CV, 198.

[44] "Ante missam completam non exeant, et verbum Dei intente audiant." *Capit. Herardi archiep. Turon.*, c. xv. MANSI, t. xvi (Appendix), 679.

[45] "Ut nullus in die dominico, cum ad missam venerit, aut in ecclesia fuerit audeat placitare: sed potius verbum Dei in ipsa die intente audire." *Concil. incerti loci et temporis in Normannia*, c. viii. MANSI, t. xviii, 433.

THE FIRST COMMANDMENT

observed by all, it admits of a more and more detailed application; it is granted, for example, that, in case one is obliged to start on a journey, simple assistance at mass suffices, but ordinarily mass is but the nucleus of a more complete observance and of further religious exercises, which begin Saturday night.[46]

Such are the classical texts on the matter, the only ones cited in the collections of Regino and Burchard. They form the basis of the examination of conscience which the priest used to make for his penitents before confession, and also of the questions which the bishop in synod had to ask his priests: Does everyone faithfully attend Matins and Mass and Vespers on Sundays and the principal feasts?[47] Are there persons so impious and so estranged from God, that they do not come to church at least on Sundays?[48] Do the swineherds

---

[46] "Die solis ... si accidat ut proficisci debeat, tunc potest ... ea conditione ut *missam* suam et preces suas non negligat. ... Oportet etiam omnem christianum, qui hoc perficere potest, die saturni ad ecclesiam venire, et luminare secum adferre, ac ibi cantum vespertinum audire et noctu laudes nocturnas, et mane cum oblationibus suis venire ad missarum solemnitatem." *Liber legum ecclesiasticarum* (about the tenth century), c. xxiv, Mansi, t. XIX, 186.

[47] "Si ad matutinas et ad missam et ad vesperas his diebus impraetermisse omnes occurrant." Regino, *De ecclesiasticis disciplinis*, l. II, c. v, no. 57. *P. L.*, t. CXXXII, 285. Cf. Burchard, *Decretum*, l. I, c. xciv, *interrog.* 57. *P. L.*, t. CXL, 577.

[48] "Si aliquis est tam perversus et a Deo alienus ut saltem dominica die ad ecclesiam non veniat." Regino, *ib.* no. 63. Burchard, *ib.*, interrog. 62.

and other herdsmen come to church on Sunday to hear Mass?[49] Are there promoters in each parish, dispersed through the farming centers, loyal and God-fearing men, who admonish the others to come to church, to assist at Matins, Mass and Vespers?[50] The way in which this obligation is considered during this epoch can be summed up as follows: the sanctification of the Sunday by works of religion, prayer, etc., performed in church, is considered of grave obligation for all those who can fulfill it with reasonable facility. The most important among these works of religion, and the one that dominates all the others, is assistance at mass, at the whole mass, and in particular at consecration and communion. The faithful are strongly exhorted to do their duty and the masters to make its accomplishment possible for even the most destitute of their bondmen.

Temporal Sanctions.—After the year 1000, the Church had greatly developed in power, so that many temporal rulers counted themselves her vassals and, to a greater extent than ever before, placed the "secular arm" at her disposal in the enforcement of her discipline. We now behold the

[49] "Si porcarii et alii pastores dominica die ad ecclesiam veniant et missas audiant." *Ib.*, no. 64.

[50] "Si in unaquaque parochia decani sunt per villas constituti, viri veraces, et Deum timentes, qui ceteros admoneant, ut ad ecclesiam pergant ad matutinas, missam et vesperas." *Ib.*, no. 68; Burchard, *interrog.* 68.

THE FIRST COMMANDMENT

strictly spiritual obligation of assisting at mass upheld by the threat of temporal penalties. Let us open the Collection of Ecclesiastical Constitutions written in Hungary in the reign of King St. Stephen; in this book not only the legitimate causes exempting from assistance at mass were provided for, but the chastisement due to a culpable and stubborn disobedience is also set forth: only those who are obliged to tend to fires are excused from attending church on Sunday; whoever else dares to neglect this Christian duty shall have his head shaved and be handcuffed.[51]

That a country but lately converted from pagan barbarism, should adopt this rather forcible manner of introducing the customs and practices of Christianity is somewhat remarkable. Towards the end of the same century, the same sanctions were renewed in a synod against those who did not attend church on Sunday.[52] Some restrictions were added: if the distance is too great, each family will only be held to send one representative

[51] "A sacerdotibus vero et comitibus commendatur omnibus villicis ita ut ipsorum jussu omnes concurrant die dominica ad ecclesiam, majores et minores, viri et mulieres, exceptis illis qui ignes custodiunt. Si quis vero obstinatus remanebit, ob negligentiam vapulet et depiletur." *Constitutiones ecclesiasticae sub S. Stephano rege Hungariae conditae circa ann. 1016*, c. vii. MANSI, t. XIX, 371.

[52] "Si quis in dominicis diebus, . . . ad ecclesiam non venerit parochialem, verberibus corripiatur." *Conc. Szabolchen.* (1092), c. xi, MANSI, t. XX, 763.

charged with offering three loaves and a candle at the altar.[53]

The régime of coercion instituted by the Church of Hungary was, except for minor modifications, applied also outside that country in the following centuries, and its two essential elements ("obligatory assistance at the parochial mass" and "temporal punishment for obstinate delinquents") proved quite effective. The temporal penalty took the place of corporal punishment and was imposed without scruple in the beginning of the thirteenth century, in the south of France, where a fine was substituted for blows. At Pamiers this new discipline attained a rare degree of ingeniousness: The parishioners had to come every Sunday to church to hear mass and a sermon; every house-owner who, without reasonable excuse, such as sickness, absence, etc., missed mass, had to pay a fine of six *deniers tournois,* which was to be equally divided between the landlord, the pastor, and the church.[54] At this time the Albigenses

---

[53] "Si vero illae remotae fuerint, et ad ecclesiam suam parochialem villani venire non potuerint, unus tamen ex eis nomine omnium baculo ad ecclesiam veniat, et tres panes, et candelam ad altare offerat." (*Ib.*)

[54] "Parochiani cogantur venire ad ecclesiam dominicis . . . et ibidem missam et praedicationem ex integro audire; ita quod si dominus vel domina cujuslibet domus ad ecclesiam non venerint, et in villa praesentes fuerint nulla praepediti infirmitate, aut alia causa rationabili, persolvent sex denarios turonensis monetae, quorum medietas erit domini villae, et alia medietas per medium sacerdotis et ecclesiae." *Conc. Apamien.* (1212), c. vii. MANSI, t. XXII, 357.

held sway in Languedoc and the prescriptions of Pamiers did not at once obtain the desired success; they were consequently renewed seven years later by a synod held near Toulouse,[55] and confirmed at Toulouse, A. D. 1229,[56] and Beziers, A. D. 1233.[57]

The Parochial Mass.—The second element of the precept proclaimed by the Hungarian Council imposed the obligation not only of assisting at mass, but at the parochial mass, that is, the one celebrated in the parish church. In the Middle Ages, obligations were in general personal rather than territorial, and, from the ecclesiastical point of view, the parish was the equivalent of the seignorial castle. It was at the parish church that the Christian paid his duties to God, as it was at the castle that he rendered homage to his feudal lord. The Council of Nantes, presumably held in 658, enjoined every parish priest to expel from his

[55] "Statuimus, quod parochiani, dominus et domina cujuslibet domus, dominicis . . . teneantur ad ecclesiam venire, audituri ex integro praedicationem et divinum officium, nec inde recessuri donec missa compleatur omnino. Quod si alter illorum absens fuerit extra villam, vel alia legitima causa praepeditus, alter saltem teneatur, dummodo sint in villa praesentes, nulla infirmitate seu alia rationabili causa detenti, duodecim denarios turonenses solvere quilibet teneatur; quorum medietas sit domini villae, et alia sacerdotis Ecclesiae." *Statuta in concil. apud Tolosam promulgata per dom. Romanum, s. Angeli Card. diacon.* (1219), c. ii. *Ib.*, 1135.

[56] *Conc. Tolosan.* (1229), c. xxv. MANSI, t. XXIII, 200.

[57] *Conc. Biterren.* (1233), c. v. *Ib.*, 271.

church on Sundays and feast-days any stranger who pretended to fulfill his Christian duty there, and in order to make it possible for the parishioners of each parish to hear mass, a capitulary of Charlemagne ordered the priests to celebrate mass in their churches on Sundays and feast-days and forbade the wealthy to invite them to say it in their castles.[58]

The parishioner was therefore attached to his church as the bondman or vassal to his lord. It was no more allowable for a pastor to accept another's parishioners than for a lord to accept another's bondmen or vassals, or to give them refuge. Such was the situation from time immemorial. But in the course of the thirteenth century a number of prescriptions appear which seem to be part of a defensive movement. The Council of Rouen of 1235 recalls the obligation of the pastor to see before saying mass on Sunday, whether there are outsiders in his church, and to expel them unless they are travelers or well-known persons. Priests without parishioners are forbidden to admit anyone to their mass on that day.[59] The

[58] "Ut in diebus festis vel dominicis omnes ad ecclesiam veniant; et non invitent presbyteros ad domus suas ad missam faciendam." *Duplex legationis edictum*, c. xxv. Capitularia (Boretius), t. I., p. 64.

[59] "Quolibet die dominico quaerant [sacerdotes] si sint parochiani extranei inter suos; et ante missae ingressum ejiciant extraneos diebus praedictis, nisi sint aliquae notae personae transeuntes. Item qui nullos habent Parochianos, nullos recipiant

same prohibition is renewed three years later by a Council of Treves.[60]

Bination.—In order to render it possible for the parishioners to assist at the Sunday mass, the new law admitted exceptions to the rule made by the Council of Seligenstadt and by Pope Alexander II,[61] and permitted the celebration of more than one mass a day. Innocent III [62] recognized the right of the priest, even outside the feast of Christmas, to say more than one mass in case of necessity. An ancient custom already permitted priests to say mass twice on great feast-days when the rush was so great that many could not enter the church. St. Leo had confirmed this traditional privilege by a famous letter to the Patriarch Dioscurus of Alexandria.[63] Consequently, since

diebus solemnibus praedictis. Item, parochianus existens in parochia, si tribus diebus dominicis continuis ad missam non venerit, excommunicetur: et hoc frequenter in ecclesiis publicetur." *Nova precepta domni Petri de Colle medio* (1235). MANSI, t. XXIII, 403.

[60] "In parochialibus ecclesiis pulsentur horae canonicae et de villis cum adjacentibus et capellis attinentibus compellantur homines Dominicis diebus ad missam venire ad matricem ecclesiam." *Conc. Treviren.* (1238), c. xxx, *ib.*, 482.

[61] C. *Sufficit*, 53, D. I, *De Consecratione.*

[62] C. *Consuluisti*, 3, X, *de celebratione Missarum.*

[63] "Ut autem in omnibus observantia nostra concordet, illud quoque volumus custodiri, ut cum solemnior quaeque festivitas conventum populi numerosioris indixerit, et ea fidelium multitudo convenerit, quam recipere basilica simul una non possit, sacrificii oblatio indubitanter iteretur; ne his tantum admissis ad hanc devotionem, qui primi advenerint, videantur hi, qui postmodum confluxerint, non recepti, cum plenum pietatis atque rationis sit, ut

that period, bination, which in ordinary circumstances would have been simply permitted or tolerated, began to assume the character of an obligation whenever the people could not otherwise fulfill the precept of hearing mass. The result was that priests endured great fatigues in order to say the Sunday mass for the faithful living at a distance from the parish church; for example, Gregory of Tours tells of a priest (Severus) who, after having said mass at his residence, travelled twenty miles every Sunday in order to say another at a church which he had built in an outlying village.[64]

The Precept as Observed in the Thirteenth Century.—The ecclesiastical discipline had thus, in course of time, gradually determined the exact limits of the precept of hearing mass on Sundays. A synodal statute of Chichester and one adopted by a Council at Oxford give us the precept in a summary form. The former obliges all the faithful, except in case of sickness or necessity, to as-

quoties basilicam, in qua agitur, praesentia novae plebis impleverit, toties sacrificium subsequens offeratur." *Epist.* IX, *ad Dioscor. Alexandrin.*, c. ii. Migne, *P. L.*, *t.* LIV, 626.

[64] "In rure domus Sexciacencis, quod in ejus sessione subsistebat, ecclesiam aedificavit: exinde iterum in alia villa aedificavit templum Dei . . . cum autem dies dominicus advenisset, celebratis missis uno in loco, ad alium pergebat. Erat autem inter utrasque ecclesias spatium, quasi millium viginti. Hoc ei erat opus per singulos dominicos dies." *De Gloria Confessorum*, c. 1. *P. L.*, t. LXXI, 865.

sist at mass on Sundays and solemn feasts, lest the omission of this duty might harden their hearts.[65] The latter urges parish priests to remind their people that if they do not assist at mass in their church on Sundays and feast-days, but absent themselves habitually, they shall be punished by the bishop.[66]

These texts, together with those previously quoted, furnish us with all the elements of the precept concerning Sunday observance, to wit: the sanctification of Sunday by works of religion, assiduous and fervent prayer, hearing of the mass in its entirety from the beginning to the priest's benediction, and the disposition of going to a certain amount of trouble and even of modifying one's habits in order to be faithful to these obligations. There was further the duty of assisting at the evening office, which, however, like the offices themselves, later fell into desuetude. By a logical consequence another element was added to the obligation of Sunday observance, which gradually

[65] "Volumus quod fideles laici diebus dominicis et aliis solemnibus, saltem intersint celebrationi divinorum, nisi valetudine aut aliqua causa necessaria fuerint occupati, ne forte, propter hoc quod ab auditione divinorum cessaverint, corda eorum indurescant." *Statuta synodalia Richardi Cicestrien. episc. anno 1246, in synodo edita.* MANSI, t. XXIII, 714.

[66] "Ut parochianos suos moneant diligenter et efficaciter inducant: ut ecclesiam *suam* festis diebus, praesertim dominicis, studeant frequentare, divinum officium audituri, . . . qui si ex consuetudine se absentaverint, per locorum ordinarios puniantur." *Synod. Oxonien.* (1287), c. xxv. MANSI, t. XXIV, 812.

disappeared later on, *viz.*, the obligation of assisting at mass in one's own parish church, and its corollary,—the obligation on the part of the pastor to celebrate mass in his parish church.[67]

Dispute Between the Parish Priests and the Regular Clergy.—This last-mentioned obligation was kept strictly enough by the clergy, but that of the laity to assist at mass in their parish church fell little by little into desuetude, though not without much struggling and vigorous resistance.

As long as the prohibition of admitting outsiders to the parish mass was meant only to regulate the ordinary rights of pastors, the situation was simple and obedience easy. Every parish priest had a chance of profiting some day or other by this at times irksome measure; and the bishop possessed the necessary power to enforce it. The struggle began only when the rights of the secular clergy were threatened by the mendicant Friars. The latter were accused of trying to draw to their own chapels the people devoted to them, thus preventing the parish priests from exercising their right of inspection over these deserting parishion-

[67] On this last point we will only cite the following ordinance of a council of Benevento: "Statuimus, et ordinamus, et mandamus, quod quilibet ecclesiarum rector, sive capellanus civitatis, dioecesis, et provinciae Beneventanae ecclesiae parochiali in propria persona deserviens, teneatur singulis diebus dominicis missarum solemnia, in ecclesia cui deserviat, celebrare sub poena per nos, aut nostros suffraganeos, eidem nostro, vel eorum arbitrio infligenda." *Conc. Benevent.* (1331), c. lxii. MANSI, t. XXV, 969.

ers and giving rise to the fear that negligent individuals might easily dispense themselves from the law of Sunday observance and, by falsely affirming that they attended the Friars' chapels, exempt themselves altogether from their duty and incur the danger of falling into deplorable ignorance. Perhaps also these deserters, by the attachment and respect which they manifested for the regulars, showed too plainly a contempt for the pastor, holding him to be less perfect than the monks, and for the people faithful to their parish.

About the middle of the thirteenth century, no change had been made in the established doctrine. Hostiensis affirms, without hesitation and without giving the slightest hint of the existence of any controversy on the matter, that while the parishioners may on other days, for any cause whatever, hear mass where they will, on Sundays and feast-days they are obliged to hear it in their parochial church.[68] Soon after, the first symptoms of disquietude appear in the prescriptions of the Council of Buda (1279), which insists on the obligation of the faithful to attend mass in their own parish churches, to the exclusion of churches administered by religious orders, even though they be parish

[68] "Parochiani singulis diebus dominicis et festivis debent ad propriam ecclesiam convenire, aliis vero diebus videtur, quod possint missam ex causa audire ubi voluerint." *Summa aurea*, in tit. *De parochiis et alienis parochianis*, no. 3 (Lugduni, 1588), fol. 206, col. 2 r°.

churches. Abuses had already crept in, for the council imposes severe penalties both on the faithful who have gone to hear the dominical mass outside of their own church, and on the priests who have admitted extraneous parishioners into their churches. The former are deprived of participation in the sacraments, the latter are suspended *ipso facto* from the exercise of their orders.[69]

How did these abuses originate? The Mendicant Orders, having obtained the permission of the Pope for the faithful to hear mass in their churches, interpreted the concession in its broadest sense, according to the legal axiom: *privilegium principis amplissime interpretari debemus;* and deduced from it the conclusion that anyone fulfilled his Sunday duty who assisted at mass in their churches. The parish priests objected to this interpretation as an unjust derogation from the decrees of councils and an encroachment upon

[69] "Praecipimus, ut ecclesiarum parochiani singulis diebus dominicis . . . ad divina officia, specialiter ad *missam*, vadant ad *suas parochiales ecclesias*, ibique divina officia, prout Deus dederit, audiant diligenter: nec ipsi parochiani, relicta sua parochiali ecclesia vel contempta, ad alias ecclesias, cujuscumque sint ordinis, religionis, aut status, sive hujusmodi ecclesiae sint parochiales, sive non, ad audienda divina officia, et specialiter missam, praesumant accedere . . . Parochiani vero, contra constitutionem hujusmodi venientes, a perceptione sacramentorum; illi autem, qui contra constitutionem hujusmodi parochianos alienos receperint ad divina, vel eis administraverint ecclesiastica sacramenta, ab executione suorum ordinum se noverint suspensos." *Conc. Buden.* (1279), c. xxiii. MANSI, t. XXIV, 286.

THE FIRST COMMANDMENT

their own authority. After many vicissitudes, which it would take too long to relate,[70] the quarrel grew worse. Finally, in 1478, two centuries after the Council of Buda, Pope Sixtus IV intervened in Germany to establish peace between the parish priests on the one side, and the Friars-Preachers, Friars Minor, and Carmelites on the other. By the constitution *Vices illius* he forbade the Mendicant Friars to tell their parishioners that they were not obliged to hear mass each in his parish church on Sundays and feast-days, since this obligation was imposed upon all by law.[71]

In spite of this intervention the quarrel continued; the tendency of the public mind was to throw off parochial feudalism as well as all other feudal authority. Then again, too, other popes took the opposite position to that of Sixtus IV. In opposition to the entire previous discipline Leo X answered the reiterated applications of the Mendicant Friars with a new privilege. Henceforth,

[70] We note only the 6th chapter of the synodal statutes of Avignon (1365) which prescribes assistance at mass in one's parish church on Sundays and feastdays ("veniant ad ecclesiam suam parochialem") under penalty of a fine of one pound of wax for each offense ("et hoc sub poena unius librae cerae pro qualibet vice"). Martène, *Thesaurus Anecdotor.*, t. IV, 571.

[71] "Quod fratres mendicantes non praedicent populo, parochianos non teneri audire missam in eorum parochiis diebus festivis et dominicis, cum jure sit cautum, illis diebus parochianos teneri audire missam in eorum parochiali ecclesia, nisi forsan ex honesta causa ab ipsa ecclesia se absentarent." Extravag. *Vices illius.* 2, *de Treuga et pace*, inter *Communes*.

by papal decree, anyone who on Sundays and feast-days assisted at mass in the churches of the Mendicant Friars, provided his motive was not contempt for his pastor, satisfied the commandment of the Church and committed no sin.[72] Here the controversy ended so far as the Friars were concerned.

However the question re-arose in connection with other religious. New religious congregations came into existence, and the common law, except where modified by custom, continued to govern them. The common law obliged the faithful to hear the parish mass on Sundays wherever a contrary custom had not established itself. But the contrary custom made rapid progress; by the end of the sixteenth century it extended over the greater portion of Christendom. The moralist Azor, who does not conceal his preference for the common law, gives a positive testimony. To the usual question: "Is the common law, which obliges

[72] "Intelleximus quosdam in dubium revocare, et perinde timoratis conscientiis scrupulum injicere, si christifideles, qui dominicis et festis diebus extra ecclesias suas parochiales, missas audiunt in ecclesiis Fratrum Ordinum Mendicantium, Ecclesiae praecepto de missa audienda satisfaciant. Nos ... ambiguitatem hujusmodi penitus tollere volentes ... auctoritate apostolica praesentium notum facimus, omnes christifideles utriusque sexus, (qui non contempto proprio sacerdote parochiali), in ecclesiis Fratrum Ordinum Mendicantium, dominicis et festis diebus missas audiunt, satisfacere praecepto Ecclesiae de missa audienda, nec in aliquam labem mortalis peccati poenamve incurrere." Leo X, Bull *Intelleximus*, Nov. 13, 1517.

THE FIRST COMMANDMENT

everyone to hear mass in his parish, abrogated by custom?" he answers: "Many so affirm; as for myself I doubt it, and in certain dioceses of Flanders, Germany, and France, the pastors still oblige their parishioners to assist at the parochial mass; it is not to be doubted, however, that in many dioceses the contrary custom prevails and mass may be heard on Sundays and feast-days outside of one's parish."[73]

This custom continued to spread. Everything seemed to favor its extension. The Council of Trent, while it recommended the clergy to tell the people to attend at their parish church at least on Sundays and great feast-days,[74] did not insist on this point as strongly as former synods, and hence no very marked result was obtained. Some years later Clement VIII, by his decree of December 22, 1592, granted the Jesuits the same privileges that Leo X had accorded to the Mendicant Orders.[75]

[73] "An jus commune, quo quisque in sua parochia rem divinam audire debet, sit consuetudine abrogatum? . . . ego tamen dubito, num ita generalis consuetudo sit hactenus introducta; nam alicubi, ut in quibusdam dioecesibus Flandriae, Galliae et Germaniae, parochi contendunt, his in locis contrariam esse consuetudinem, cujus vi cogunt parochianos ad suas parochias accedere. Non tamen dubito quin in multis provinciis sit usu receptum ut extra parochiam diebus festis et dominicis res divina audiatur." *Institut. Moral.*, l. VII, c. vi, q. 5.

[74] "Moneant populum, ut frequenter ad suas parochias, saltem diebus dominicis et majoribus festis accedant." Sess. XXII, *Decretum de observandis et evitandis in celebratione missae.*

[75] "Praesenti nostro decreto sancimus, licere saecularibus,

About 1650, Busembaum said that the precept of hearing mass could be fulfilled in any place,—in the parish church, the cathedral, the churches of the regular clergy, and even in private oratories,[76] and this teaching appeared to him so well established that he considered it useless to substantiate his conclusions by erudite quotations. Pontas, who employed greater erudition in his *Cas de Conscience,* was however constrained to admit that absolution cannot be refused to a penitent who, without formal contempt for the Church or his pastor, habitually hears Sunday mass at another than the parish church of the place where he lives.[77] This point, then, is settled. Whatever may be inferred from the texts of ancient councils, the first commandment of the Church no longer obliges the faithful to assist under pain of mortal sin at the parochial mass.

Conformity or Non-Conformity of the Mass with the Rubrics.—There was less difficulty in solving another question in which not so many interests were involved. To fulfill the precept, was it neces-

Christique fidelibus universis missas diebus dominicis et festis aliis majoribus audire in ecclesiis tam Fratrum Praedicatorum, quam aliorum Mendicantium, nec non etiam collegii Societatis Jesu, juxta eorum privilegia et antiquas consuetudines, dummodo id in contemptum parochialium ecclesiarum non faciant." I quote the text according to Busembaum, *Theologia Moralis,* l. III, c. i, dub. iv.

[76] *Id.,* dub. iii, no. 10.

[77] *Dictionnaire des Cas de Conscience,* Messe, cas LIII (édit. 1730), t. II, p. 1446.

THE FIRST COMMANDMENT

sary to hear the mass of the respective day or Sunday as prescribed by the rubrics, or would any other mass serve the purpose just as well? At the present day we can hardly believe that this question could have been raised or that a pretense could have been made to impose upon the faithful assistance at a certain mass under pain of mortal sin. Yet the theory had its defenders. Angelo de Chivasso (better known as Angelo de Clavasio), unhesitatingly affirmed that one could not fulfill the precept of hearing mass by assisting at a mass other than that of the day. He based his assertion on the Chapter: *Quidam laicorum*, X, *De Celebratione Missarum*, but admitted that the majority of the people [78] were excused by ignorance. Other authorities took a milder view. Fagnani cited St. Antoninus, Silvestre, Navarrus, and Soto against Angelo de Clavasio and concluded that there was no obligation for anyone to hear the mass proper to the day, or in conformity with the office.[79] His conclusion was borne out by the few moralists who

[78] "Unde missas peculiares audiens, non satisfacit praecepto de audienda missa; quia illa quae praecipitur est missa de festo vel quae secundum officium debet dici . . . Credo tamen quod seculares propter ignorantiam excusentur: sed non celebrantes." *S.v. Missa*, n⁰ 33. *Summa Angelica de Casibus Conscientie*.

[79] "Conclude igitur neminem obligari . . . ad audiendam missam propriam illius diei seu de officio currenti, sed satisfacere praecepto Ecclesiae audiendo quamlibet missam peculiarem seu votivam." In cap. *Quidam laicorum*, X, *De Celebr. missar.*, n⁰ 2 sq.

deemed it worth while to examine the question once more in the following years. Now, for a long time, it has been a dead issue.

Assistance at Vespers.—No sooner had the theologians agreed that the dominical precept did not strictly require assistance at the parish mass, than a new theory came forth. It was especially upheld in France and Belgium, where, as we have noted, the obligation to assist at mass in one's parish church to the exclusion of all other churches and private oratories was maintained longer than elsewhere.

This new theory affirmed that the first commandment of the Church involved the obligation to assist at Vespers, at the sermon, etc. The champions of this theory were divided into two camps. The extreme right, to employ a parliamentary term, taught that the faithful must not only assist at mass, but pass the rest of the day in religious exercises, and that it would even be a mortal sin to miss Vespers. Such was the opinion of Natalis Alexander. After citing various texts of the Councils of Milan (1573), Rheims (1583), Aix (1585), and Aquilea (1596) he concludes: "Although it is not a mortal sin to miss Vespers and the sermon on Sundays and holy-days, as it is a mortal sin to miss Mass, still one is not altogether blameless if he neglects to attend, unless he is excused by a just cause. A holyday must be sanc-

THE FIRST COMMANDMENT

tified in its entirety and the afternoon as well as the forenoon must be consecrated to God. Sometimes it is even a mortal sin to miss Vespers, namely, if the time be employed in eating, playing, dancing, etc., so as to give scandal."[80]

But this opinion appeared too rigorous and rested on too uncertain a basis to secure general approval. It postulated a divine or an ecclesiastical precept which did not exist. Doubtless many councils had advised the faithful to sanctify Sundays and feast-days by assisting at Vespers in particular, but there was no proof to show that it was a strict obligation, and the only conclusion that could legitimately be drawn was that of the Conférences d'Angers: "As the forenoon of Sundays and holy-days is sanctified by hearing mass, so the afternoon is sanctified by assisting at Vespers,"[81] and that of Bishop Montazet: "It takes barely half an hour to hear mass; common sense

[80] "Quamvis ergo concioni, et Vespertinis officiis non adesse dominicis et festis diebus, lethale peccatum non sit, sicut lethale peccatum est missam integram sacris illis diebus non audire: non tamen nullum peccatum est deesse verbi Dei auditioni, cum sacra concio habetur, et vespertinis officiis, nisi justa causa quis praepeditus sit: quia solidus dies festus sanctificandus est, nec matutinis dumtaxat, sed pomeridianis horis Deo vacandum. *Et quandoque lethale peccatum est a Vesperarum officio abesse,* si quis verbi gratia commessationi, ludo, choreis, cum scandalo vacet, quo tempore celebratur." *Theolog. Dogmat. et Mor.,* l. IV, c. v, art. 6, reg. 10.

[81] *Conférences d'Angers sur les Commandements de Dieu,* April, 1714, third question.

protests that this is not sufficient for Christians, because it is not even the twentieth part of a day."[82] Billuart and Pontas unhesitatingly affirm that to miss Vespers is but a venial sin, and they base the obligation of assisting thereat on custom: "Such is the custom of the faithful, who all understand this duty, but regard it as somewhat less binding than that of assisting at mass."[83] This principle afforded a juridical basis on which the question could be discussed to good advantage. Nay, more, the fact of attributing such a foundation to this obligation made it possible to determine from the same custom the degree of culpability incurred by the negligent faithful. To-day the theologians whom we have cited would be astonished at the laxity of the solution which we base on their own principle. Fr. Marc writes that there is no obligation, in the

[82] "In missa audienda vix consumitur media hora: atqui clamat sensus communis, non satis esse ut Christiani Deum per mediam tantum horam colant, cum ne vigesimam quidem diei partem efficiat." *Compend. Institut. Theologic. quae, anno 1780, Lugduni editae sunt. De Praeceptis Ecclesiae*, t. II, c. II, p. 235.

[83] "Obligantur fideles *sub peccato veniali* adesse Vesperis diebus dominicis et festis . . . quia sic fert consuetudo populi christiani, nec est ullus, saltem in his partibus, qui aliquam obligationem audiendi Vesperas his diebus non apprehendat, minorem tamen obligatione audiendi missam, et ideo de hujusmodi omissione se accusant, distinguendo tamen inter omissionem missae et vesperarum." BILLUART, *Tract. de Religione*, dissert. 6, art. 3, § Dico 4º.— PONTAS, *Dictionnaire des Cas de Conscience*, vº DIMANCHE, cas II.

THE FIRST COMMANDMENT

strict sense, of assisting at Vespers, though the faithful should be urgently exhorted to come.[84] Lehmkuhl is of the same opinion [85] and it is the common teaching of theologians.

Summary.—We have shown how the precept of assisting at the Sunday mass came to be adopted in its present form. Moralists have minutely discussed all the circumstances in which a Christian can find himself regarding this precept, but that is a question of casuistry which leaves the precept itself unchanged. We have seen that the precept was imposed little by little, beginning in the primitive Church, by the force of circumstances and without a juridical sanction; how the Council of Elvira threatened those who missed mass on three consecutive Sundays with excommunication; how later on efforts were made to enforce assistance at the entire mass by every Christian, even the bondmen, and, as one council says, the *idiotae;* how the bishop exercised the right of punishing delinquents and the secular power gave him support. At the time when the feudal power reigned supreme, the parish too was necessarily a feudal

[84] "Nulla est obligatio, per se et directe urgens, assistendi Vesperis; ita communiter theologi.—Verumtamen, multum fideles adhortandi sunt ut assistant." *Institut. Morales,* p. II, sect. II, tract. III, c. I, nº 657.

[85] "Praeter assistentiam missae nihil aliud proprie praecipitur, ita ut neque devotionis pomeridionalis, neque concionis assistentia ex se obligatoria sit." *Theolog. Moral. Specialis,* p. I, c. iv, art. 2, § 2, t. I, no. 556.

center: mass had to be heard at the parochial church under pain of not fulfilling the precept; for a time it even looked as if the rubrics were to be raised to the dignity of a civil law binding all, the learned as well as the ignorant. However, circumstances and custom gradually returned to what had constituted the essence of the commandment from the beginning, *viz.* assistance at an entire mass on Sunday.

CHAPTER III

THE FIRST COMMANDMENT (CONCLUDED)

B. ABSTENTION FROM SERVILE WORK

The First Four Centuries.—Under the Mosaic Law, the sanctification of the Sabbath essentially comprised abstention from all labor,[1] and we know to what details of casuistry the legal prescriptions gave rise. These prescriptions were observed at least in substance by the disciples of Jesus during the life-time of the Master and in the first years after His death.[2] Was the obligation simply transferred to Sunday when this day took the place of the Jewish Sabbath? We do not know. We may suppose, however, that a certain Sunday rest imposed itself probably without any legislation. Partial abstention from work was a necessity during the forenoon of Sunday when that day was consecrated (as it was in the time of Pliny) to the celebration of the holy mysteries. Besides, the Christian converts from Judaism would surely have felt as if they were showing ir-

[1] *Exod.*, xx, 10; xvi, 22-30; xxxv, 3; *Num.*, xv, 32; *Jerem.*, xvii, 21, etc.
[2] *Acts*, i, 12.

reverence toward Christ had they neglected to consecrate Sunday to His service as completely as their Jewish brethren consecrated the Sabbath to Jehovah; whilst the converts from paganism, who were accustomed to see certain feast-days observed by a cessation of manual labor,[3] must have found it quite natural that a like practice was observed by the Christians.

In Tertullian's time Sunday-rest seems to have been a well-established custom, for this famous apologist, without mentioning any law, says in many passages of his writings: We consecrate Sunday to the joy of rest.[4]

When peace was restored to the Church by Constantine, this custom had implanted itself so deeply in the public conscience, that the emperors had to take account of it in their secular legislation. In 321 a decree of Constantine, addressed to Elpidius, forbade all mechanical work and every kind of legal procedure on Sunday. However, tilling fields was allowed; for man on this point depended too much on weather conditions not to take advantage of the propitious days when they came. Such are the motives indicated by the

[3] "Affirmabant sacerdotes pollui ferias, si indictis conceptisque opus aliquod fieret. Praeterea regem sacrorum flaminesque non licebat videre feriis opus fieri: ideo per praeconem denuntiabatur, ne quid tale ageretur; et praecepti negligens multabatur." Macrob., *Saturnal.*, l. I, c. xvi.

[4] *Ad Nation.* I, 13; *Apolog.*, 16.

THE FIRST COMMANDMENT (CONCLUDED)

Emperor in his edict: "Let all, judges, villagers, and artisans of every trade, rest on Sunday; but the farmers may continue their work, as it often happens that there are no other days when sowing can be done under favorable conditions and the harvests depend largely on the weather."[5] It has been maintained that as this prohibition lacked penal sanction, it was not observed in practice,[6] and consequently was of no avail. The logic of this argument is questionable; supposing that the law was not observed, that would not prove that it had no binding force; and, besides, how are you going to prove that it was not observed? It is true that a subsequent constitution promulgated by Valentinian, Theodosius, and Arcadius makes no mention of Sunday beyond saying that judicial proceedings on that day are prohibited; but the constitution in question was professedly directed against these transactions only, as is indicated by the opening words: "Omnes dies jubemus esse juridicos," etc.[7]

[5] "Omnes judices urbanaeque plebes, et cunctarum artium officia venerabili die solis quiescant: ruri tamen positi agrorum culturae libere libenterque inserviant: quoniam frequenter evenit ut non aptius alio die frumenta sulcis, aut vineae scrobibus mandentur, ne occasione momenti pereat commoditas coelesti provisione concessa." *Cod. Justinian.*, l. II, tit. XII, *De feriis*, lex 3a.—Cf. Euseb., *Vita Constantini*, l. IV, c. xviii; Sozom., I, c. viii.

[6] E. Löning, *Geschichte des deutschen Kirchenrechts*, t. II, c. v, p. 454.

[7] *Cod. Justinian.*, l. II, tit. XII, lex 7a.

We must confess, however, that the obligation of abstaining from labor on Sunday was not as rigorous as it became later on. The Council of Laodicea, which mentions it, does so in extremely moderate terms; it prohibits cessation from work on Saturday, but enjoins rest on Sunday only so far as possible: "Christians must not imitate the Jews and be idle on the Sabbath, but they must work on that day; let them honor the day of the Lord in Christian fashion by abstaining *as much as possible* from work on that day."[8]

Two centuries later, in the poor Nestorian communities of Mesopotamia, very little more was required; the councils, after having mentioned the good example of "some faithful" who "refrain from work or travel on Sunday until the church service is ended," left it to the bishops to issue practical decisions befitting the case of the pearl-divers who often had to work on Sunday: "so that they (the divers) would, if possible, neither sin nor suffer loss."[9]

---

[8] "Ὅτι οὐ δεῖ Χριστιανοὺς ἰουδαΐζειν καὶ ἐν τῷ σαββάτῳ σχολάζειν, ἀλλὰ ἐργάζεσθαι αὐτούς ἐν τῇ αὐτῇ ἡμέρα· τὴν δὲ κυριακὴν προτιμῶντας, εἴγε δύναιντο σχολάζειν ὡς χριστιανοί." C. xxix. Bruns, *Canones Apost. et Concilior.*, t. I, 76.

[9] Synod of Jesuyahb I (585), c. xix, *Synodicon Orientale*, published by J. B. Chabot, Paris, 1902, p. 447-448. The Syriac *Didascalia* (fourth century?), ch. xiii, express themselves on this subject, though the obligation they impose seems rather vague. The author, in order to put the lukewarm Christians to shame, speaks of the Jews, "who on one day out of six do not work." He adds: "If a man, under pretext of secular employment, neglects

THE FIRST COMMANDMENT (CONCLUDED)

Elsewhere, however, the discipline was more severe. We have quoted above a passage from the *Apostolic Constitutions* in which the legislation on the dominical precept is attributed to the Apostles Peter and Paul,[10] and pointed out that the beneficiaries of the weekly rest were the slaves; no mention being made of other members of the Church nor of the labor of any but slaves.

It was natural that the prescription should be extended so as to forbid every occupation of a nature to prevent assistance at divine worship, whatever may have been the social state of those who worked. This was in conformity with the motives assigned by the *Constitutions* "for the sake of the teaching of religion." Hence it is that the texts do not mention the work of slaves until a much later date, in Gaul, and then they deal with the bondmen who were kept by their masters on estates far removed from any church.

The Fifth and Sixth Centuries.—During the fifth century, as a consequence of the barbarian invasions, a great social revolution took place and the

---

his duties, let him know that the arts of the faithful are not considered absolutely necessary works, for their true work is the fear of God." *Canoniste Contemporain*, t. XXIV, 544. It would seem, therefore, that for the faithful, for whom the *Didascalia* was intended, there was no other obligation of abstaining from work on Sunday but the one consequent on that of assisting at Mass.

[10] *Constit. Apost.*, l. VIII, c. xxxiii, *P. G.*, t. I, 1133.

former landlords were forced to take up tilling the soil themselves. Shortly afterwards a new element was introduced into the theory of Sunday-rest, *viz.* the rigorous application to the first day of the week of the prescriptions of the Mosaic Law concerning the Sabbath. St. Caesarius of Arles, whose influence in Gaul at the beginning of the sixth century is well known, when speaking of the dominical obligations, always cites the biblical texts concerning the Sabbath. His leading idea is: If the Jews are so scrupulous in the observance of the Sabbath, should not Christians be even more so in regard to Sunday? [11]

This is not merely his own theory, but he says it is the teaching of the holy doctors, who have bestowed upon Sunday all the honors formerly attached to the Jewish Sabbath; [12] and he completes the assimilation by reckoning the day from night to night, thus making the obligation to rest begin with Saturday night and continue till Sunday night.[13]

[11] "Omni die dominico ad ecclesiam convenite. Si enim infelices Judaei tanta devotione celebrant sabbatum, ut in eo nulla opera terrena exerceant; quanto magis Christiani, in die dominico soli Deo vacare, et pro animae suae salute debent ad ecclesiam convenire." *Serm.*, 265, inter Oper. s. Augustini. Migne, *P. L.*, t. XXXIX, 2238.

[12] "Sancti doctores Ecclesiae decreverunt omnem gloriam judaici sabbatismi in illam [diem dominicam] transferre." *Serm.*, 280; *ib.*, 2274.

[13] "Observemus ergo diem dominicam, fratres, et sanctificemus

THE FIRST COMMANDMENT (CONCLUDED)   69

This teaching was repeated by the priests who preached and even exaggerated St. Caesarius' sermons [14] and succeeded at times in misleading the consciences of the faithful to such an extent that it became necessary to react against the Judaic rigor with which many observed the dominical rest. The Third Council of Orleans deemed it necessary to correct these false views, and declared: "People believe that it is unlawful to travel with horses, oxen, or any kind of vehicle on Sunday; to prepare food, or to devote to home and person the care which they require; all of which is more Judaic than Christian; we therefore decree that it is lawful to do whatever was formerly permitted on Sunday. However, all agricultural labor, such as ploughing, tilling vines, mowing, harvesting, pruning, and felling trees must be omitted, and should anyone be found doing these forbidden

illam *sicut antiquis praeceptum est de sabbato*, dicente Legislatore: *a vespere usque ad vesperam celebrabitis sabbata vestra* (*Levit.*, xxiii, 32) . . . a vespera diei sabbati usque ad vesperam diei dominici sequestrati a rurali opere et ab omni negotio, soli divino cultui vacemus. Sic quoque sanctificamus rite sabbatum Domini, dicente Domino: *omne opus non facietis in eo.*" (*Ib.*, 36.) Cf. on the same point the *Didascalia* of Our Lord, according to the Greek text, which is later than the Syriac *Didascalia* (seventh to tenth century), published and translated by Fr. Nau, ch. vi: "Worthy is the man who observes the holy Sunday, beginning at the night hour of Saturday. . . . Woe to those who work on Sunday." *Revue de l'Orient Chrétien*, 1907, p. 245.

[14] Cf. *Vita Caesarii*, l. I, c. v, no. 42; Migne, *P. L.*, t. LXVII, 1021.

things, it rests with the priest alone to correct and chastise him."[15]

This synodal decision was of very great importance, inasmuch as it furnished the basis for all future decrees.[16] Soon, too, the secular power (*districtio laici*) intervened to enforce the penalty inflicted by the priest (*castigatio sacerdotalis*). This became a necessity owing to the too great success with which the first part of the decree had met. It is against the tendency to work on Sunday that the later councils had to struggle. The Council of Mâcon, A. D. 585, emphatically protests against the profanation of Sunday by manual labor and judicial proceedings. It pictures the Christian populace as contemning the Sunday by working on it as on any other day, and directs each bishop to remonstrate with his people and give them warning that anyone who disobeys, exposes

[15] "Quia persuasum est populus die dominico agi cum caballis, aut bubus, et vehiculis itinera non debere, neque ullam rem ad victum praeparare, vel ad nitorem domus vel hominis pertenentem ullatenus exercere (quae res ad judaicam magis quam ad christeanam observantiam pertinere probatur), id statuimus, ut die dominico, quod ante fieri licuit, liceat. De opere tamen rurali, id est arata vel vinea, vel sectione, messione, excussione, exarte vel sepe, censuimus abstenendum, quo facilius ad ecclesiam venientes orationis gratiae vacent. Quod si inventus fuerit quis in operibus supra scriptis, quae interdicta sunt, exercere, qualiter emendari debeat, non in laici districtione sed in sacerdotis castigatione consistat." *Conc. Aurelian.* (538), c. xxx. Maassen, p. 82.

[16] Cf. in particular *Conc. Vernense* (755), c. xiv. Capitularia (Boretius), t. I, p. 36, which merely reprints the text of Orleans.

THE FIRST COMMANDMENT (CONCLUDED) 71

himself to the chastisement of God. Then, addressing the people themselves, the Council says: "Observe Sunday, the day on which we have been redeemed from all our sins. Let no one among you engage in law suits, let no one place himself in the necessity of working. It is the day on which our hands should be raised to God." Then, passing on to the sanctions, it adds: "If you do not observe these prescriptions, the lawyer shall lose his case, the peasant or bondman shall receive blows, the cleric or monk shall be separated from his brethren for six months." [17] To render the decisions of the Council more efficacious, the secular power intervened and forbade all judicial pro-

[17] "Videmus populum christianum temerario more die dominica contemtui tradere et sicut in privatis diebus operibus continuis indulgere. Propterea per hanc sinodalen nostram epistolam decernimus, ut unusquisque nostrum in sacrosanctis ecclesiis admoneat sibi subditam plebem. ... Custodite diem dominicam, quae nos denuo peperit et a peccatis omnibus liberavit. Nullus vestrum litium fomitibus vacet, nullus ex vobis causarum actionis exerceat, nemo sibi talem necessitatem exibeat, quae jugum cervicibus juvencorum imponere cogat. ... Si quis vestrum proximam habet ecclesiam, properet ad eandem et ibi Dominico die semetipsum precibus lacrymisque afficiat. Sint oculi manusque vestrae toto illo die ad Deum expanse. ... Si quis itaque vestrum hanc salubrem exortationem parvi penderit aut contemtui tradiderit, sciat se pro qualitatis merito principaliter a Deo punire et deinceps sacerdotali quoque irae implacabiliter subjacere; si causedecus fuerit, irreparabiliter causam amittat; si rusticus aut servus, gravioribus fustium ictibus verberabitur; si clericus aut monachus, mensibus sex a consortio suspendetur fratrum." *Conc. Matiscon.* (585), c. i. Maassen, p. 165.

cedure and all corporal works excepting those necessary for the preparation of food.[18]

Sanctions Imposed by Secular Legislation.— The decree of the Council of Mâcon and that of King Guntram inaugurated a new system of repression. Up to this time the law of dominical rest was considered to have a sufficient sanction in the more or less informal chastisement by the priest and in the divine punishments, which, if the tales of the time are to be believed, were not infrequent. The writings of Gregory of Tours are full of such tales, which must have made his contemporaries tremble with fear. Now the fire of Heaven consumes the profaners,[19] now the unfortunate peasants with suddenly contracted hands grasp the tools which they tried to use on Sunday,[20] or run their nails into the palm of their hands.[21] A peasant who tried to bring in his hay on Sunday, so as to save it from a threatening rainstorm, was afflicted in his feet and eyes,[22] and even excessive attention to toilet was punished, as in the case of a young coquette, the teeth of whose comb, in arranging her hair, entered the palm

[18] *Edictum Guntramni,* "De celebrando die dominico." Capitularia (Boretius) t. I, p. 10.

[19] *Histor. Francor.,* X, 30. Migne, *P. L.,* t. LXXI, 562.

[20] *De miraculis S. Juliani,* c. xi, *ib.* 808; *De miraculis S. Martini,* l. III, c. iii, vii, xxix, lv, etc.

[21] *De miraculis S. Martini,* l. II, c. xl.

[22] *Ib.,* l. IV, c. xlv.

THE FIRST COMMANDMENT (CONCLUDED)

of her hand, causing her excruciating pain.[23]

However, as these divine punishments became less frequent, there were found at times men who were sceptical, and for such, if they belonged to the lower classes, were devised corporal punishments, while others had to pay pecuniary fines. Thus the Council of Narbonne, 589, confirmed by King Recared, decided that for all work done on Sunday without necessity, the guilty person, whether he be Goth, Roman, Syrian, Greek or Jew, should pay a fine of six sous if a free man, and if a bondman, receive a hundred blows with a whip.[24] In Gaul, in the kingdom of Childebert, the law was just as strict: the guilty Frank had to pay fifteen sous and the Roman seven and a half sous, while the bondman could choose between receiving blows or paying a fine of three sous.[25]

[23] "Puella quaedam, die dominico cum suum caput componeret, pectine apprehenso, credo ob injuriam diei sancti, in manibus adhaesit, ita ut affixi dentes tam in digitis quam in palmis magnum ei dolorem inferrent." *Vitae Patrum*, c. viii, *ib.*, 1040. Cf. the malediction of the Greek *Didascalia:* "Woe to the women who have adorned their hair on the day of the Holy Sunday." C. xvii. *Rev. de l'Orient Chrétien*, 1907, p. 249.

[24] "Ut omnis homo tam ingenuus quam servus, Gothus, Romanus, Syrus, Graecus, vel Judaeus, die dominico nullam operam faciant, nec boves jungantur, excepto si immutandi necessitas incubuerit: quod si quisque praesumpserit facere, si ingenuus est, det comiti civitatis solidos sex, si servus, centum flagella suscipiat." *Conc. Narbon.*, c. iv, Bruns, t. II, 60.

[25] "De die dominico similiter placuit observare, ut si quicumque ingenuus, excepto quod ad coquendum vel ad manducandum pertinet, alia opera in die dominico facere praesumpserit, si

The most complete, practical, and detailed secular decisions on this subject are those attributed to King Dagobert I. They contain the expression *servile works,* which we have not found so far, and which designates, not the work of bondman or slave, or the subjective quality of the work, but rather its objective aspect of corporal and hard labor. The first of these decisions is as follows: "Let no one dare to do servile works on Sunday, for the law forbids it and the Bible is opposed to it. If any bondman is found doing them, let him be soundly beaten; if a free man, let him be reprimanded three times. If after three reprimands he is found once more in fault, he shall lose a third of his possessions. If then he does not reform and is again found dishonoring the Sunday by performing servile works, he shall be led before the Count, and his offense being juridically proved, the Duke shall make him a bondman: [26] since he did

Salicus fuerit, solidos quindecim componat; si Romanus, septem et dimidium solidi. Servus vero aut tres solidos reddat, aut de dorsum suum componat." *Childeberti II decretio,* c. xiv. Capitularia (Boretius), t. I, 17.

[26] "Die dominico nemo *opera servilia* praesumat facere: quia hoc lex prohibuit, et sacra scriptura in omnibus testatur. Si quis servus in hoc vicio inventus fuerit, vapuletur fustibus; liber autem corripiatur usque ad tertium. Si autem post terciam correpcionem in hoc vicio inventus fuerit et Deo vacare die dominico neglexerit, et opera servilem fecerit, tunc terciam partem de hereditatem sua perdat. Si autem super haec inventus fuerit ut die dominico honore non impendat, et opera servilem fecerit, tunc coactus et probatus coram comite, ubi Dux tunc ordinaverit, in servicio tra-

THE FIRST COMMANDMENT (CONCLUDED)

not wish to serve God, he shall remain a bondman forever."

The second is still more severe, not to say brutal: "If anyone performs any servile work on Sunday, he shall be reprimanded twice, and if he does not amend, but continues to work on Sunday, and if he be a free man who hitches his oxen to his cart and goes on a journey, he shall lose the ox on the right side; if he mows, or gathers in the harvest, or performs any other servile work on Sunday, he shall be reprimanded twice, and if he does not amend, and again continues to work on Sunday, one-third of his goods shall be taken from him; in case of a further relapse, he shall lose his liberty, because he did not want to be free on the holy day. If he be a bondman, he shall be beaten; if he repeat the offense, he shall lose his right hand, for those acts which excite the anger of God and draw calamities and miseries upon us, must be forbidden. Journeys on Sunday are also forbidden, be they in chariots or by boat: one should wait till Monday before resuming his journey; if he disobey, he shall be fined twelve sous, and if he repeat the offense, the penalties stated above shall be inflicted." [27]

datur; et qui noluit Deo vacare, in sempiternum servus permaneat." *Lex Alamannorum*, l. I, c. xxxviii. PERTZ, *Legum*, t. III, 57.

[27] "Si quis die dominico *operam servilem* fecerit: liber homo, si bovem junxerit, et cum carro ambulaverit, dextrum bovem

Outside the Frankish States, and in countries which had reached an equal degree of civilization, the same ideas were expressed in analogous decisions, with, however, attenuations in favor of the slave or bondman who had been forced to work by a wicked master. In such cases, in England at least, it was the master who paid the fine, the amount of which varied between thirty and eighty sous. If the slave or bondman works of his own initiative, he is beaten unless he pays a compensating fine. If he be a free man, the sanction varies, according to locality, between the loss of liberty and a heavy fine, one-half of which is sometimes given to the informer; if the guilty person

perdat. Si autem secaverit fenum, vel collegerit, aut messem secaverit aut collegerit, vel aliquid opus servile fecerit die dominico, corripiatur semel vel bis, et si non emendaverit, rumpatur dorso ejus quinquaginta percussiones. Et si iterum praesumpserit operare die dominico auferatur de rebus ejus tertiam partem. Et si nec cessaverit, tunc perdat libertatem suam, et sit servus, qui noluit in die sancto esse liber. Servus autem pro tale crimine vapuletur. Et si non emendaverit, manum dextram perdat. Quia talis causa vetanda est quae Deum ad iracundiam provocat, et exinde flagellamur in frugibus, et penuria patimur. Et hoc vetandum est in die dominico et si quis in itinere positus cum carra, vel cum nave, pauset die dominico usque in secunda feria. Et si noluerit custodire praeceptum Domini, quia Dominus dixit: *Nullum opus servile facias in die sancto, neque tu, neque servus tuus, neque ancilla tua, neque bos tuus, neque asinus tuus, neque ullus subjectorum tuorum*. Et qui hoc in itinere vel ubicumque observare neglexerit, cum duodecim solidis condemnetur; et si frequens hoc fecerit superiora sententia subjaceat." *Lex Bajuwariorum. Monumenta Germaniae*, PERTZ, *Legum*, t. III, p. 335-336.

THE FIRST COMMANDMENT (CONCLUDED)

be a priest, his fine is double that of others.[28] The same regulations were enforced in Hungary under the ecclesiastical constitutions of St. Stephen. But here it was the priest or Count who had to enforce the dominical rest: anyone detected working on Sunday was driven from his work; if he used an ox at his work, it was taken from him and killed, and given to the inhabitants of the village to eat; if he used horses, one horse was taken from him, though he could redeem it by giving an ox which was butchered and distributed as above; and all the instruments he made use of were taken from him, together with his clothes, which however he could purchase back by submitting to a whipping.[29]

[28] "Si servus homo die dominica operatur jussu domini sui, liber sit, et dominus debeat xxx solidos pro poena. Si autem servus absque ejus scitu operetur, verberibus caedatur, vel cutis pretium solvat. Si autem liber eo die operetur absque domini jusso, perdat libertatem suam, vel sexaginta solidos; et sacerdos duplum debeat." *Leges ecclesiasticae Inae regis Occiduorum Saxonum*, c. III. Mansi, t. XII, 57. Cf. the decisions of the Council of Berkhampsteadt, c. x: "Si servus ex mandato Domini opus servile praestiterit a vespera diei solis post occasum ejus usque ad occasum vesperae diei lunae (note that the day begins at night), octoginta solidos illud dominus compenset." C. xi: "Si servus hoc faciat proprio motu, eo die sex [solidos] ipse domino pendat aut cutem suam." C. xii: "Si liber homo id fecerit tempore vetito, sit reus collistrigii, et qui eum detulit, habeat mulctae et aestimationis capitis dimidium." Bruns, t. II, 312. Cf. *Leges presbyteror. Northumbrien.*, c. lv, lvi. Mansi, t. XIX, 69; *Leges ecclesiasticae Canuti regis*, c. xiv, *ib.* 562.

[29] "Si quis presbyter, vel comes, sive aliqua alia persona fidelis die dominica invenerit quemlibet laborantem, abigatur: si vero

In spite of these rather barbarous penalties, the observance of the dominical rest was never perfect. The Council of Chalon (639–654) found it necessary to recall the discipline of the Council of Orleans of 538.[30] On the other hand the *Penitentials* show that the Church did not restrict herself to the prescriptions of the civil law, that custom aimed not only at servile works, but at others of a less material character, and lastly that the real fault was punished in the forum of conscience by a penance of seven days.[31]

Prohibition of Court Sessions and Markets on Sunday.—From the eighth century onward, both the civil and ecclesiastical laws emphasize abstention from court sessions and markets as an im-

cum bobus, tollatur sibi bos, et civibus ad manducandum detur: si autem cum equis, tollatur equus, quem dominus bove redimat, si velit; et idem bos manducetur, ut dictum est. Si quis aliis instrumentis, tollantur instrumenta, et vestimenta, quae, si velit, cum cute redimat." *Constitutiones ecclesiasticae sub S. Stephano rege Hungar. circa ann. 1016*, c. vi. Mansi, t. XIX, 370. Cf. *Conc. Szabolchen.* (1092), c. xii. Mansi, t. XX, 765.

[30] *Conc. Cabilonen.*, c. xviii. Maassen, p. 212.

[31] "Die dominico Graeci et Romani navigant, equitant, panem non faciunt, nec in curru ambulant, nisi ad ecclesiam tantum, nec balneant. Graeci non scribunt in publico, tamen pro necessitate seorsum in domo scribunt. Qui operantur die dominica, eos Graeci prima vice arguunt, et secunda tollunt aliquid ab eis, tertia vice tertiam partem de rebus tollunt, aut vapulant, vel VII dies poeniteant. Lavacrum capitis potest esse in dominica, et in lixivio pedes lavare licet." *Poenitentiale Cummeani*, c. xii, n° 3, 4, 5, 6. Schmitz, *Die Bussbücher und die Bussdisciplin der Kirche*, t. I, p. 640. Cf. *Poenitentiale Theodori*, I, xi, 1; II, viii, 1, 2, 8, *ib.*, p. 533, 543, 544.

portant feature of Sunday observance. True, the emperors Constantine, Valentinian and Theodosius had already prohibited judicial transactions on Sunday, and the Council of Mâcon (A. D. 585) had mentioned law-suits among the works forbidden on that day; but the enactments concerning manual labor had held the first place. From now on, however, the decrees concerning law-suits and the holding of markets claim our attention, for it is to these operations that the legislators for many centuries directed their efforts. And, in spite of prohibitions and penalties, they never succeeded in obtaining full obedience, and this finally led to that laxity which developed into our present conditions. There were peculiar difficulties to overcome. Since the Christian legislation regarding Sunday labor was founded, at least in part, on the Mosaic Law, it might seem that its text was to be strictly adhered to; but the Old Law was not meant to regulate public gatherings. On the other hand, how could men who met once a week, and whose work absorbed the other days of the week, be prevented from taking advantage of their weekly gatherings to treat on that day questions of interest? How was it possible to forbid the mutual exchange of ordinary commodities between the tenants of farms widely separated? In how far was such exchange opposed to the precept of hearing Mass and of abstaining from work? This was undoubtedly the people's way of looking at it, and they struggled against the prohibitions and were often victorious in opposing them.

At first markets were probably forbidden because there could be no supply of the necessary goods without previous labor, without transportation and display of merchandise.

As to the holding of court sessions, it was at first forbidden to hold hearings where a capital crime or a grave offense was to be judged. Such is the decision of the Synod of Compiègne, which was reaffirmed in the decree of Burchard, and renewed by the Council of Mayence, A. D. 813;[32] other decrees allow court proceedings to establish the peace,[33] and in a Carolingian capitulary it is noted that the holding of court is permitted in case of urgent necessity, or to take measures to repulse an enemy.[34] The Council of Rheims, A. D. 813, mentions public donations as servile works prohibited on Sunday.[35] In England the

[32] "Omnes dies dominicos cum omni veneratione observare decrevimus et a servili opere abstinere, et ut mercatus in eis minime sit nec placitum, ubi aliquis ad mortem vel ad poenam judicetur." *Conc. Moguntin.*, c. xxxvii. *Mon. German., Concilia*, t. II, 270.

[33] Burchard, *Decretorum*, lib. II, c. lxxxi. Migne, *P. L.*, t. CXL, 640 and c. lxxxv, col. 641.

[34] "Ut in dominicis diebus conventus et placita publica non faciant, nisi forte pro magna necessitate, aut hostilitate cogente." *Capitulatio de partibus Saxoniae*, c. xvii, Boretius, t. I, p. 69.

[35] "Ut diebus dominicis secundum Domini praeceptum nulla opera servilia quilibet perficiat nec ad placita conveniat *nec etiam*

holding of markets was punished by a heavy fine; [36] the same in Hungary.[37]

In brief, action was taken everywhere with a view of prohibiting whatever was apt to prevent or diminish the sanctification of the Lord's Day.[38]

From the Ninth to the Twelfth Century.—Every effort thus far had obtained only temporary results. The attempts had to be incessantly renewed, and the same energy was always applied, so convinced were all that, without Sunday observance, no Christian life was possible. At his annual or bi-annual synod as well as in his parochial visitations the bishop asks: Is there anyone in the parish who works on Sunday? [39] Pope Nicholas I reminds the Bulgarians that they must ab-

donationes in publico facere praesumat neque mercata exerceat." *Conc. Remen.* (813), c. xxxv. *Monument. German., Concilia*, t. II, p. 256. Cf. *Capitula Herardi Turonen.*, c. ii. Mansi, t. XVI (appendix), 677.

[36] "Si quis die dominica mercari praesumat, perdat mercatum et duodecim oras apud Danos, et triginta solidos apud Anglos." *Leges ecclesiasticae Eduardi senioris reg. Anglor.*, c. vii. Mansi t. XVIII, 238. Cf. *Leges presbyteror. Northumbr.*, c. lv. Mansi, t. XIX, 69.

[37] *Conc. Szabolchen.*, c. xvi. Mansi, t. XX, 770.

[38] Cf. *Conc. Arelaten.* (813), c. xvi: "Ne in dominicis diebus mercata neque causationes disceptationesque exerceantur et penitus a rurali et servili opere cessetur, his solummodo peractis, quae ad Dei cultum et servitium pertinere noscuntur." *Monum. Germ., Concilia*, t. II, 252; *Conc. Turonen.* (813), c. xl, *ib.*, 292; *Conc. Roman.* (853), c. xxx. Mansi, t. XIV, 1007.

[39] "Est aliquis qui in die dominico vel in praecipuis festivitatibus quidquam operis faciat?" Regino, *De ecclesiasticis disciplinis*, l. II, c. v, no. 57. Migne, *P. L.*, t. CXXXII, 285.

stain from all work on Sunday.⁴⁰ The chastisements which the anger of heaven inflicts upon those who profane the Sunday are recalled, for example a thunderbolt falling upon men who worked on that day.⁴¹ An attempt was made to substitute, in place of the sanctions given by the civil laws, and undoubtedly unapplied because of their severity, purely penitential sanctions which are themselves gradually mitigated, *e.g.* where the Penitential of Regino imposes seven days of penance,⁴² that of Burchard imposes only three.⁴³

However, the bishops were not discouraged. To the works formerly forbidden they added others, *v.g.*, hunting, and along with the rather masculine works that we know of, they enumerate feminine occupations as likewise prohibited on Sunday. The *Capitula* of Rodulf of Bourges furnish us with the following complete exposition of the dominical discipline: On that day outside the labor necessary for the preparation of food, no one should take up any occupation whatsoever but all should

---

⁴⁰ "Dominico die a labore terreno cessandum est." *Ad consulta Bulgaror.* Mansi, t. XV, 406.

⁴¹ "Quorum relatu didicimus quosdam in hac die ruralia opera exercentes fulmine interemptos." *Concil. Parisien.* (829), l. I, c. L. Mansi, t. XIV, 568.

⁴² "Operatus es aliquid in dominica die, *septem dies* poeniteas." *De ecclesiast. discip.*, l. I, c. ccc. Migne, *P. L.*, t. CXXXII, 251.

⁴³ "Operatus es aliquid in dominica die? Si fecisti, *tres dies* in pane et aqua poenitere debes." *Decretor.*, l. XIX, c. v. Migne, *P. L.*, t. CXL, 976.

THE FIRST COMMANDMENT (CONCLUDED)

devote their time to assistance at mass and prayer. Servile and agricultural works must be abstained from, such as tilling, plowing, harvesting, mowing, clearing shrubbery, felling trees, cutting stone, building, dressing a garden, preparing the ground, holding court sessions, and hunting, unless such work be necessary to earn a living or to protect oneself against the cold. Women must abstain from weaving, knitting, sewing, washing, beating flax, carding wool, and shearing sheep.[44]

It was realized, however, that it was becoming quite impossible to maintain the ancient prohibitions in all their vigor. Little by little they became modified according to times and countries. The *Lex Bajuvariorum,* as we know, had ordered travellers both on land and sea to discontinue their voyage on Sunday, under pain of a pecuniary fine; in the tenth century a collection of ecclesiastical laws permits, in certain cases which are not specified, the starting of a journey on Sunday, on con-

[44] "Tanta ergo hujus diei [dominicae] debet esse observantia ut praeter orationes et missarun solemnia, et ea quae ad vescendum pertinent, nihil aliud fiat. Videlicet ut *nec opera servilia* in eo agantur, nec viri *ruralia exerceant,* nec vineas colant, nec campos arent, nec messem metant, nec foenum secent, nec sepem ponant, nec silvas stirpent, nec arbores caedant, nec in petris laborent, nec domos construant, nec hortum faciant, nec terram moveant, nec ad placita conveniant, nec *venationes exerceant,* nisi tantum cibi vel frigoris necessitate. Item *feminae* opera textrilia non faciant, nec vestimenta capulent, nec consuant, nec vestimenta lavent, nec liniant nec linum battant nec lanam carpere praesumant, nec barbices tondcant." *Capit. Rodulfi Bitur.,* c. xxvi. Mansi, t. XIV, 955.

dition that neither assistance at Mass nor the ordinary prayers be omitted.[45]

Another text, attributed by Regino and Burchard to a council held "apud S. Medardum, praesente Carolo imperatore," permits certain trucking to be done on Sunday, for war, for food and for husbandry services for the prince, and even, if necessary, burying the dead;[46] whereas a Council of Bourges, in the eleventh century, repeating the ancient prohibitions, forbids this kind of work on Sunday except where the love of God, the fear of an enemy, or a great necessity require it to be done.[47] In Rome, some years later, Pope Nicholas II shows himself more liberal, for he allows the annual fair to be held on Sunday.[48] In Spain, on

[45] "Si accidat ut proficisci debeat [homo]; tunc potest sive equitare, sive navigare, sive eam viam aggredi, quae ad iter illius conducit, ea conditione ut missam suam et preces suas non negligat." *Liber legum ecclesiasticarum,* c. xxiv. Mansi, t. XIX, 186.

[46] "Tria carraria opera licet fieri in dominica die, id est hostilia carra, victualia, vel angaria, et si forte necesse sit, corpus cujuslibet duci ad sepulcrum." Regino, *op. cit.,* l. I, c. ccclxxii. Migne, *P. L.,* t. CXXXII, 264; Burchard., *op. cit.,* l. II, c. lxxxii. *P. L.,* t. CXL, 641.

[47] "Ut in die dominica vectigalia non fiant, quod carregium vel sagmegium dicitur, nisi amore Dei, vel timore hostium, vel propter magnam necessitatem." *Conc. Bituricen.* (1031). c. xv. Mansi, t. XIX, 505.

[48] "Ut dominicis diebus mercata non fiant, exceptis annuis feriis, et quae ad victum pertinent." *Decretum Nicolai II Papae,* c. x. Mansi, *ib.,* 876.

THE FIRST COMMANDMENT (CONCLUDED)

the contrary, voyages are again forbidden, unless they be for the purpose of ending a pilgrimage, burying the dead, visiting the sick or helping the king against Saracen invasions.[49]

We must also mention another prohibition of a very particular kind, on which much emphasis was laid for two or three centuries, and which later on was almost completely dropped; *viz.* that of marital cohabitation. This prohibition was based on the idea, dear to the Church even before the time of St. Augustine, that the marital act, even though it be legitimate, is not a good preparation for prayer and for the reception of the sacraments. Reference was made to the Old Testament, where the priest had to abstain from cohabiting with his wife during the time of service. This prohibition is mentioned in the Penitential Books together with the penalty to which it rendered one liable,[50] and the councils did not omit to point it out.[51] This

---

[49] "Opus servile non exerceant, nec sectentur itinera, nisi orationis causa, aut sepeliendi mortuos, aut *visitandi infirmos*, aut *pro regis secreto*, pro Saracenorum impetu." *Conc. Coyacen.* (1050), c. vi, *ib.*, 788.

[50] Cf. the text *Poenitentiale Theodori*, l. I, c. xiv, 20: "Qui nupserit die dominico, petat a Deo indulgentiam et I vel II vel III dies poeniteat." Schmitz, *op. cit.*, p. 536. Regino, *op. cit.*, l. 1, c. ccc; Burchard, *op. cit.*, l. XIX, c. v. There is no doubt that the word *nubere* here signifies the consummation of the marriage, as plainly appears from nos. 21 and 22.

[51] Cf. *Concil. Forojulien.* (796-797), c. xiii: "Diem dominicum . . . cum omni reverentia et honorifica religione venerari omnibus

interdiction is again mentioned as of counsel by some few theologians;[52] but beginning with the thirteenth century the decrees make no further reference to it. Hostiensis, who gives a rather detailed list of works forbidden on Sunday, does not mention it.[53]

On all other points we may believe the Church was more faithfully obeyed, for, during the twelfth century, in the whole of western Europe, it rarely became necessary to recall the prohibition to do servile work or to transact business on Sunday. The question hardly ever arises of court sessions; for the social and political evolution had suppressed them to a great extent; however, we will meet later on with *assisiae* (assizes) which resembled the ancient court sessions and for this reason were likewise forbidden.

Strange to say, it is during the thirteenth century, at a time when the social power of the Church seems greatest, that the episcopal councils and statutes are obliged to recall more often the interdictions against Sunday work formulated during the preceding centuries. Such statutes, are, *e.g.*,

mandamus christianis, abstinere primum omnium ab omni peccato et ab omni opere carnali, etiam a propriis conjugibus . . ." *Mon. German., Concilia*, t. II, 194.

[52] Cf. De Graffiis, *Decisiones aureae* (De diebus festis, no. 24), pars II[a] (Anvers, 1604), p. 139.

[53] It appears among the admonitions in the missal at the end of the mass *pro sponso et sponsa*, which the pastor is expected to give the newly wedded pair by way of counsel.

the ecclesiastical *capitula* for Paris,[54] and Rouen;[55] the *customs* of the Count de Montfort;[56] a council of Scotland,[57] and another council of Rouen, which forbids under pain of excommunication *ipso facto* the holding of assizes by bailiffs, provosts, mayors and other secular judges.[58] In the country of the Albigenses, to preserve the faithful from bad example, Jews were forbidden to work publicly on Sunday.[59] In spite of all these precautions, however, relaxation becomes more pronounced and even the clergy are accused of furthering this decadence, because of their lack of vigilance, which is blamed and punished. "The priests shall denounce culprits to the bishops under pain of suspension," says a council of Bourges.[60]

Legal Introduction of Dispensations.—A century before the Council of Bourges, during the

[54] *Conc. Parisien. a Roberto Corceone* (beginning of the thirteenth century), pars IV, c. xviii, Mansi, t. XXII, 843.

[55] *Conc. Rothomagen.* (1214), pars. III, c. xix. *ib.*, 920.

[56] *Consuetudines quas dnus comes Montisfortis stabilivit apud Pamias* (1212), c. iv, *ib.*, 856.

[57] *Conc. Scoticum* (1225?), c. xxix, *ib.* 1230.

[58] *Conc. Rothomagen.* (1299), c. ii. Mansi, t. XXIV, 1204. Cf. *Concil. Copriniacen.* (1262?), c. xxvi and xxxvi. Mansi, t. XXIII, 872; *Conc. Biterren.* (1310), c. xv and xvi. Mansi, t. XXV, 363-364.

[59] *Conc. Albien.* (1254), c. lxviii. Mansi, t. XXIII, 851.

[60] "Quod dies dominici et festa . . . cum omni cura et vigilantia praecipiantur ab omni servili opere observari: et quod sacerdotes, sub poena suspensionis, contravenientes denuntient ordinariis, qui eos puniant, prout viderint faciendum." *Conc. Bituricen.* (1286), c. xxxii. Mansi, t. XXIV, 641.

pontificate of Alexander III, there occurred an event which, though it was not perhaps the first of its kind, was the first of which we have knowledge. This event is of interest for two reasons, first because it shows that fishing was among the prohibited works, and secondly, that a dispensation from the prohibition could be had only from the Pope.

The crops having failed that year, the Archbishop of Drontheim, in Norway, wrote to the Pope to ask permission for the people of his diocese to catch fish on Sunday. The Pope granted the desired permission on condition that, if the draught be plentiful, a suitable share should be given to the neighboring churches and the poor.[61] It is only at a much later date that we see that the *permission of the priest* is mentioned among the conditions required for working on Sunday. A Spanish council of the fourteenth century gives us the first declaration of this kind.[62]

Systematization of the Theory.—To the synodal

[61] "Indulgemus, ut liceat parochianis vestris diebus Dominicis . . . si alecia terrae se inclinaverint, eorum captioni, ingruente necessitate intendere: ita quod post factam capturam Ecclesiis circumpositis et Christi pauperibus congruam faciant portionem." C. iii, X, l. II, tit. IX, *de Feriis*.

[62] "Statuimus, ut nullus in diebus dominicis et festivis agros colere audeat, aut artificia manualia exercere praesumat, nisi urgente necessitate, vel evidenti pietatis causa, et tunc de *speciali licentia sacerdotis*." *Conc. apud Vallem Oleti Valentinae dioecesis* (1322), c. iv. Mansi, t. XXV, 698.

THE FIRST COMMANDMENT (CONCLUDED)

texts regarding works permitted or forbidden on Sunday little was added in the following centuries. But canonists and theologians began to comment on the older texts and prescriptions, and to search for the motives underlying them. Doubtless this and similar questions had been proposed long before the thirteenth century; but from this time forward the inquiry was carried on along different lines.

The first point now taken up was whether it was true, as had been maintained ever since Caesarius of Arles, that the law of Sunday rest was a positive divine law. St. Thomas held that it was merely an ecclesiastical precept growing out of the practice of the faithful.[63] Hence the obligation of the precept did not emanate from the ancient law concerning the Sabbath, but was based on an adaptation of that law by the Christian people, confirmed by the Church. The ancient law of itself had no binding force for Christians, but it could furnish a directing rule to determine what was lawful and what unlawful on Sunday. The Angelic Doctor teaches that the first obligation on Sunday is to attend divine worship, and the second, to abstain from all servile work, as the Scripture prescribes.[64]

---

[63] "Observantia diei dominicae in nova lege succedit observantiae sabbati, non ex vi praecepti legis, sed ex constitutione Ecclesiae, et consuetudine populi Christiani." *Summa theol.*, IIa IIae, qu. CXXII, art. 4, ad 4um.

[64] "Aliud est cessatio operum quae significatur cum subditur:

The work forbidden on Sunday therefore, according to St. Thomas, and his teaching agrees with that of the Doctors and the councils for many centuries before him, is *servile work*. But what, precisely, is servile work? The *Summa* gave a complete theory which was unanimously accepted by theologians. There are three kinds of servile work, as there are three kinds of servitude; that of sin, that of man (by which one man is the servant of another), and that of God. Servile work of the last-mentioned kind (*latria*) is not forbidden on Sunday. To sin, however, is to profane the Lord's Day. As for the corporal works, those which are performed in the service of God do not deserve the name "servile." Others are not, strictly speaking, all servile, some being common to slaves and free men, *e.g.* to provide for one's own needs or those of others, when there is question of safeguarding or recovering the health of the body, or of avoiding loss of property.[65]

septima die Domini Dei tui non facies omne opus: sed de quo opere intelligatur, apparet per id quod exponitur (Lev. 23): *Omne opus servile non facietis in eo.*"

[65] "Opus servile dicitur a servitute: est autem triplex servitus: una quidem, qua homo servit peccato . . . et secundum hoc omne opus peccati dicitur servile: alia vero servitus est, qua homo servit homini . . . et ideo opera servilia secundum hoc dicuntur *opera corporalia*, in quibus unus homo alteri servit: tertia autem est servitus Dei; et secundum hoc opus servile potest dici opus latriae, quod pertinet ad Dei servitium: si autem sic intelligitur opus servile, non prohibetur in die sabbati; quia hoc esset contrarium fini observationis sabbati. Opera servilia ad spiritualem Dei cul-

THE FIRST COMMANDMENT (CONCLUDED)

This explanation in no way modified the existing practice. The works that custom had permitted on Sunday remained permissible in the same degree. The value of St. Thomas's teaching lay in furnishing a logical theory to support the traditional practice. Hence its great vogue, which still continues. Among the conclusions deduced from this theory are the following: Works permitted on Sunday are (1) those which in any way refer to divine worship; (2) those necessary to satisfy the absolute needs of life, and to repel immediate danger to one's person or property; works prohibited on Sunday are those by which one becomes the servant of the devil, or the servant of men, outside of certain exceptions.

There is reason to believe that this theory was not an invention of St. Thomas but that he found it prevailing in the Schools. That part of it relating to sin as forbidden work on Sunday, is based on a text of St. Augustine which St. Thomas quotes in the *Summa*. Cardinal Henry of Susa, better known as Hostiensis (+1271), uses it to explain why court sessions, markets, and the taking of oaths are forbidden on Sunday. Commenting on

tum non pertinentia in tantum servilia dicuntur, in quantum proprie pertinent ad servientes: in quantum vero sunt communia servis et liberis, servilia non dicuntur; quilibet autem tam servus, quam liber tenetur in necessariis providere non tantum sibi, sed etiam proximo: praecipue quidem in his quae ad salutem corporis pertinent . . . secundario autem etiam in damno rerum vitando." *Ib.*, ad 3um.

the title *de Feriis* of the Decretals, he asks two questions: (1) What is to be done on these days? (2) What is not to be done? and answers the latter by saying that markets and courts and the taking of oaths are forbidden. The holding of markets is prohibited for reasons which show that he has no great esteem for merchants, *viz.*, because it is difficult, in transactions between buyer and seller, to keep free from sin, a thing to be avoided above all on Sundays. Court sessions, though quite lawful in themselves, should not be held because they are not becoming. Oaths should not be taken because their motive is the incredulity of the wicked.[66] This theory was not however peculiar to him, and the system met with further success, for we find the same reasons serving as the basis for like solutions more than three hundred years later, in the *Decisiones aureae* of James de Graffiis, who prohibits business transactions on Sunday and refuses to admit a contrary custom as lawful, because, he says, though commercial bargaining is not in itself a sin, nevertheless it is a proximate occasion of sin, and it is hardly possible that no

[66] "Ideo autem *mercatum* his diebus fieri non debet, quia difficile est inter ementis et vendentis commercium non intervenire peccatum . . . quod praecipue his diebus vetandum est, nam tempus peccatum aggravat . . . Ideo etiam a *placitis* abstinendum est, quia quamvis liceat placitare, non tamen expedit . . . et a juramentis . . . quia a malo non credentium fiunt." Hostiensis, *Summa*, in tit. *de Feriis*, nº 5. Cf. Rather. Veronen., *Epist. synod. ad Presbyter.*, nº 2. Migne, *P. L.*, t. CXXXVI, 555.

sin be committed either by sellers or buyers, and for this reason business transactions are forbidden on Sundays and feast-days.[67]

This exposition marks the last palmy days of this curious theory. If market holding remained almost universally forbidden on Sunday for a long time afterwards, it was because of other motives, because it was apt to keep people away from Mass, or because the cares of noisy traffic appeared incompatible with the holy thoughts which should occupy Christians on that day.

Regarding judiciary proceedings, the practice of the Church was extremely broad where she was queen and mistress. All proceedings in which the salvation of souls was at stake, such as matrimonial cases, maintaining or bringing about peace, and the cases of "the poor and the miserable" could be begun and carried on on Sundays.[68]

The solutions of Hostiensis, who well knew the practice of the Roman Court, were generally accepted. When the Church practically lost the jur-

[67] "Nam licet mercatura in se non sit peccatum, tamen de facili in mercatura incurritur peccatum, cum difficile sit inter ementes et vendentes non intervenire peccatum, . . . unde propter propinquitatem ad peccatum, prohibetur saltem his temporibus." De Graffiis, *Decisiones aureae*, pars II^a, c. xiii, *de diebus festis*, no 13 (Antwerp, 1604), p. 137.

[68] "Causae matrimoniales et aliae in quibus vertitur periculum animarum . . . et pro pace, vel necessitate alia, vel utilitate his diebus jurare possumus . . . Item videtur, quod causae miserabilium et debiliorum personarum his diebus tractari possunt." *Summa Hostiensis, l. cit.*

isdiction which she had exercised for a long time over the "miserabiles et debiliores personae," these solutions were still maintained in their favor, and, in that field, the judiciary works permitted formerly were probably more numerous than would be tolerated to-day.

From the Thirteenth to the Seventeenth Century.—It was the corporal works called servile that the moralists now discussed more frequently. This was a practical question; the State did not interfere nor legislate on the subject, and the faithful had to act each according to his own conscience.

Since the forbidden servile works were, in the main, sin and certain corporal works, all labor was permitted which pertained principally to the mind, to the military and scholastic sciences, etc., in a word the practice of the liberal arts. As to the servile works, the exceptions mentioned by St. Thomas were accepted as well as that regarding fishing, permitted by Alexander III.[69]

It is by the same theories that De Graffiis also

[69] "Ea quae pertinent ad disciplinam militarem, vel scholasticam, proprie liberales artes peragi possunt, ergo studere possum. . . . Item ea quae pertinent ad agriculturam vel putationem vinearum vel fossuram earum . . . et est ratio ne modico momento pereat commoditas coelesti provisione concessa. . . . Licet piscari etiam diebus dominicis ad alecia, ut cum facta collectione seu captione congrua portio ecclesiis circumpositis et Christi pauperibus fiat. . . . Et generaliter quandocumque necessitas vel pietas exigit." *Ibid.*

THE FIRST COMMANDMENT (CONCLUDED)

permits application to intellectual work on Sunday; for this sort of work contains nothing that smacks of the relation of slave and master. It was therefore permitted to teach, to give consultations, to preach by word of mouth or in writing, to write lectures for one's pupils, to correct books, and to take down notes for one's lectures or sermons.[70]

De Graffiis, like so many other writers of his time, seems to have considered only the needs of clerics and scholars devoted to purely intellectual pursuits. One of his contemporaries, Azor (+1607), takes a broader view. He puts the question: "What works are permitted on feast-days?" and answers it as follows: "Everybody admits that we must abstain from servile works, from business and court proceedings, but not from works proper to free men. However it is not sure what the works proper to free men are and what those proper to slaves and what the common works; for it cannot be truthfully said that all that concerns the body is servile work, and all that concerns the mind is the work of free men, and what relates

[70] "Talis [operatio spiritualis] cum sit secundum spiritum, sive mentem, secundum quam homo non est servus hominis . . . [licet] docere, consulere, praedicare verbo aut scripto . . . lectiones scholaribus notare . . . etiam publicas disputationes facere pro veritatis dilucidatione, . . . in lectionibus libros corrigere . . . sine magno tamen labore . . . scribere aliquid, ut colligendo aliqua utilia ad legendum vel praedicandum." De Graffiis, *op. cit.*, nos 31 et 32.

to both body and mind is common work."[71] The practical solutions which he gives show traces of his theoretical incertitude. He permits study and teaching on Sunday, but he seems to believe that it is servile work to write mainly for gain; not that the fact of working for a salary renders servile a work that is of its nature liberal, but writing is a work of uncertain character: liberal if done to improve oneself or to teach others, servile if done for the sake of pecuniary profit. The same solution is given on the question whether it is permissible to copy manuscripts. Fishing and hunting are forbidden, fishing in particular, when carried on as a trade. Travelling is allowable but not the loading of vehicles. Evidently these solutions are not very scientific, especially those which appear, contrary to the author's declaration, to make pecuniary gain the distinguishing mark of servile work.

Binsfeld in his *Enchiridion theologiae pastoralis et doctrinae necessariae sacerdotibus curam*

[71] "Quaenam opera die festo jure fiunt?—In hoc conveniunt omnes, cessandum esse ab operibus, ac laboribus, quae servilia dicuntur; a forensibus item causis atque negotiis: non tamen ab iis operibus quae sunt propria hominum liberorum. *Sed dubiae est et incertae quaestionis, quae sint opera propria liberorum, et quae propria servorum et quae communia.* Neque enim vere dici potest, omnia quae ad corpus spectant, esse propria servorum; quae ad animum, esse propria liberorum: quae ad utrumque vero pertinent, esse communia." *Institution. moral.*, pars IIa, *De tertio Decalogi praecepto*, c. xxvii.

THE FIRST COMMANDMENT (CONCLUDED)

animarum administrantibus, in spite of its practical character, is rather vague on the subject of servile work. Servile works, he says, are forbidden; and he defines them as those which are distinctively the work of servants.[72] This statement hardly adds anything to our knowledge. Diana, a writer of greater authority, and, in general, more complete than Binsfeld, is equally unsatisfactory when he speaks of servile works; he allows writing, copying, setting type for the printing press, and whilst he does not absolutely forbid hunting, he is less favorably disposed towards fishing.[73]

Escobar deserves credit for opposing the theory more or less unconsciously accepted by Azor, *viz.,* that pecuniary profit is one of the characteristic marks of servile work. A work does not become servile, he says, because done with an intention of gain, if not servile by nature.[74] Consequently it is not forbidden to study the mechanical arts in order to gain knowledge or to teach. Unfortunately the solutions he deduces from these principles are not always unexceptionable. Thus he doubts whether copying manuscripts is a servile work, but affirms that painting *is.* He

---

[72] "Omnia opera servilia prohibentur: qualia sunt illa quae proprie servientibus conveniunt . . . non autem illa quae communia sunt tam iis qui serviunt, quam illis, quibus serviunt." *Enchiridion,* pars III, c. x.

[73] *Summa,* sub verbo *festum servare.*

[74] *Liber Theologiae moralis, Leges, Examen quintum,* c. ii.

holds travelling to be a servile work if done with baggage or burden; likewise hunting, if carried on as a trade.[75]

Moralists were indeed unfortunate in dealing with the question of servile work. Laymann, ordinarily very interesting, offers nothing original on this point except a questionable exegesis of the texts which forbade labor under the old law, especially those which, to his mind, apply to the new.[76]

A Tentative Reaction During the Sixteenth and Seventeenth Centuries.—In the midst of this casuistry, owing to arbitrary decisions rendered by confessors, and to the circumstances of the time, laxity made rapid progress. About the end of the sixteenth century a reaction was attempted in France and northern Italy. The Councils of Milan, held during the episcopate of St. Charles Borromeo, the councils of Rouen (1581), Tours (1583), Aix (1585), and royal ordinances of Orleans and Blois (concerning especially the prohibiting of market and court holding), inaugurated a return toward the severer discipline of former days. In the seventeenth century, Alexander

[75] "Transcribere etsi probabile sit servile est, contrarium probabilius affirmo. . . . Pingere servile ex suo genere. Itineratio minime, nisi fiat cum oneratis jumentis, vel deferantur humeris onera. Venatio si fiat ex officio, servile est, ut pictura, ob voluptatem et recreationem minime." *Ibid.*

[76] *Theologia moralis*, l. IV, tract. VII, c. ii.

Natalis quoted, along with the decisions of the new councils, older texts, which he sometimes strained, in view of reëstablishing the austere morals of a former time.[77] This with other factors led to a sharpening of ecclesiastical discipline in France, where, moreover, secular laws helped to secure the observance of the prescriptions laid down by the national councils. But the contrary current could not be stayed nor banked. The greatest council of modern times, the Council of Trent, simply exhorted the bishops to watch over the pious and religious observance of the feast-days.[78] This looked like a refusal to make legislation uniform and a suggestion to trust Christian piety. Now everywhere people were inclined towards leniency. The result was that instead of giving a more precise and more practically complete definition of servile work than that of the old theologians, opinions, more or less discordant, on the works which were permitted and on those which were not, continued to be ventilated, so that the law which originated from custom, continued to be of custom, and to be modified slowly like other such laws.

Triumph of the Lenient Tendency.—One of the theologians who exercised a profound influence in the matter was P. Busembaum, S. J. He enunci-

[77] *Natalis Alexander*, l. IV, De Decalogo, art. VI, reg. 1.
[78] Sess. XXV, *Decretum de mortificatione carnis, jejuniis et diebus festis.*

ated the general theory on servile works in terms which simply echoed the common doctrine, *viz.*, that servile labors are forbidden on feast-days, and that servile works are those which are exercised on matter and belong to the mechanical order, such as sewing, artisan's work, and work expected only of workmen and servants,[79] and added that the motive of gain, the amount of fatigue involved, the length of time occupied did not modify the nature of the work performed. This theory was not new and the solutions given by Busembaum were all borrowed from the great theologians of the Society of Jesus; but the author had the advantage of summing up briefly the lengthy expositions of his forerunners, and for that reason his book was destined to serve as a text for the commentaries of many of his successors, among whom the most prominent were Claude Lacroix, S. J., and St. Alphonsus de' Liguori. Through the former his doctrine in the north of France and in the Low Countries struggled against the rigorist tendencies of Natalis Alexander and other moralists of the same school; through the latter, it obtained a success which has not yet died out, and which, after the upheaval caused in France by

---

[79] "Die festo prohibentur omnia opera servilia, hoc est, quae et versantur circa materiam externam; et vel mechanica, et illiberalia sunt, v. gr. suere, fabricare: vel requirunt tantum laborem corporis, et ab operariis tantum, et servis fieri solent." *Medulla theologiae moralis*, l. III, tract. III, c. i.

the revolution of 1789, supplanted not only the theology of Archbishop Montazet of Lyons (which appears inoffensive enough as regards our subject), but also those of Bailly and Bouvier, and was finally naturalized by Gousset, who established it definitively in France. One of the points by which Gousset enters into the true tradition of the Church and takes the opposite stand to Natalis Alexander, is where he affirms the legitimacy of custom in matter of Sunday rest; for example in the following passage: "But on holydays merchandise must not be carted, unless there is some necessity, or unless custom authorizes it." And further, in dealing with the work of millers: "On that point the custom of the place must be lived up to; custom can excuse those who on Sunday take their grain to be ground even without necessity." [80]

For a time, at the beginning of the nineteenth century, it was deemed possible to rebuild by means of authority a discipline that had fallen into desuetude. In France, after the fall of Napoleon, the government of the Restoration, by recognizing the Catholic religion as the State religion, and by a special law of November 18, 1814, again put into force the old ordinances on the observance of Sundays and feast-days. A similar revival of Christian legislation manifested itself in various other

[80] *Théologie morale*, Du Décalogue, c. ii, art. 1, t. I, no. 563.

countries of Europe. But it was soon realized that the awakening of the Christian spirit, upon which the reformers had counted, was not as strong as they had supposed. What neither the Church nor the secular governments could maintain before the Revolution, they were equally unable to restore after it. The new sanctions could not be effectively applied. Abstention from work on Sunday became more and more dependent on custom, and custom was daily becoming less rigorous.

To-day the tendency everywhere is towards leniency, especially in the countries which are supposed to be pre-eminently Christian. Open the work of any modern theologian, Lehmkuhl for example, or Berardi, and you will find what an important place the theory of legitimate dispensations from Sunday work occupies, and how great is the rôle assigned to custom.

But it seems that, as far as theory is concerned, a new evolution is under weigh. Not that present-day theologians are attempting a new definition of servile work, but the consideration of salary, which Escobar and Busembaum had opposed, is now the main factor which determines the character of certain works of doubtful nature, or excludes as forbidden some works, in themselves liberal. Berardi, who invokes the common sentiment of the faithful in favor of his opinion, thus expresses himself: Works of a liberal nature of themselves

THE FIRST COMMANDMENT (CONCLUDED)

are allowed, *i.e.*, those which formerly were performed by free men and in which the mind is employed more than the body; but if they are done to make money, or as a trade, the common sense of the faithful considers them servile and illicit;[81] hence it would be illicit for anyone, who does so as a trade or profession, to teach, to set type, to paint or to go hunting.

It cannot be denied that many of these solutions run counter to the teaching of past centuries, though conformable to the tendencies of the public spirit of our time. Agriculture, centuries ago, was the daily and regular occupation and the means of livelihood for the majority of men; the trades or professions were organized in such a way that their members, shielded against unlimited competition, lived in more or less easy circumstances, and in any case could always make a living because work ordinarily was not lacking. Hence they considered the dominical rest a necessary and regular relaxation needed by the body. But in our age of feverish competition, when irregular and sometimes prolonged lay-offs affect the trades of the poor; when life is becoming

[81] "Per se licent opera liberalia, ea videlicet quae antiquitus a solis liberis exercebantur, et in quibus magis mens quam corpus occupatur. *Ista tamen, si modo mercenario, seu ad modum artis, atque ad lucrum faciendum exerceantur, communi fidelium sensu tanquam servilia et illicita habentur.*" *Praxis confessar.* (2nd ed.), t. I, n. 370 ff.

more and more costly and at the same time more uncertain; the loss of gain looms up as a most vital consideration. The theology of the older moralists seems immoral to many who deem it wrong to allow opportunities for gain on Sunday to those whom easier circumstances have enabled to choose a liberal career, and to deny these opportunities to those who have to work hard for a living. Of course, there is another legitimate reason for allowing Sunday work to the latter, the motive, recognized from the first centuries, of necessity. But people prefer to have recourse to another motive now-a-days, *viz.*, custom; and to this fact we thought it our duty to call attention.

Of late years a new movement has been on foot which aims at the weekly rather than the dominical rest. What the government of the Restoration could not obtain by legislative appeal to Christian principles, public opinion in France has obtained by an appeal to the social sense. The protagonists of this new legislation were undoubtedly Christians, but they could not have succeeded had it not been for the Socialist party. And it is rather in consideration of social utility than in order to obey the Church that the law of July 13, 1906, imposed the so-called "repos hebdomadaire." Its champions insisted that the workingman needs a day's rest from his labors each week, for his bodily health as well as for his moral and intellectual development. The law, aiming at rest for rest's sake, has not fixed it invariably on Sunday. It declares Sunday to be the usual day of rest, not because it is consecrated to divine worship, but because it was already established and respected by the majority of citizens, and consequently offered a better opportunity than any other day to all the members of a family to gather together. However, in consideration of the special needs of particular industries it was granted that the day of rest could be fixed each day of the week in rotation.

On the other hand, the law, having for its object the protection of salaried workmen, does not impose a weekly rest on those who work at home, either alone or with their family. While the employees rest, the employers are at liberty to continue their work.

Yet, as a matter of fact, under the influence of various sentiments, partly of a Christian and partly of a social origin, people go beyond the requirements of the law, and ever since its enforcement the observance of the dominical rest has become much more pronounced in France. Christians cannot but congratulate themselves because of the new facilities which the law thus places at their disposal for observing the precept of the

Church; they should sanctify by divine worship a rest that was given to them for altogether different motives.

At What Time Did Sunday Rest Begin?—Custom also determined the hour at which the obligation of Sunday rest was to begin. As the reader may have noticed in the texts we have cited, during the Middle Ages the period of Sunday rest began on Saturday night. Let us add to the proofs already given some new ones. The Council of Berkhampstead fined any master eighty sous who made his bondman work from Sunday evening after sunset until Monday evening.[82] In order to better insure the observance of the Sunday rest precept, the cessation from work was at times made to begin earlier. An Anglo-Saxon law orders the Sunday rest to begin at three o'clock Saturday afternoon.[83] Later on, the ecclesiastical day of rest was made to coincide in general with the common day, *viz.*, midnight to midnight; yet in the seventeenth century, the old custom was still known, and, in certain places, the obligation of rest began on Saturday at sunset. Laymann is aware of this custom and admits its perfect legitimacy;

---

[82] Cf. *supra*, p. 72, and *Conc. Francofurten.* (794), c. xxi: "Ut dies dominica a vespera usque ad vesperam servetur." *Mon. Germ., Concilia*, t. II, 168.

[83] "Dies sabbati ab ipsa diei saturni hora pomeridiana tertia usque in lunaris diei cubiculum festus agitur: quit non celebrarit, poenas in judiciali libro descriptas pendito." *Leges ecclesiasticae regis Edgardi*, c. v. Mansi, t. XVIII, 513.

in these places, he says, one can resume work on Sunday, right after sunset.[84]

Summary.—In the early days of Christianity a certain abstention from work, of unknown duration and undoubtedly adapted to the needs of the various communities, was established under the influence of either the Mosaic legislation concerning the Sabbath, or of certain pagan customs attached to the celebration of feast-days. In the second century Sunday seems to have been kept as a day of complete rest. In the fourth century the influence of the Christian custom is sufficiently strong to inspire the Constantinian decree forbidding judiciary proceedings and works of trade (*cunctarum artium officia*) on Sunday; agricultural work only is permitted. Later on, the compiler of the Apostolic Constitutions attributes to the Apostles Peter and Paul the institution of that rest by which even the slaves could benefit. In the sixth century, the sermons of St. Caesarius and the statutes of the Third Council of Orleans show that nearly all the rigors of the Sabbath had come to be imposed on the Christian Sunday. The Council of Orleans so successfully combated this practice that henceforth there was no need of further efforts in this direc-

[84] "Ubi consuetudo viget festa inchoandi a vespera tanquam ex obligatione, non ex libera devotione, ita observandum est. Quare, adveniente vespera, videlicet ad solis occasum, talibus locis laborare concessum erit." Laymann, *op. et loc. cit.*

tion, but the need soon arose of combating the opposite extreme, *viz.*, laxity. To remedy this the secular arm intervened and inflicted severe penalties, such as fines, corporal chastisements, incarceration, etc. At the same time the expression *servile work* came to be applied not only to the work of slaves, but also to the corporal and hard work of the body which, though ordinarily the work of the slave, may nevertheless be performed by anyone. The rigorous laws imposed by the civil codes of the newly converted nations in their first fervor (in Gaul, England, Hungary) soon fell into desuetude; the ecclesiastical penalties were replaced by stated and more lenient penances. Little by little, certain material works of a servile nature were permitted.

As to business transactions and judiciary acts, they were first prohibited, but in course of time exceptions arose and, becoming more and more numerous, finally established a contrary custom.

In vain the councils of France and Milan, in the sixteenth, and the theologians, particularly of France, in the seventeenth century, tried to restore the old-time severity; but they were powerless in opposing a deeply rooted custom. As the Church gradually lost its influence, laxity increased; the last efforts of secular legislation proved unsuccessful; the laws passed were eluded or remained a dead letter. Finally the modifications introduced into social life by the modern economic régime modified the popular ideas concerning Sunday work; many now regard rest above all as a loss of gain, a new cause of privations added to those that already make the life of the poor so precarious, and it seems that justice will not be satisfied unless Sunday labor be forbidden to the rich, whether their profession be servile or liberal.

There is another noticeable phenomenon; in all this process the Church legislates only through particular councils; the popes enact no general laws; Nicholas I, Nicholas II, Alexander III, accept prevailing custom without altering or extending it; and the Council of Trent, which legislated on so many subjects, barely mentions the matter of Sunday rest. The law of the Sunday rest has remained what it was from the beginning, —a law of custom, and this consideration furnishes the key to the attitude of the moralists, who, instead of continually condemning, bear with the vicissitudes of a practice constantly growing less rigorous.

CHAPTER IV

THE SECOND COMMANDMENT

Les fêtes tu sanctifieras
Qui te sont de commandement.

The feast-days shalt thou sanctify,
Which are for thee appointed.

In the Baltimore Catechism this commandment is mentioned under the First Commandment: To hear Mass on Sundays and holydays of obligation.

The institution of feasts is not peculiar to any one religion; it is, even more than the observance of Sunday, a practice common to all nations and religions. Every nation has various categories of feasts, some movable like the course of the heavenly bodies, phases of which they celebrated (*e.g.* feasts of the new moon; solstices, etc.), others stable like the anniversary of the foundation of the empire, of the birth of the sovereign, of a great victory won over the enemies of a nation or tribe, and their celebration implied, besides the offering of sacrifices, a certain abstention from servile labor.[1]

[1] Macrobius, *Saturnalia*, l. I, xv and xvi.

The Jews knew this double category of feasts and celebrated them with special ceremonies.

If the institution of feasts is a trait common to all religions, we must not be surprised that Christianity too has its feasts, especially if we consider that Christianity has elements common to all religious cults.

The kinship is closest between the Jewish and Christian feasts; it is from Jewry that our Christian feasts have sometimes borrowed not only the day, but even definite modes of celebration.

Some of the Jewish feasts were particularly solemn and holy; and they lasted several days, the holiest of which were the first and the last. Such was the case with the Pasch, which lasted seven days and which found in Pentecost something like the conclusion of an octave of weeks; the feast of the Tabernacles, which lasted eight days, each celebrated by joyous sacrifices. On the three principal feasts every Jew had to appear before the Lord on the first day, or at least, come on one of the remaining six, and offer a personal sacrifice.

Such was the distribution of the Jewish feasts. They existed in addition to the weekly Sabbath, and the Lord said to His people after enumerating them: "These are the feasts of the Lord which you shall call most solemn and most holy; you shall offer on them oblations to the Lord, holocausts and libations, according to the rite of each day." [2]

The First Christian Feasts.—Such was the pattern after which the Christian feasts were modeled, and hence it is easy for us to realize the origin of the great solemnities with octaves celebrated later on.

The Apostles and the first Christians converted from Judaism quite naturally continued to celebrate the Jewish feasts of their compatriots just as they continued the observance of the Sabbath. By and by, as they separated themselves from Judaism (considered as a nation), they allowed the peculiarly national feasts to drop, preserving only the Pasch and Pentecost, which they Christianized by a twofold commemoration: Easter by the remembrance of the Resurrection of Christ, Pentecost by the commemoration of the descent of the Holy Ghost on the Apostles. This twofold memory being historically attached to the dates of the Jewish feasts, the same date was preserved at first for the Christian feasts.

It is not unlikely that on these feasts, as on the Sabbath, the people came together to celebrate the liturgy and that they observed the Jewish precept of abstaining from servile labor as far as possible; but there is no decisive proof for this assumption; on this point, as on many others, we have no legislative texts of the first centuries.

[2] *Levit.*, xxiii, 37.

For a long time Easter and Pentecost remained the only Christian feasts. Later, when the leaders of the Church sealed the testimony they gave of Jesus Christ with their blood, the flock celebrated the day of their birth in Heaven, as the *dies natalis* of the emperors were celebrated in civil life. By the middle of the second century this is an established custom, as is evidenced by the letter of the Church of Smyrna which narrates the martyrdom of its bishop, St. Polycarp. After having told how they succeeded in seizing some relics of the martyr's body and placing them in a becoming location (*ubi decebat*), the letter adds that there, in that becoming spot, all wish to gather in the future, in order to celebrate with joy and happiness the anniversary of the holy martyr, to honor the relics of those who have fought, and to inspire and prepare future combatants.[3]

A hundred years later we find the custom raised to the dignity of an institution and inculcated as a duty. After the time of Tertullian, who mentions the offering of the Eucharist on the anniversary day of the martyrs,[4] some well-known passages in St. Cyprian's letters point to the celebration of the

[3] "Quo etiam loci nobis, ut fieri poterit, in exsultatione et gaudio congregatis, Dominus praebebit, *natalem martyrii ejus diem* celebrare, tum in memoriam eorum qui certamina pertulerunt, tum ut posteri exercitati sint et parati." *Eccles. Smyrnen. de martyrio Polycarpi, epist.* XVIII. Migne, *P. G.*, t. V, 1043.

[4] *De corona*, III. Migne, *P. L.*, t. II, 79.

anniversary of the martyr as a constant practice. Eulogizing the ordained Lector Celerinus, Cyprian declares that the family of the young man is well known, for his relatives have given testimony of Jesus Christ by their blood and their anniversary is celebrated every year.[5] Speaking of the martyrs of the persecution which was still raging, he recommends that the day on which they render their souls to God be noted, so that, later on, oblations and sacrifices may be offered on the day of the anniversary.[6]

We have no intention of giving an account of the institution of various feasts; we simply wish to explain how, to the two primitive feasts, borrowed from Judaism and Christianized by the memories they honored, the piety of the faithful soon added others. These were not attached to a variable, though definite, day of the lunar cycle, but to anniversaries strictly defined according to the Julian or solar calendar. It is probable that the general outlines of the Jewish ceremonial for the feasts of

[5] "Sacrificia pro eis semper, ut meministis, offerimus, quoties martyrum passiones et dies anniversaria commemoratione celebramus." *Epist.* XXXIV, 3. Migne, *P. L.*, t. IV, 323.

[6] "Denique et dies eorum quibus excedunt annotate, ut commemorationes eorum inter memorias martyrum celebrare possimus . . . Tertullus . . . significet mihi dies quibus in carcere beati fratres nostri ad immortalitatem gloriosae mortis exitu transeunt, et celebrentur hic a nobis *oblationes et sacrificia*, ob commemorationes eorum, quae cito vobiscum, Domino protegente, celebrabimus." *Epist.* XXXVII, *ib.* 328-329.

the Pasch and Pentecost were adapted to the needs of the Christian Church.

This rudimentary cycle was gradually filled out. It was made up of two parts, one comprising the feasts of the whole Christian people, the other the feasts peculiar to each diocese; *viz.* the anniversaries of the martyrs, of dedications of churches, of ordinations and burials of bishops, and feasts of confessors. The first part, comprising the common or universal feasts, was soon enriched by the addition of Christmas, placed on the 25th of December by some, and on the 6th of January by others; of feasts destined to commemorate the leading Apostles and certain ancestors of the Saviour, St. John the Baptist, the Holy Innocents, the Machabees, of the feast of the Ascension, of the feasts of the Blessed Virgin, Mother of God, and of others, of which many first appeared as feasts of a particular church, and spread either throughout the entire Church or through one of the great divisions of the Christian world, the East or the West.

How those feasts were introduced into the calendar is difficult to say. Some of them were introduced by the express authority of councils, others merely through custom or by local legislation.

The history of each feast, which in many cases it would be impossible to tell and which at all events would be altogether too lengthy, interests us much less than the following points: Was there an obligation for all the faithful to celebrate those feasts? and how was this obligation satisfied?

Obligation for the Faithful to Celebrate Feasts. It is impossible to quote a text of the Fathers or of councils—at least we know of none—instituting this obligation. It was, however, established firmly enough in the second half of the fourth century. We have proof of it in a text of civil law. A rescript of the emperors Valentinian, Theodosius, and Arcadius, enumerates among the days on which legal action could not be taken, the principal Christian feasts, *viz.*, Easter, with seven days either preceding or following the feast, Christmas and Epiphany, and the feasts of the Apostles Peter and Paul; all these feasts were added to the Sunday.[7]

The Manner in which Feasts were Sanctified. Assistance at the Liturgy.—The feasts of the Church were sanctified from the very beginning by liturgical celebrations. The letter of St. Cyprian, which we have just cited, is positive. "We

[7] "Sacros quoque Paschae dies qui septeno numero, vel praecedunt vel sequuntur. Dies etiam Natalis atque Epiphaniarum Christi, et quo tempore commemoratio Apostolicae Passionis totius Christianitatis Magistrae a cunctis jure celebratur. In eadem observatione numeramus et dies solis, quos Dominicos rite dixere majores." *Cod. Justinian.*, 1. II, tit. XII, lex 7a. Is not this text a dear proof that on the feast days people abstained from work as much as possible, in order to devote themselves entirely to divine worship?

offer sacrifices," he says, "every time we celebrate the passions of the martyrs"; "so we celebrate oblations and sacrifices here to commemorate them." The celebration of the liturgy was an integral part of the feast, so much so that in Asia Minor, where the liturgical synaxis during Lent was only held on Saturday and Sunday, the Council of Laodicea transferred the celebration of the anniversaries of the martyrs to these days.[8]

The great feasts were celebrated in church. The Apostolic Constitutions mention Easter, Ascension Day, Pentecost, Christmas, Epiphany, and the feasts of the Apostles and of St. Stephen and say that Christians spend these days in church to receive religious instruction.

It was at church also, on the anniversaries of the martyrs and on great feasts, that the bishops addressed their homilies and catechetic instructions to the people.

The Obligation of Assisting at Mass.—What was the precise nature of this obligation in the early Church? To answer this question is very difficult; the extant documents do not touch on the juridical nature of the precept. To judge by the texts and practice of this period, it seems that the obligation was not considered uniformly binding,

[8] "Quod non oporteat in Quadragesima natalitia celebrari, sed eorum sancta commemoratio in diebus sabbatorum et dominicorum fieri conveniat."—*Conc. Laodicen.* (about 381?), c. li. Mansi, *Concil.*, t. II. col. 572.

and that there were notable differences in the solemnization of the various feasts.

St. Gregory of Nazianzus in a celebrated passage tells how the Emperor Julian, when accompanied by his guards he entered the Church of Caesarea on the feast of the Epiphany during the divine service, beheld "an ocean of people," whose psalmody "struck his ear with the sound of thunder."[9] The whole narrative gives us a picture of a great multitude fervently fulfilling a sacred duty.

This is also the impression left on us by the sermons St. Augustine preached on the great feasts of his church. Easter eve, the great bishop begins his instruction in these terms: "I must tell you why we celebrate this nocturnal vigil with such great solemnity."[10] The same with Epiphany: "The time of the year invites me to tell you what renders particularly important the solemnity of this day, so well known all over the world."[11] The feast of the Ascension is placed in the same rank as that of Easter.[12] Both are celebrated

[9] *Eulogy of St. Basil*, c. LII, edition of F. Boulenger, p. 162 sqq.

[10] "Dicendum est cur tanta celebritate hodierna potissimum nocte vigilamus." *Sermo* 221, *In vigil. Paschae*, III. *P. L.*, t. XXXVIII, 1087.

[11] "Hodierni diei per universum nota solemnitas quid nobis afferat solemnitatis . . . tempus admonet ut loquamur." *Sermo* 202, *In Epiphan. Domini*, IV, *ib.*, 1033.

[12] "Festus nobis dies uterque." *Sermo* 263, *De ascensione Domini*, III, *ib.*, 1209.

throughout the world.[13] Nor are the feasts of Our Lord the only ones thus solemnized. When preaching on the feast-day of the Apostles Peter and Paul, he thus begins: "We ought certainly to celebrate the feast-days of these great martyrs, the Apostles Peter and Paul, by a more numerous attendance. If the attendance is numerous on the days we celebrate the lambs, how much greater should it be on the day we celebrate the feast of the rams?"[14] The attendance is just as large on the feast of the great martyr of Africa, St. Cyprian, "this grandeur on a day so pleasing and so enjoyable, that happy and pleasant feast of the triumph of so great a martyr";[15] it is a very holy and solemn day;[16] as is also the feast of the twenty martyrs.[17] I can hardly believe that, if they had not been pressed by a real obligation, the Christians of Hippo would have gathered together in

[13] "Ecce celebratur hodiernus dies toto orbe terrarum." *Sermo* 262, no. 3, *ib.* 1208.

[14] "Debuimus quidem tantorum martyrum diem, hoc est sanctorum Apostolorum Petri et Pauli, majore frequentia celebrare. Si enim celebramus frequentissime natalitia agnorum, quanto magis debemus arietum?" *Sermo* 298, *In natal. Apostolor. Petri et Pauli*, IV, *ibid.* 1365.

[15] "Diei tam grati laetique solemnitas, et coronae tanti martyris tam felix et jucunda festivitas." *Sermo* 312. *In natali Cypriani martyris*, IV, 1, *ibid.*, 1420.

[16] "Sanctissimus et solemnissimus dies." *Sermo* 313, 1, *ibid.*, 1423.

[17] "Eorum dies solemnissimos celebramus." *Sermo* 325, *ibid.*, 1447.

such numbers in the churches on all these feast-days.

Still, on certain days the obligation was undoubtedly less strict and less imperative, for the Christian assembly is less numerous and the preacher, who well knew how to show great energy against negligence of duty, laments the small attendance, though without saying anything which would imply that the absentees have committed any fault by not coming. For instance, here is the exordium of a sermon for the feast of St. Lawrence: "The martyrdom of the Blessed Lawrence is celebrated in Rome, but not here, so few do I behold present. . . . Well, small flock, listen to these few words . . .,"[18] and that is all. If there had been a strict obligation for his diocesans to assist at the services of the day, would not the holy doctor have instructed the faithful more plainly? And can one see in this calm and melancholy exordium a reproach intended to censure a real fault?

We cannot, therefore, draw any solid conclusions from the few indications contained in St. Augustine's sermons. They show that these feast-days were celebrated by assemblies and liturgical services; but they do not tell us the nature of the obligation compelling the faithful to assist. Perhaps many of these feasts were simply what we

[18] "Beati Laurentii illustre martyrium est, sed Romae, non hic; tantam enim video vestram paucitatem. . . . Ergo, pauci audite pauca . . ." *Sermo* 303, 1, *ibid.*, 1393.

to-day call *feasts of devotion*. The first words of a sermon delivered by St. Augustine on the calends of January point in that direction: "We see, brethren, that you have come to-day, as if it were a day of solemnity, and in greater numbers than usual." [19]

Such was the discipline of the African Church. It must have been about the same in the rest of the Latin world; but the sermons of the other Fathers of the time, Maximus of Turin, Peter Chrysologus, and Eucherius give us no information on the subject. Everywhere we behold the celebration of more or less numerous feasts, some common, others differing according to dioceses. Those which were preceded by a vigil [20] were undoubtedly counted as more obligatory; but it seems impossible to prove from those texts that the obligation of celebrating those feasts was a clearly codified duty. The petition made to the emperor by an African council to close the theatres and other play houses on Sundays and solemn feast-days, only proves that the spectacles given there endangered the sanctification of those holydays.[21]

[19] "Admonemus charitatem vestram, fratres, quoniam vos quasi solemniter hodie convenisse conspicimus, et ad hunc diem solito frequentius congregatos." *Sermo* 198, no. I, *ibid.*, 1014.

[20] Cf. for the diocese of Tours the vigils instituted by St. Perpetuus for the feasts of St. Martin, St. Lidorius, etc. Gregor. Turonen., *Historia Francorum*, l. X, c. xxxi, no. 6. *P. L.*, t. LXXI, 566.

[21] "Necnon et illud petendum, ut spectacula theatrorum ceteror-

122 THE COMMANDMENTS OF THE CHURCH

In the Sixth Century.—Not until the sixth century do we find a firmer and more definite discipline. The first expression is furnished by the Council of Agde, which gives the list of the more solemn feasts and imposes severe penalties on those clerics who stayed away from the liturgy on those days. A cleric who absented himself from church on Christmas, Epiphany, Easter or Pentecost, and occupied himself with temporal gain rather than with the service of the Church, was to be excluded from communion for three years.[22] The same penalty is inflicted upon the people who do not come to celebrate these feasts in the episcopal city,[23] and, in order to enforce their presence, it is forbidden on those days to celebrate mass in the oratories or country chapels under

umque ludorum die dominica vel ceteris religionis christianae diebus celeberrimis amoveantur, maxime quia sancti Paschae octavarum die populi ad circum magis quam ad ecclesiam conveniunt, debere transferri devotionis eorum dies si quando occurrerint." *Codex Canonum Ecclesiae Africanae*, c. LXI. BRUNS, t. I, 170.

[22] "Si quis in clero constitutus ab ecclesia sua diebus solemnibus defuerit, id est, nativitate, epiphania, pascha, vel pentecoste, dum potius saecularibus lucris studet quam servitio Dei paret, convenit ut triennio a communione suspendatur." *Conc. Agathen.* (506), c. lxiv. BRUNS, *Canones et Concilia*, t. II, p. 158.

[23] *Ibid.*, lxiii. The same obligation is imposed for the feasts of Christmas, Easter, and Pentecost, but without punishment, by the first Council of Orleans (511), c. xxv. Maassen, *Concilia*, p. 8; it is imposed under pain of excommunication by the Council of Clermont (535) c. xv, *ibid.*, p. 69. Cf. *Conc. Aurelian.* IV, (541), c. iii, *ibid.*, 88.

THE SECOND COMMANDMENT

pain of excommunication for the celebrant.[24] If there had not been a real obligation, could the penalty have been so severe?

At about the same time Caesarius of Arles instructs his people that there is the same obligation for them to sanctify the solemn feast days as to sanctify Sundays, by hearing an entire mass.[25] However, this is only for the great feasts, for he seems to place the feasts of the saints a little below Sunday, as shown by the following passage: "Know, my very dear brethren, that if our holy fathers have ordered the Christians to rest and to cease all earthly occupations on the feasts of the saints and especially on Sunday, it is in order to prepare them and render them better disposed for divine worship."[26]

As time goes on, the obligation becomes more strict. At the end of the same century, in the region of Mâcon, it made a great step forward. Perhaps this was a consequence of the principle

[24] *Conc. Agathen.*, c. xxi. Bruns, *op. cit.*, p. 150. Among the great feasts is enumerated that of St. John the Baptist.

[25] "Rogo vos, fratres charissimi, et paterna pietate commoneo, ut quoties aut in die dominico, aut in aliis majoribus festivitatibus missae fiunt, nullus de ecclesia discedat, donec divina mysteria compleantur." *Sermo* 281, *inter opp. S. Augustini* (appendix). Migne, *P. L.*, t. XXXIX, col. 2276.

[26] "Sciendum est, fratres charissimi, quod ideo a sanctis patribus nostris constitutum est christianis et mandatum, ut *in solemnitatibus sanctorum et maxime in dominicis diebus* otium haberent et a terreno negotio cessarent: ut paratiores et promptiores essent ad divinum cultum." *Sermo* 280, *ibid.*, 2274.

we have seen applied to servile labor on Sunday, *viz.* the transfer of the prescriptions of the old law regarding the feasts of Judaism to the Christian feasts. What makes it likely, is the fact that the feast of the Pasch lasts about the same length of time as with the Jews, and that during the six days of the celebration (from Holy Thursday to the Tuesday after Easter, inclusive) the faithful are constantly urged to assist at the morning synaxis and the offices of the day.[27]

Since that period, a great number of feasts, the most solemn ones in fact,—those inscribed on the special catalogue of each church,—were celebrated like Sunday, and the assimilation is complete between the Jewish Sabbath and Sunday, between Sunday and the feast days.

Abstaining from Work.—This was not, strictly speaking, a novelty. The Apostolic Constitutions, in a passage cited above, had imposed for the great feast days the same obligations regarding mass and servile work, as for Sunday. Those feast days comprised the holy week preceding Easter, Ascension, Pentecost, Christmas, Epiphany, the feasts of the Apostles, of St. Stephen, and others not explicitly mentioned.[28] Barely a century later,

[27] See note given below, p. 125.

[28] "Tota magna hebdomada, et proxima sequenti vacent, . . . die Assumptionis vacent, . . . in Pentecoste vacent, . . . in die festo Natalis, . . . in die festo Epiphaniae, . . . in diebus Apostolorum, . . . in die Stephani protomartyris item vacent ac re-

THE SECOND COMMANDMENT

Pope St. Leo in one of his sermons describes the faithful as donning their best attire on feast days, an unmistakable sign that they abstained from work on those days.[29]

We can easily understand now why St. Caesarius, in imposing rest from servile work, appeals to the constitutions of the Holy Fathers,[30] and how the Fathers of the Council of Mâcon, when they codified the obligations of the six days of Easter, seem rather to renew an ancient discipline than to institute a new one.[31]

The Church authorities were exacting at this time, and as the feasts were still few in number, the possessors of large domains could be forced to permit their lowliest servants, cowherds and swineherds, to sanctify these days.[32]

liquis diebus sanctorum martyrum, . . . qui Christum vitae suae anteposuerunt." *Const. Apost.*, VIII, xxxiii. Migne, *P. G.*, t. I, col. 579-582.

[29] "Rationabile et quodammodo religiosum videtur per diem festum in vestitu nitidiore prodire, et habitu corporis hilaritatem mentis ostendere." *Sermo* 41, *De Quadragesima*, iii, 1. Migne, *P. L.*, LIV, 272.

[30] Cf. *Sermo* 280, *supra citat*.

[31] "Pascha itaque nostrum . . . debemus omnes festivissime colere . . . . ut illis sanctissimis sex diebus nullus servile opus audeat facere, sed omnes simul quoadunati, himnis paschalibus indulgentes, perseverationis nostrae praesentiam cotidianis sacrificiis ostendamus." *Conc. Matiscon.* II (585), c. ii. Maassen, *Concilia*, p. 166.

[32] Cf., for the limited number of feasts, *Statuta Synodalia Eccles. Remens.* per Dominum Sonnatium (about 630, doubtful both as to date and authenticity), c. xx. Mansi, t. X, 599. I

In the eighth century the number of feasts is multiplied and the manner of sanctifying them better defined. To observe a feast day properly means to assist at mass and abstain from work. Thus the great Apostle of Germany, St. Boniface, issued the following prescription: "Let the priests announce that people must not work on the Sundays of the year; at Christmas they must not work for four days, nor must they work on the feast days of the Circumcision, Epiphany, and Purification, nor on Easter day, and the three days following the feast; and on the feast days of the Ascension, of the Nativity of St. John the Baptist, of the death of the Blessed Apostles Peter and Paul, of the Assumption and Nativity of the Blessed Virgin, of the death of the Holy Apostle Andrew, they must rest one day." [33]

We must be careful, however, not to draw from these various texts proofs of a uniform and universal legislation; for they are usually only dioce-

have already cited the text of the Council of Rouen in favor of cowherds and swineherds. Bruns, t. II, 271.

[33] "Adnuncient presbyteri diebus dominicis per annum *sabbatizandum* ... in Natale Domini VIII Kalendas Januarias, dies quatuor, in circumcisione Domini, in Epiphania, in purificatione S. Mariae, diem unum. In Pascha Domini, post dominicam, dies tres, in Ascensione Domini, ... in natale sancti Joannis Baptistae, in passione sanctorum apostolorum Petri et Pauli, in Assumptione S. Mariae, in passione S. Andreae apostoli, diem unum." *Statuta S. Bonifacii, archiep. Mogunt. et Mart.*, c. xxxvi. Mansi, t. XII, 386.

THE SECOND COMMANDMENT

san or provincial laws, and rarely national, though they manifest national tendencies.

What is universal, however, is the increase of the number of feasts honored by rest from work.

In the Ninth Century.—From the ninth century on, not only is the time of rest lengthened, but many new feast days are added, thereby increasing the days of rest. This process of development, however, was not uniform. Thus the Council of Mayence (813) prescribes rest on Easter Sunday and the whole week following, on the day of the Ascension, the whole week of Pentecost as at Easter, on the feasts of St. Peter and St. Paul, on the Nativity of St. John the Baptist, on the Assumption of the Blessed Virgin, on the dedication of St. Michael, on St. Remi's day, St. Martin's, St. Andrew's, on four days at Christmas, on the days of the Circumcision, the Epiphany, and the Purification; on the feasts of the martyrs and confessors whose relics are in the parish church, and on the anniversary of the dedication of that church.[34] These decisions were extended to a

[34] "Festos dies in anno celebrare sancimus, hoc est diem dominicum Paschae cum omni honore et sobrietate venerari, simili modo totam ebdomadam illam observare decrevimus, diem Ascensionis Domini pleniter celebrare, in Pentecosten similiter ut in Pascha, in natali apostolorum Petri et Pauli diem unum, nativitatem sancti Johannis Baptistae, adsumptionem sanctae Mariae, dedicationem sancti Michahelis, natalem sancti Remigii, sancti Martini, sancti Andreae, in natali Domini dies quattuor, octavas Domini, Epiphan-

great part of the Carolingian empire by the bishops united at Aix-la-Chapelle in September of the same year, as the document called *Concordia Episcoporum* attests.[35] Elsewhere, a capitulary of the same period added to those feast days the octave of the Epiphany, the Long Litany (the day of St. Mark), suppressed others, and left the feast of the Assumption in doubt.[36]

Along with these feasts, which appear to have been celebrated everywhere in the Frankish Empire, the diocesan records mention those of local saints, *e.g.:* Ursicinus, Austregisillus and Sulpitius at Bourges;[37] Euvertus, Aignan, Benedict, Mesmin, Lisard, and the Finding and Exaltation

iam Domini, purificationem sanctae Mariae et illas festivitates martyrum et confessorum observare decrevimus, quorum in unaquaque parrochia sancta corpora requiescunt, similiter etiam dedicationem templi." *Conc. Moguntin.* (813), c. xxxvi. *Mon. Germ., Concilia,* t. II, 269-270.

[35] "De observatione dierum festorum per anni circulum et de veneratione et reverentia Paschalis solemnitatis, quae per totam ebdomadam cum omni veneratione celebranda est, ita omnes observandum decrevimus, sicut in Mogonciacensi conventu decretum est." C. xvii, *ibid.,* 299.

[36] "Haec sunt festivitates in anno quae per omnia venerari debent: natalis Domini, sancti Stephani, sancti Johannis evangelistae, Innocentum, octabas Domini, Epiphania, octabas Epiphaniae, purificatio sanctae Mariae, Pascha dies octo, Litania major, Ascensa domini, Pentecosten, sancti Johannis Baptistae, sancti Petri et Pauli, sancti Martini, sancti Andreae. De adsumptione sanctae Mariae interrogandum reliquimus." *Capitula ecclesiastica,* c. xix (810-813 ?). Boretius, t. I, 179. Cf. *Capitul. Ansegisi,* i, 158, *ibid.,* 413.

[37] Cf. *Capitula Rodulfi Bituricen.* (841-866), c. xxvii. Mansi, t. XIV, 956.

of the Cross at Orleans;[38] others again were indicated by the head of each diocese, who had the necessary power to institute new feasts; whilst some were introduced by custom.

However, if all those days were celebrated by abstention from servile work, they were not all so observed in an equal degree. It goes without saying that the solemnity of Easter was the greatest. During the whole Easter octave, says the Council of Meaux of 845, all kinds of work are forbidden: agriculture, blacksmithing, carpentry, masonry, painting, women's occupations, hunting, judiciary affairs, commerce, and even the taking of oaths; all are forbidden under pain of excommunication.[39] As for the lesser feasts they were to be honored becomingly according to each one's devotion.[40]

This discipline left a wide margin to diocesan regulations; only the great feasts, *viz.* Easter,

[38] *Capitula Walter. Aurelianen.* (after 869), c. xviii. Mansi, t. xv, 508.

[39] "Dies octo sacrosanctae paschalis festivitatis omnibus christianis feriatos esse definimus. Ab omni opere rurali, fabrili, carpentario, gynaeceo, caementario, pictorio, venatorio, forensi, mercatorio, audientiali ac sacramentis exigendis. . . . Quod si quis temerarie praesumpserit, excommunicetur." *Conc. Melden.* (845), c. lxxvii. Mansi, t. XIV, 840.

[40] "Ceteras festivitates sanctorum apostolorum, martyrum, confessorum atque virginum *congruo honore* celebrandas esse censemus." *Capitula Rodulfi, loc. cit.*—Cf. BURCHARD, *Decretor.*, l. II, c. lxxvii: "Reliquae vero festivitates per annum *non sunt* cogendae ad feriandum nec prohibendae." (*Ex conc. Lugdunen.*, c. iv). *P. L., t.* CXL, 640; Hettonis, *Capitular.*, viii. *P. L.*, t. CV, 764.

Ascension, Pentecost, Christmas, and a few others, were universally celebrated, and they are the only ones which Pope Nicholas I imposed on the Bulgarians in addition to their own.[41] And as to Easter week, the variants of certain manuscripts give the text of Mayence, which we have just cited, a turn of particular significance: it is permitted, from Thursday inclusive, to plough before Mass, to sow, to till the vineyard or the garden, and surround one's property with palisades. After mass, however, no more work is to be done.[42] It is true that, later on, when Christianity became more firmly established among these nations, stricter rules and absolute rest from work were made obligatory.[43]

[41] "Nec non et in eorum sanctorum natalitiis, quorum *apud vos*, Deo favente memoria celebris et dies festivus habebitur." *Ad consulta Bulgar.*, c. xi. Mansi, t. XV, 407.

[42] "Diem dominicum Paschae cum omni honore et sobrietate venerari, similiter feriam secundam, tertiam et quartam, a feria quinta ante missam licentia sit arandi vel seminandi et ortum et vineam excolendi et sepem circumcludendi, ab alio vero opere cessare decrevimus, post missam autem ab opere vacare." *Concil. Moguntin.* (813), *loc. cit.*—A Bavarian council at the end of the eighth century, quoted by Regino (*De ecclesiast. discip.*, l. I, c. ccclxxviii), had made a similar decision, with this difference, however, that work was not allowed on Thursday, any more than on the previous days. Cf. *Conc. ad Rispach*, c. ii. *Monum. German.*, t. cit., p. 197. Baluze, in his notes, remarks that in his time work was allowed on certain feast days no longer before, but after mass. Migne, *P. L.*, t. CXXXII, 439.

[43] "Ut paschalis hebdomada festive tota celebretur, et in Pentecosten secunda, tertia, quarta feria, non minus quam dies dominicus honorentur." *Conc. Engilenheimen.* (948), c. vi. Mansi, t. XVIII, 421.

THE SECOND COMMANDMENT

The Rest on Feast Days in England.—A tendency can now be noticed in some countries, especially England, not to multiply the number of feasts of obligatory rest beyond measure. The Council of Cloveshow (747), introducing the feasts of St. Gregory the Great and St. Augustine into its provincial cycle, and prescribing that they be celebrated by all with befitting honor, adds that both are meant for ecclesiastics and monks.[44]

It was realized that poor workmen should be permitted the right of earning their livelihood more easily; and a distinction was often made between the bondmen and the *ingenui*. We read, *v. g.*, in the laws of Alfred the Great: "Here are the days of rest except for the bondmen or the laborers: twelve days at Christmas, the day when Christ defeated the demon, the day of St. Gregory, seven days preceding and seven following Easter, one day at the feast of SS. Peter and Paul, in autumn one complete week before the feast of the Blessed Virgin Mary, one day before All Saints' day, and the four Wednesdays of the four weeks of fast."[45]

---

[44] "Constitutum est, ut dies natalitius beati papae Gregorii, et dies quoque depositionis, qui est septimo Kalendas Junii, sancti Augustini archiepiscopi atque confessoris, qui genti Anglorum missus a praefato papa et patre nostro Gregorio, scientiam fidei, baptismi sacramentum, et coelestis patriae notitiam primus attulit, ab omnibus, sicut decet, honorifice venerentur. Ita ut uterque dies ab ecclesiasticis et monasterialibus feriatus habeatur." *Conc. Cloveshov.* II, c. xvii. Mansi, t. XII, 400.

[45] "Omnibus ingenuis hominibus dies hi sint remissi, exceptis servis et operariis. Duodecim dies in Natale Domini, et dies

The Council of Enham,[46] however, held in the same period, did not modify the common discipline of Christian countries; and the ecclesiastical laws of Canute in favor of Sunday rest were most strict, and to work on feast days exposed freemen and bondmen to severe corporal punishments.[47]

Nevertheless the principle produced new fruit in time. In the thirteenth century England developed a very special discipline in this matter. A Council of Oxford divides the feasts into three series from the viewpoint of rest. The first series comprises the feasts on which all work is forbidden; *viz.* five days at Christmas, the Circumcision, the Epiphany, all the feasts of the Blessed Virgin, except that of the Conception, which is not obligatory, the Conversion of St. Paul, the Chair of St. Peter, the feasts of all the Apostles, St. Gregory's feast day, Good Friday and four days after Easter, the Ascension, four days at Pentecost, St. Augustine's feast day in the month of May, two feasts of the Cross, the translation of St. Thomas mar-

ille in quo Christus diabolum superavit et S. Gregorii dies memorialis, et septem dies ante Pascha, et septem post, et unus dies in festo S. Petri et S. Pauli, et in autumno plena septimana ante festum beatae Mariae, et unus dies ante celebrationem Omnium sanctorum, et quatuor dies mercurii in quatuor septimanis jejunialibus, omnibus hominibus sunt remissi." *Leges ecclesiasticae Alfredi M. regis Anglor.*, c. xviii. Mansi, t. XVIII, 35.

[46] *Conc. Aenhamen.* (1009), c. xv. Mansi, t. XIX, 308.

[47] *Leges ecclesiasticae Canuti regis* (saeculare consilium), c. xiv, *ibid.*, 562.

tyr, the two feasts of St. John the Baptist, the feasts of St. Margaret, St. Mary Magdalen, St. Peter in Chains, St. Lawrence, St. Michael, St. Edmund Confessor, St. Edmund king and confessor, St. Catharine, St. Clement, St. Nicholas, and the dedication and the feast of the Patron Saint of each church. On the feasts of the second series, heavy works are absolutely forbidden, the light works are regulated according to custom; this class includes the feast days of SS. Fabian and Sebastian, St. Agnes, St. Vincent, St. Blasius, St. Agatha, St. Felix, St. George, St. John before the Latin Gate, St. Dunstan, St. Alban, St. Emeldrida, the Finding of the Cross, St. Stephen, St. Jerome, St. Faith, the dedication of St. Michael, St. Denys, the feast of All Souls, St. Cecilia, St. Lucy, and St. Leonard. In the third series are enumerated the feasts on which it is permissible to cultivate the ground, but only after mass; *viz.* the octave of Epiphany, the feasts of SS. John and Paul, the translation of St. Benedict, and the translation of St. Martin.[48]

[48] "Statuimus quod festa subscripta sub omni veneratione serventur, videlicet omnes dies dominici, quinque dies natalitii. . . . Volumus etiam ut alia festa a rectoribus ecclesiarum et capellanis in obsequio divino et laude devotissime celebrentur, minoribus operibus servilibus, secundum consuetudinem loci, illis diebus interdictis, festum sanctorum Fabiani et Sebastiani. . . . Haec sunt festa, in quibus post missam opera rusticana concedimus: sed antequam, non. Octava Epiphaniae, sanctorum Joannis et Pauli, translatio sancti Benedicti, translatio sancti Martini." *Conc. Oxonien.* (1222), c. viii. Mansi, t. XXII, 1153.

Although it was the intention of the Council of Oxford to bring about certain needed reforms in England, its decisions were not universally applied and did not suppress all the local usages even in the sanctification of feasts. Indeed a synod held at Worcester in 1240, shows the diversity of custom that then existed together with the unity of doctrine and discipline in general. So instructive do the prescriptions of this council regarding feasts appear, that we think it useful to cite them. In the first place, many categories of feasts which are given, are not those of Oxford. Secondly, the feasts of the first category are not absolutely the same; a rather striking fact that in the same country, between two dioceses not far from each other, and in twenty years' time, there should be such differences. Besides, among the feasts of the first series given by Oxford, Easter and Pentecost had four days' rest; here they have only three. On the feasts of the second order, carting is the only work allowed. The third series, comprising only feasts of female saints, *e.g.* St. Agnes, St. Margaret, St. Lucy, St. Agatha, forbids only feminine works. Lastly, other feasts are celebrated in the churches without involving any obligation of rest.[49]

[49] "Haec sunt ferianda in toto episcopatu Wigorniae . . . (The council enumerates at least forty-four days, not counting Sundays.) Haec sunt ferianda in omnibus praeterquam in carucis: sancti Vincentii martyris. . . . Haec sunt ferianda in operibus mulierum tantum, videlicet sanctae Agnetis. . . . Festa sanctorum

THE SECOND COMMANDMENT

In Hungary.—There was less leniency in Hungary. On the forty feasts to be celebrated every year, in addition to Sundays, rest seems to have been of equal obligation. On each feast one had to assist at Mass or send a representative; even hunting, if done with dogs, was forbidden, under pain of having one's horse taken away or being forced to buy it back with an ox; or for priests and clerics, of being deposed from their orders.[50] The secular law was just as severe. All sales made on a feast day obliged the guilty to pay fourfold in addition to the penance imposed. Every man who did not celebrate the prescribed feasts was punished with a three days' penance if he was free, and with seven blows if he was a bondman.[51]

Dominici, Francisci et Edmundi confessoris in ecclesiis cum novem lectionibus celebrari volumus. Nolumus tamen per haec opera fidelium impediri." *Synod. Wigornien.* (1240), Mansi, t. XXIII, 547. Also cf. the synod of Oxford (1287), c. xxiii, and its prescriptions, made expressly to bring about complete uniformity in the diocese. Mansi, t. XXIV, 812.

[50] *Conc. Szabolchen.* (1092), c. xxxviii. Mansi, t. XX, 779; cf. c. xi. "Si quis . . . ad ecclesiam non venerit parochialem, verberibus corripiatur" . . . c. xii: "Si quis in his diebus venatus fuerit canibus, equo careat sed equum bove redimat. Si vero presbyter aut clericus fuerit venatus, ab ordine descendat, usque ad satisfactionem." *Ibid.*, 763-766.

[51] "Si quis festo vendiderit, pretium acceptum quadruplo restituat, ipse vero poenitentiae subjaceat. Si quis descriptas festivitates non celebraverit, sic judicetur in eum: ut si liber est, tribus diebus poeniteat, si servus, septem plagis mulctetur." *Constitut. ecclesiast. Colomanni regis* (1103), l. II, c. vii et viii. Mansi, *ibid.*, 1180. Cf. *Synod. Strigonien.* (1114), c. viii. Mansi, t. XXI, 102.

The Sanctification of Feasts in France.—It has been seen above what success the régime of compulsion instituted in Hungary, obtained in France during the remaining portion of the Middle Ages. What has been said concerning Sunday is true also of feast days, since the measures urging the celebration of Sunday applied, according to the same texts, to the sanctification of feast days.[52]

Rest was rigorously enforced in Le Mans, where the Monday of the Quasimodo (lunae post Quasimodo), the Conception of the Blessed Virgin Mary (in December), and Corpus Christi were counted among the solemnized feasts;[53] in Mayence, where the conversion of St. Paul was celebrated;[54] and at Arles, where St. Trophimus was placed in the same rank.[55] In Narbonne, it was forbidden, under pain of the interdict and excommunication, to transport and cart wood, wheat, hay, straw, or any other kind of salable merchandise, except that which was to be consumed that very day.[56] Ap-

[52] "Parochiani cogantur venire ad ecclesiam dominicis et festivis diebus, in quibus cessatur ab operibus ... si non venerint ... persolvent sex denarios Turonensis monetae." *Convent. Apamien.* (1212), c. xvii. Mansi, t. XXII, 857. Cf. *Statuta ... ap. Tolosam* (1219), c. ii, *ibid.*, 1135-1136; *Conc. Tolosan.* (1229). c. xxv. Mansi, t. XXIII, 200.

[53] *Statuta Cenomanen.* (1247). Mansi, t. XXIII, 764.

[54] *Conc. provinc. Moguntin.* (1261), c. xxxi. Mansi, *ibid.*, 1091.

[55] *Conc. Arelaten.* (1260), c. vi, *ibid.*, 1006.

[56] "In festivitatibus beatae Virginis et Apostolorum, et S. Joannis Baptistae et aliis praecipuis solemnitatibus, opera servilia

THE SECOND COMMANDMENT

peals to the secular arm were made when the need arose.

In Cognac the simple act of going to market on feast days was forbidden under pain of excommunication *ipso facto*.[57]

If work and commerce were forbidden, such also was naturally the case with court sessions, lawsuits, and judgments, which are everywhere placed on a level with manual labor and business transactions.[58]

A half-century later, at Béziers, it was permitted to sell, in case of necessity, on Sundays and feast days, other things than eatables; but merchants were forbidden to keep their shops open when the articles exposed for sale were not eatable.

Return to a More Lenient Discipline.—But there

non exerceant; nec ligna, bladum, vel foenum, vel paleas, aut alias res venales, exceptis his quae ad esum illius diei pertinebunt, transferre, seu juxta vulgare quod dicitur *carrejare*, non praesumant. Et post dictas tres monitiones omnes qui ex tunc contra fecerint, nominatim denuntientur interdicti. . . . Et si eorum creverit contumacia, eosdem anathematizare proponimus, et invocare contra ipsos, si opus fuerit, brachium saeculare." *Statuta Domini Guidonis, archiep. Narbonen.* (about 1260), iv. Mansi, t. XXIII, 1032.

[57] "A macellis publicis abstineant diebus praedictis, et aliis solemnitatibus et festis: nec ad mercatum eant, aut nundinas, in eisdem vendituri aliquid aut empturi. Qui vero contra haec facere praesumpserint, excommunicationis sententiae subjaceant ipso facto." *Conc. Copriniacen.* (1262), c. xxxvi, *ibid.*, 874-875.

[58] Cf. *Conc. apud S. Mariam de Prato, juxta Rotomag.* (1313), c. iii. Mansi, t. XXV, 526; *Conc. Florentin.* (1346). Mansi, t. XXVI, 33.

was already under way in France what many undoubtedly called a relaxation, and what might more exactly be termed a wise moderation. Though continuing to institute new feasts, the authorities, following the example of England, did not make them feasts of complete rest.

We have noted that the principal feasts enumerated by the Council of Oxford in its first category, included Good Friday. Little by little it was generally felt that this rest, when added to that of the following week, was very burdensome, hence many worked on this day. A council of London tried to combine respect for discipline with the regard due to the poor, and framed the following decision to secure this combination: the obligation of rest remained for all those who were not poor, or who did not work for the poor on that day. "By the authority of the present council," said the bishops, "we rigorously forbid all persons to give themselves over to servile works on that day, or to any work foreign to piety. Still by this prohibition we do not impose an obligation on the poor, nor forbid the rich to pay the poor for their work, or to give by charity the accustomed help."[59]

[59] "Auctoritate praesentis concilii, districtius inhibemus, ne de cetero quispiam servilibus, ipsa die, intendat operibus, vel quaevis alia exerceat, quae a pietatis cultu fuerint aliena. Per hoc tamen legem pauperibus non imponimus, nisi (nec?) divitibus prohibemus, quin ad agriculturam pauperum promovendam, suffragia consueta, caritatis intuitu subministrent." *Conc. Londinen.* (1327), c. i, *ibid.*, 829. At Dublin, on the contrary, the feast of

THE SECOND COMMANDMENT

In France the calendars of the dioceses of Rodez, Cahors, and Tulle comprised more than fifty feasts on which work and business had to be suspended, without counting the other days on which local custom prescribed rest. Wishing to form a code of local customs regarding what was called the common feasts of the departed, which were ordinarily celebrated on the morrow of All Saints', the morrow of St. Hilary's, and, in some places, the morrow of the octaves of Easter and Pentecost, it was decided that the celebration of these feasts should last only till after mass.[60] This was an opportune and a prudent measure. Everywhere laxness increased. The devotion of many had been exhausted by the introduction of so many new feasts. La Fontaine's cobbler murmured in his stall:[61]

> The worst of all I must confess
> Is that the days are made so many
> In which we cannot earn a penny.

the Immaculate Conception of the Blessed Virgin was imposed as a feast of obligation, and absolute abstention from work required in express terms: ". . . *ab omni opere servili, rurali et manuali prorsus abstinendo.*" *Conc. Dublinen.* (1351), c. ii et c. vi, Mansi, t. XXVI, 119.

[60] "Celebrantur haec festa defunctorum usque post missas." *Synodalia statuta Cadurcen. Ruthenen. et Tutelen. Ecclesiarum* (1289), c. xxxi. Mansi, t. XXIV, 1054.

[61] Qu'il faut toujours chômer: on nous ruine en fêtes.
L'une fait tort à l'autre; et Monsieur le curé
De quelque nouveau saint charge toujours son prône.
LA FONTAINE *Fables,* viii, 2.

> The sorest ill the poor man feels:
> They tread upon each other's heels,
> Those idle days of holy saints!
> And though the year is shingled o'er
> The parson keeps a-finding more.[62]

It was time to moderate an over-ardent zeal. So, when the Council of Prague, in 1355, once more enumerated the list of days of rest, it added that repose on the more recent ones should last only till after mass.[63]

In Provence, on the contrary, near the pontifical court, the clergy strongly inveighed against the looseness of manners, especially with regard to the observance of feast days. The Council of Apt, of 1365, appealed to the secular arm to enforce the Church law, as the archbishop of Narbonne had done a hundred years earlier.[64]

We do not know whether this display of energy

[62] Translation by E. Wright.

[63] "Item, in diebus beatorum Marci et Lucae Evangelistarum, et quatuor doctorum Ecclesiae, Gregorii, Ambrosii, Augustini, et Hieronymi, quorum festivitates felicis memoriae Bonifacius papa mandavit in universis ecclesiis, sub officio duplici solemniter venerari. Et populus in sua parochiali ecclesia divino officio peraudito, ad sua opera licite se convertit." *Synod. Pragen.* (1356), c. xlvi. Mansi, t. XXVI, 398.

[64] "Cupientes tali morbo pestifero obviare, statuimus praesentis auctoritate concilii, per Ordinarios juris remediis provideri, et si non obtemperaverint, temporalem curiam per quemlibet nostrum in dictis nostris dioecesibus requirendam, quae subditos ipsos compescat talibus poenis et remediis aliis quibus videbitur expedire." *Conc. Apten.* (1365), c. xiii. Mansi, *ibid.*, 450-451.

THE SECOND COMMANDMENT

obtained the desired success; to tell the truth, we doubt it somewhat.

In Spain, on the contrary, the authority of the Church kept growing stronger, and after the pattern of a council of Albi, which we have cited above, the authorities felt themselves possessed of sufficient power to forbid even the Saracens and the Jews to work or trade on Sundays or feast days. Lay judges received orders to assist the bishops in enforcing these precepts.[65]

This was the last effort of the ecclesiastical authorities towards adding to the precept. Thenceforth they were satisfied to maintain the acquired positions. The various councils of Cologne and Ireland in the fifteenth century, and those of Poland in the sixteenth, did not go beyond this. The Council of Trent likewise was satisfied with the existing prescriptions.[66] It was thought for a time that the authority of this council would supply a basis for the right of the bisops to introduce new feast days of precept in their respective dioceses, but a bull of Urban VIII, while not deciding against the existence of that right, counselled that no use be made of it,[67] and at the same time suppressed a number of ancient feasts.

[65] *Conc. Palentinum* (1388), c. vi. Mansi, *ibid.*, 744.

[66] *Sess.* XXII, *Decretum de observandis et evitandis in celebratione missae;* cf. Sess. XXV, c. xii, *de Reform.*, and *Decretum de mortificatione carnis, jejuniis et diebus festis.*

[67] Bull *Universa*, 22nd of December, 1642.

142   THE COMMANDMENTS OF THE CHURCH

The Bull "Universa" and the Reduction of Feast Days.—Urban VIII's bull "Universa" demands special attention because it confirms with sovereign authority the historical exposition into which the impartial study of documents has led us, and also establishes a definite and universal law on the matter.

"The number of feasts and their diversity are such," says the Pope, "that many do not know any more which are to be observed *ex praecepto*, and which are purely devotional. Their very number begets lukewarmness among Christians. Nay more, the poor clamorously lament that the excessive multiplication of feast days deprives them of the means of sustinence; while others take advantage of it to abandon themselves to an idleness that is full of perils; for, instead of using those days for praising God in church, they consume them in worldly and pernicious pleasures, and change what was instituted to facilitate their eternal salvation into occasions of sin and damnation." [68]

---

[68] "Multi jam dubitare videantur quaenam ex praecepto, quaeve ex libera cujusque voluntate, sint servanda, pietatis fervore ob nimiam eorumdem numerositatem tepescente; quinimmo et clamor pauperum frequens ostendit ad nos eamdem multitudinem ob quotidiani victus laboribus suis comparandi necessitatem, sibi valde damnosam conquerentium, et quod summopere dolendum est, magno cum animi nostri moerore didicimus tanta saepe saepius malignatum inimicum in Sancto, ut ipsa multitudine non ad aedificationem, et ad laudandum in ecclesiis Deum populi utantur,

The Pope indeed knew better than anyone how urgently from all parts of the Church in Germany, in England (where a reduction of feast days had been so often called for, particularly under Henry VIII), in Italy, and in brief, throughout Christendom, a reform was demanded. So Urban VIII modified the traditional list. Among the feasts of Our Lord that remained obligatory were Christmas, Easter, and Pentecost, and the two days following both Easter and Pentecost, the Circumcision, Epiphany, Ascension, Trinity, Corpus Christi, and the Finding of the True Cross; among those of the Blessed Virgin, the Purification, Annunciation, Assumption and Nativity; among the feasts of the saints, those of St. Michael (May 8), the nativity of St. John the Baptist, SS. Peter and Paul, St. Andrew, St. James the Greater, St. John, St. Bartholomew, St. Thomas, SS. Philip and James, St. Matthew, SS. Simon and Jude, St. Mathias, St. Lawrence, St. Sylvester, St. Joseph, St. Ann, All Saints', and the feast of the Patron Saint of each particular region.

While the number of feasts was henceforth fixed and uniform, it was not notably reduced, because to the thirty-four days just enumerated, and which could fall on any day of the week, had to be

sed ad otia, vanitates et vitia frequenter abuti non formident, ita ut quae ad glorificandum divinum nomen sunt primitus instituta, temporis decursu inimicus homo corruperit et in magnam illius offensionem, gravemque jacturam converterit animarum."

added all the Sundays. Complaints naturally continued.

But in order to keep as close as possible to old traditions, instead of completely suppressing the feasts, the authorities maintained the obligation of assisting at Mass, while they permitted the faithful to devote the remainder of the day to their work.[69]

Benedict XIV, who issued the canonical statement quoted in the note, was frequently urged, when Pope, to grant the bishops the power of reducing the too numerous feasts which still remained after the modifications made by Urban VIII. The Bishop of Calahorra brought to his notice the fact that because of the excessive increase of feasts, the poor could no longer earn their livelihood, and received permission, by a special indult, to reduce the number of feasts in his diocese to nineteen.[70] For the other feasts only the obli-

[69] "In nonnullis dioecesibus numerus dierum festorum de praecepto ... eatenus est imminutus, ut nempe in aliquibus festis christifideles et missam audire, et ab operibus servilibus abstinere debeant; in aliis vero populo permissum sit opera servilia exercere, firma remanente obligatione audiendi missae sacrificium ..." Benedict. XIV, Constitut. *Cum semper*, 19 August, 1744.

[70] "Hominibus, (qui manu et labore in sudore vultus vescentes pane suo, ob ingentem festorum numerum, obtenta alendae vitae necessitate, vetitis laboribus jam late aperuerunt), si per omnes dies festos hujusmodi a servilibus operibus abstineant, ad vitam lucro sustentandam haudquaquam tempus sufficiat." Const. *Cum sicut*, § 1, September 3, 1742.

gation of hearing mass remained; after mass all could work without scruple.⁷¹

Poland was given a further favor. Two indults, to the bishops of Vilna and of Posen, gave permission for the benefit of the peasants to transfer to the Sunday following the feasts of precept which fell on week days during the months of July, August, and September; the feast of the Assumption alone was excepted.⁷²

But these partial concessions did not seem sufficient. Public opinion demanded more. Benedict XIV himself narrates how, under pressure, he asked the advice of forty theologians and canonists of repute, among them many cardinals, and thirty-three declared a reduction of feast days to be necessary or highly expedient. Fifteen begged him to order this reduction by a special constitution for the entire Church, while eighteen believed that it would be better to wait for action on the part of the bishops. The Pope followed this latter advice; but at the same time, in order to obtain

⁷¹ "In reliquis diebus festis . . . praeceptis, audita missa, laboriosis suorum artium exercitationibus, servilibusque operibus, sine ullo prorsus conscientiae scrupulo vacare possint, auctoritate nostra Apostolica concedas . . ." *Ibid.*, § 2. The concession is about the same for the diocese of Nice. Constit. *Inter sollicitas*, April 11, 1745. Also, in 1742, 1743, 1744, 1745, similar constitutions were issued for different dioceses in Spain.

⁷² Const. *Nuper pro parte tua*, September 1st, 1745, and *Ut per tres*, May 27th, 1743.

as much uniformity as possible, decided to grant an indult to a diocese only when the neighboring dioceses had manifested the same desire. The discussions raised by this affair became so animated that the Pope had to forbid the publication of books on the subject.[73]

Ferraris [74] gives a list of cities and dioceses which, in 1748, had reduced the number of feast days, as far as abstaining from servile labor was concerned; this list must have increased rapidly.

The reduction bore mainly on those feasts which had been added to the calendar last. In France it reached its limit on the occasion of the Concordat, when only four feasts remained with the double obligation of assisting at Mass and abstaining from servile labor. These four feasts were: Christmas, the Ascension, the Assumption, and All Saints'; the others were either completely suppressed, or, what was practically the same thing, so far as the people were concerned, transferred to the following Sunday.

Regarding the transferred or suppressed feasts, one part of the discipline was, however, maintained, *viz.* the obligation of the pastor to say Mass *pro populo,* which had been introduced as a correlative to the obligation of the faithful to assist at mass.[75] The pontifical constitutions which re-

---

[73] Constit. *Non multi*, November 14th, 1748.
[74] *Prompta Bibliotheca Canonica*, etc., v. Festa, n. 140.
[75] Benedict XIV, Const. *Cum semper.*

duced the observance of feasts, while maintaining the obligation of assisting at Mass, took care to add that the obligation still existed for the pastor to say Mass *pro populo*.

On May 3, 1858, Pius IX, by the Constitution *Amantissimi*, renewed in express terms the declaration of several of his predecessors that the obligation of celebrating Mass *pro populo*, not only on Sundays but also on the feast days suppressed since the Constitution of Urban VIII, remained in full force.[76]

However, the popes did not ignore the fact that this part of the law, like the preceding one, was of ecclesiastical institution, and that the supreme legislator has the power to modify or abrogate what custom or law has created. When needs like those which had led to a reduction of the feast days in favor of the people, manifested themselves in matters concerning the general welfare of the Church, the popes consented to similar reductions. Thus, in order to provide the necessary pecuniary resources, various indults now al-

---

[76] "Declaramus, statuimus atque decernimus, Parochos aliosque omnes animarum curam actu gerentes sacrosanctum Missae sacrificium pro populo sibi commisso celebrare et applicare debere tum omnibus dominicis aliisque diebus, qui ex praecepto adhuc servantur, tum aliis etiam qui ex hujus Apostolicae Sedis indulgentia ex dierum de praecepto festorum numero sublati ac translati sunt, quemadmodum ipsi animarum curatores debebant, dum memorata Urbani VIII Constitutio in pleno suo robore vigebat, antequam festivi de praecepto dies imminuerentur et transferrentur."

low pastors to receive, under expressly stated conditions, for the celebration of Mass on the days of suppressed feasts, stipends which they have to devote to diocesan purposes.

Summary.—Such was the development of what is called the second commandment of the Church. The origin of our Christian feasts goes back to the earliest days of the Church, to the very Resurrection of Christ, which forms the keystone of Christianity, and to Pentecost, which gave the Church her first converts. As these feasts fell on Sunday, they added no new obligation, but merely made Sunday more solemn. Later were celebrated the anniversaries of the martyrs on the day on which they happened to fall; the birth or Epiphany of Our Saviour, the dedication of churches, and some other feasts which usually fell on a week day.

Hence, from the beginning there were universal and local feasts, more solemn feasts, *viz.* Christmas, the Ascension, Epiphany, the anniversary of the great diocesan or national martyrs, *e.g.* St. Cyprian in Africa, St. Martin in France, etc.; and less solemn feasts, *e.g.* the anniversaries of the other martyrs. These were celebrated with the same rites as Sunday, *viz.* liturgical services and abstention from servile labor. But there remains no legislative text to indicate the nature of the corresponding obligation on the part of the faithful.

In proportion as the Church obtains a greater

control over souls, the obligation of sanctifying the feast days becomes more precise and spreads. However, each diocese preserves a certain large measure of independence; feasts are hardly ever imposed upon a diocese by universal law, but rather by provincial councils, by particular memories, or by fraternal exchange with neighboring dioceses.

Little by little the multiplication of feasts reaches the point of taking away from manual labor more than a hundred days a year in certain dioceses; and the poor who have to earn their daily bread consequently suffer. Considerateness for them caused councils or custom to create certain categories of feasts on which rest is restricted. This measure of mercy does not, however, prevent the growth of laxity, which increases in proportion as the influence of the Church diminishes. It was necessary to make a further reduction to insure the complete observance of the principal feasts, and leave the others to the devotion of the more pious among the faithful.

Many undoubtedly considered this progressive decline of venerated institutions a sort of profanation. We may indeed regret the decay into which under our economic and religious conditions many of the ancient feasts have fallen. But there is no profanation in all this. The Church, who is absolute mistress of her calendar, has simply adapted to the necessities of the present age a law which was for a long time more or less uncertain, and which she well knew how to accommodate to the requirements of the poor in the thirteenth century, and, long before, to the vacillating good will of half-converted nations. We have returned, in this regard, to the condition of the Primitive Church. The worship of God will not suffer if the Catholics of our day sanctify the limited number of feast days left to them with the same sentiments of fervor which are attributed to the Christians of the Apostolic age.

CHAPTER V

THE THIRD COMMANDMENT

Tous tes péchés confesseras,
à tout le moins une fois l'an.[1]

Confess thy sins at least once a year.

Before commencing the history of this commandment, we believe it useful to determine exactly the object of our study.

We have not to demonstrate a dogmatic thesis on the sacrament of penance or confession. That confession is of divine right; that there is a divine obligation to have recourse to it sometimes in one's life; is outside our province. Neither have we to express an opinion on the much discussed question how the sacrament of penance was administered in the first centuries. What were the sins submitted in practice to that tribunal? Was confession public or private? Was there a private along with public penance? From what period does auricular confession date? All these ques-

[1] All thy sins thou shalt confess,
Once at least each year.

In our Baltimore Catechism this is the third commandment; it reads: To confess at least once a year.

tions are outside of our pale. The only point we wish to treat is this: When did the ecclesiastical law of confessing once a year originate, and how was the obligation satisfied?

It is certain that the canon *Omnis Utriusque Sexus* of the fourth Lateran Council (1215) is the first *universal* law of the Latin Church which imposes annual confession.

But this canon was preceded by many local laws, which several centuries before had made the practice all but universal throughout the West.

Origin of the Commandment.—It cannot be accurately determined to what period the origin of this discipline goes back. If one wishes to realize fully what confession meant in olden times, he must not separate it from communion.

It is especially as a preparation for communion that the obligation of confession was imposed; the obligation of receiving the Body of Christ once a year, therefore, normally implies the obligation of preparing oneself by confession to receive Him worthily. For many centuries it was left to the conscience of the faithful to judge their own dispositions, provided no grave crime, exterior and public, exposed them as unworthy of the holy mysteries. But from the fourth century on, the preachers and Fathers of the Church insisted on the greater security given by a well-made confession. This amounted to an insistent invitation to the sinner to go to confession before receiving communion.

We shall trace in a later chapter the origin of the obligation of communicating at Easter time, or at least once a year. Since we know from St. John Chrysostom that the Lenten season, particularly at the approach of Easter, was a time of communion, we could conclude therefrom that it must have been for many a time of confession. We could even affirm it unhesitatingly should we be allowed to ground our opinion on Sermon XXV, *de S. Quadragesima,* IX, found among the works of St. Ambrose; but this text is not genuine, and its date uncertain.

We must be satisfied, therefore, for the first centuries, with the conclusion that the faithful sometimes (not as frequently as the bishops desired) had recourse to the sacrament of penance and considered it one of the safest means to obtain pardon for grave faults,—those of which St. Augustine says that, unlike the daily faults which God Himself pardons, they are "grave and mortal" sins and ordinarily can be remitted only by the power of the keys.[2]

This does not prove, however, that the faith-

[2] "Hujus vitae sunt quaedam gravia et mortifera, quae nisi per vehementissimam molestiam humiliationis cordis et contritionis spiritus et tribulationis poenitentiae non relaxantur. Haec dimittuntur per claves Ecclesiae." S. AUGUSTIN., *Serm.* 278. *P. L.*, t. XXXVIII, 2273-2274.

ful had recourse to confession once a year, or that it was considered as obligatory before each communion.[3]

Far from it; it seems that one of the most constant cares of the Fathers was not so much to invite the faithful to annual confession, as to persuade those who had committed some grave sin, not to wait until the approach of death to ask for the sacrament of Penance.[4]

Here there was undoubtedly question of public penance. Through the latter, in fact, the custom of confessing in Lent was introduced as a preparation for the paschal communion, even for those whose state of conscience did not require this sacrament.

We pass over a synodal statute of Rheims (perhaps of the seventh century,[5] 630?), which designates Lent as the time when the pastor is to hear the confessions of his parishioners; this legisla-

[3] See the sermons of St. John Chrysostom, and in particular, *Homil. III in Epist. ad Ephes.*, n. 4 and 5. *Opp. S. Joan. Chrysost.*, Migne, *P. G.*, t. LXII, 28-29.

[4] Cf. in particular the sermons of St. Caesarius of Arles, 255, 257, 258, ff., *inter Opp. S. Augustini, P. L.*, t. XXXIX, 2216, 2219, 2233, etc. That Caesarius should be so moderate in his demands concerning confession is all the more remarkable since ordinarily he was quite exacting for the service of God, and induced the Council of Agde to decide that those of the laity who missed communion on the great feasts of Christmas, Easter, and Pentecost, should not be treated as Catholics (*Conc. Agathen.*, c. xviii, BRUNS, t. II, 150).

[5] *Statuta synodalia eccles. Remen. per Dnum Sonnatium.* MANSI, t. X, 596.

THE THIRD COMMANDMENT

tion, which antedates by many centuries the Gallic and Western discipline, is really of too doubtful authenticity for the seventh century and cannot be taken as a witness of the discipline of that period.

It is from the discipline of public penance that we get the first sure testimonies of an obligatory confession which, at first, seems to have been attached to the time of Lent. Those directly affected are the persons guilty of some grave fault; but others join them in this exercise through a spirit of humility.

A description of the way penitents were treated may not be out of place here. The rite of the ceremony is explained at length in the Roman Pontifical, although for us of the present day it is only a vestige of an obsolete observance. It is also found in the *Poenitentiale Vallicellanum III*. In order to secure a more venerable authority for its prescriptions and to facilitate obedience, this Penitential claims to originate from the Council of Agde (506), which we have already mentioned. To this council it attributes the institution of the rite according to which the penitents are dismissed from church on Ash Wednesday for the whole period of Lent until Holy Thursday.

We quote from the *Vallicellanum:* "The week before the beginning of Lent, the priests convoke the people, try to reconcile by canonical authority those who live in discord, and quench dissensions; at this same period they give a penance to those who have confessed, so that, immediately before the beginning of the fast, all who have confessed may receive their penance and may say with greater fervor: Forgive us our trespasses as we forgive those who have trespassed against us.

"The priests must also notify their parishioners that every man who feels guilty of mortal sin must have recourse on the Wednesday before Lent to Holy Church, his vivifying Mother, that he must confess with humility, contrition of heart, and simplicity the wrong he has committed, and receive the remedy of penance according to the mode determined upon by the holy canons. Furthermore, not only those who have committed a mortal sin, but all who feel that they have soiled the immaculate robe of Christ, received in Baptism, shall come in haste, confess to the priest, humbly avow all their faults to him, listen piously to his advice as they would to the advice of God Himself, and faithfully observe all his directions."[6]

[6] "Ebdomada priori ante initium Quadragesimae presbyteri plebium convocent ad se populum et discordantes canonica auctoritate reconcilient, et omnia jurgia sedent et tunc primum confitentibus poenitentiam dent, ita ut antequam caput jejunii veniat omnes confessi poenitentiam acceptam habeant et liberius dicere possint: Dimitte nobis debita nostra sicut et nos dimittimus debitoribus nostris.

"Presbyteri admonere debent plebem sibi subjectam, ut omnis, qui se sentit mortifero peccati vulnere sauciatum feria IIII[a]

Such is the picture, true to life, of the discipline of annual confession with its successive developments.

But it does not seem to have been so complete from the beginning. The *Pontificale Romanum* seems to represent an earlier stage of the discipline; it mentions among those who must perform the solemn penance according to the ancient custom, only those persons guilty of particularly grave sins.[7] These are to come to the cathedral on Ash Wednesday, at the hour of Terce, barefooted, clothed in coarse garments and with downcast eyes. The bishop's penitentiary imposes a penance on them and sends them to the door of the church, where they shall remain kneeling for the rest of Lent. During the chant of None the bishop blesses the ashes, and distributes it to the people;

ante quadragesimam cum omni festinatione recurrat ad vivificatricem matrem Ecclesiam, ubi quod male commisit cum omni humilitate et contritione cordis simpliciter confessus suscipiat remedia poenitentiae secundum modum canonicis auctoritatibus praefixum. Non solum autem ille qui mortale aliquid commisit, sed etiam omnis homo, quicumque se recognoscit immaculatam Christi tunicam, quam in baptismo accepit, peccati macula polluisse, ad proprium sacerdotem festinet venire, ut cum puritate mentis omnes transgressiones omniaque peccata quibus Dei offensam se incurrisse meminit, humiliter confiteatur et quidquid a sacerdote fuit injunctum ac si ab ipso omnipotentis Dei ore esset probatum [undoubtedly a misprint for "prolatum"] intendat et cautissime observet." SCHMITZ, *Die Bussbücher und die Bussdisciplin der Kirche*, t. I, 774.

[7] "Poenitentes, quibus secundum jus vel consuetudinem, pro gravioribus criminibus solemnis est poenitentia injungenda."

and when the ceremony in church is ended, the procession of clerics goes to the door of the edifice. The pontiff imposes the ashes on the head of each penitent in the usual form, adding: "Do penance, that you may have eternal life." He then blesses the haircloths and places them on their heads. The Seven Penitential Psalms, the litany, and some prayers are sung, and the penitents are sent away with a few words of encouragement. On Holy Thursday they are solemnly reconciled; the ceremony ends with a very beautiful and expressive formula, pronouncing absolution from all sins of thought, word, and action.

Thanks to the interesting religious evolution which, since the fifth and sixth centuries, led Christians who were guilty of no fault entailing public penance to join the ranks of the penitents—an evolution of which we find traces in the text of the *Poenitentiale Vallicellanum* just quoted—the confession made at the beginning of Lent was no longer the work of penitents properly so-called, but became the practice of all good Christians.

After the Eighth Century.—Even before the middle of the eighth century, the common practice of annual confession is an established fact. Not without some difficulty, however, for a council of Bavaria, held about 740–750,[8] counsels resort to

[8] *Concil. Bajuwaricum* (740-750), c. ii. *Mon. Germ., Concilia,* t. II, 52.

confession in its strict sense only with extreme discretion; but confession is already firmly established as obligatory three times a year for the faithful, and every Saturday for the monks, under the rule of Chrodegang.[9]

However, this last prescription is perhaps the only one of its kind at this period. The Capitularies of Theodulf of Orleans mention only the confession to be made at the beginning of Lent; [10] it is also on Ash Wednesday that, according to a synodal sermon published by Mansi, the pastor was to invite his parishioners to go to confession and to impose on them a legitimate penance in conformity with the Penitentiary books.[11] On that same day, according to the statutes given by Adalard to the abbey of St. Peter of Corbie, the workmen were exempted from work, so as to be able to make their confession.[12]

[9] "In unoquoque anno *tribus vicibus,* id est in tribus quadragesimis, populus fidelis suam confessionem *suo sacerdoti* faciat, et qui plus fecerit, melius facit. Monachi in unoquoque sabbato confessionem faciant." CHRODEGANG, *Regula canonicorum,* c. xxxii. *P. L.,* t. LXXXIX, 1072.

[10] "Prima autem hebdomada ante initium Quadragesimae confessio danda est de omnibus peccatis quae sive opere sive locutione perpetrantur." THEODULPH., *Capitulare* 2dum. MANSI, t. XIII, 1017.

[11] "Feria quarta ante Quadragesimam plebem ad confessionem invitate et ei juxta qualitatem delicti poenitentiam injungite, non ex corde vestro, sed sicut in poenitentiali scriptum est." *Sermo synodalis.* (Est, says Mansi, homilia Leonis IV, quae in synodis legi solebat). MANSI, t. XIX, 314.

[12] "Similiter isti sunt dies quibus eis ab opere dominico parcen-

In the middle of the ninth century the secret confession of Lent is a well established custom. The *capitula* of Rodulf of Bourges speak of it as a received fact, having no necessary relation to the public penance. The confession to be made bears on the sins of thought as well as of action, and comprises a penance to be performed during Lent.[13]

Fifty years before Rodulf, in the days of Alcuin, it was considered wrong to communicate without previously going to confession.[14] A ritual of St. Gatian of Tours, published by Martène and at-

dum est . . . primo die jejuniorum quadragesimae, adeo ut spatium habeant confessiones suas renovare." *Statuta antiqua abbatiae S. Petri Corbeiensis*, quae monachis suis praescripsit Adalardus abbas, l. I, c. ii. *P. L.*, t. CV, 538.

[13] "Hebdomada una ante initium Quadragesimae confessiones sacerdotibus dandae sunt, poenitentia accipienda. . . . Et sic ingredientes in beatae Quadragesimae tempus mundis et purificatis mentibus ad sanctum Pascha accedant, et per poenitentiam se renovent, quae est secundus baptismus. Confessiones vero dandae sunt de omnibus peccatis, quae sive in opere, sive in cogitatione perpetrantur." *Capitula Rodulfi Archiep. Bituricen.*, c. xxxii. In the following chapter these capitula forbid, contrary to the anterior texts, the use of the penitential books, "which place cushions under the elbows of the sinners and pillows under their head" ("repudiatis ac penitus eliminatis libellis, quos poenitentiales vocant . . . qui consuunt pulvillos, secundum propheticum sermonem, sub omni cubito manus, et faciunt cervicalia sub capite universae aetatis ad capiendas animas"). *Ibid.*, c. xxxiii. MANSI, t. XIV, 958, 959.

[14] "Corpus et sanguinem Domini polluto corde et corpore, *sine confessione* et poenitentia scienter et indigne accepi." ALCUIN, *De psalmorum usu*, pars 2da, ix. Confessio peccatorum. *P. L.*, t. CI, 499.

tributed to the ninth or tenth century, shows that it is matter for confession not to have been to confession in Lent.[15]

However, if annual confession no longer had any relation to public penance, it preserved points in common with it, since it had borrowed from the discipline of public penance not only the time of going to confession, but also the delay of absolution. The penitent presented himself and made avowal of his sins on Ash Wednesday, but the absolution was normally delayed to Holy Thursday, unless particular reasons rendered its immediate bestowal advisable. The rule, therefore, was to delay absolution till Holy Thursday, even for private confession.[16]

[15] "Confiteor etiam quia Corpus et Sanguinem Domini Nostri Jesu Christi indignus,—et pollutus, et immundus, et sine confessione communicavi . . . *et in Quadragesima*, sicut constitutum est, *confessus non fui*." MARTÈNE, *De antiquis Ecclesiae ritibus*, lib. I, c. vi, art. 7, t. I, p. 279, col. 1.

[16] "Praemonere debent omnes sacerdotes eos qui sibi confiteri solent ut in capite jejunii concurrere incipiant ad renovandam confessionem. Et tunc suscepta, secundum prolatam rationis confessionem, indicet singulis congruam poenitentiam, sive observantiam usque in Coena Domini, magnopere intimans illis in praesenti, ut tunc ad reconciliandum festinare nullatenus parvipendant. Si vero interest causa aut itineris, aut cujuslibet occupationis aut ita forte hebes est, ut ei hoc sacerdos persuadere nequeat: injunget ei tam quadragesimalem, quamque annualem poenitentiam, et reconciliet eum statim." Ordo iv. Eccles. S. Gatiani Turonen. *Ordo privatae seu annualis Poenitentiae.* MARTÈNE, *De antiquis Ecclesiae ritibus*, l. I, c. vi, art. 7, t. I, p. 280, col. 1. Cf. SCHMITZ, *Die Bussbücher und die Bussdisciplin der Kirche*, t. II, 57.

Ash Wednesday was not everywhere the day of confession. In some places it was simply the day on which the priest, taking advantage of the serious thoughts inspired by the liturgical ceremonies, in particular by the imposition of the ashes, invited his people to confess their sins in the course of the week.[17] For it is always *"in capite Quadragesimae"* that one's confession must be made.[18]

From that period on the obligation of confessing annually is synonymous with that of confessing in Lent. At the annual synod, one of the customary questions that the bishop asks, in order to determine the exact religious condition of his diocese, is this: "Is there anyone who does not go to confession at least once a year, at the beginning of Lent, and does not receive penance for his sins?"[19]

Confession Three Times a Year.—How the Lenten confession developed into three confessions

---

[17] "Si feria quarta ante quadragesiman plebem sibi commissam ad confessionem invitet." REGINO, *De ecclesiasticis disciplinis. Inquisitio de his quae episcopus vel ejus ministri inquirere debeant*, nº 57, *P. L.*, t. CXXXII, 189. Cf. RATHER, *Epist. synodic. ad presbyteros*, nº 10. Migne, *P. L.*, t. CXXXVI, 562, and *Dial. Confess.*, *ib.*, 401.

[18] REGINO, *De ecclesiastic. disciplinis*, l. I, c. cclxxxviii. Migne, *P. L.*, t. CXXXII, 245; BURCHARD, *Decretum*, l. XIX, c. ii. Migne, *P. L.*, t. CXL, 949.

[19] Regino, *op. cit.*, l. II, c. v, nº 65. Migne, *P. L.*, *ib.*, 285; *item*, 457, 459, 461. Burchard, *Decretum*, l. I, c, xciv, interrog. 64, *P. L.*, t. CXL, 577, 578.

annually, and what caused this change of discipline, is not certain. We conceive it as having taken place in the following way:

At first, public penance, for which the guilty had to present themselves at the beginning of Lent, was perhaps a regulation of ecclesiastical discipline rather than a mere question of conscience. Later, when pious Christians, of their own accord and from reasons of devotion, presented themselves for the same exercises as public sinners, they evidently sought the meritorious side of penance, the purification of the soul by the twofold means of confessional absolution and penitential exercises.

For the public sinners the obligation remained above all a disciplinary one. But as confession became more frequent, the theology of the practice was studied more thoroughly. Among the nine or ten means which the Fathers and Doctors formerly enumerated as sufficient to procure the remission of sins,[20] sacramental confession with its ensuing absolution became more and more prominent. It came to be considered the normal means of regaining the state of grace; and the result was that confession for the majority of the faithful became an obligatory preparation for each communion of precept.

[20] Cf. in particular the list given by Origen, *Hom.* II *in Levit.*, n. 4. Migne, *P. G.*, t. XII, 417, and following. A great number of other references could be given to support the same teaching.

We have seen the first traces of this discipline in the rule of Chrodegang. At the beginning of the twelfth century we find it fully developed and firmly established. The obligation of communicating many times a year involved the obligation of going to confession as many times. The oldest texts establishing this dicipline, at least the oldest we know of, come from Germany. One, for instance, is that of a council of Strigony, at the beginning of the twelfth century, which clearly distinguishes between the simple faithful and the clerics, and says the former shall confess and communicate on the three principal feasts: Easter, Pentecost, and Christmas, while the clerics shall communicate on every solemn feast.[21] Hungary had then had a hundred years of Christianity, and we have already seen [22] how strictly it adhered to all Christian observances; this one, however, was not peculiar to Hungary, for it was made compulsory among the newly converted peoples as an essential point of the Church's discipline. When, shortly after, Otto of Bamberg, having passed some years among the Pomeranians, whom he had just converted, returned to his episcopal city, he recommended to his young Christians to con-

[21] "Ut omnis populus in Pascha et Pentecoste, et Natali Domini poenitentiam agat et communicet, clerici vero in omnibus majoribus festis communicent." *Synod. Strigonien.* (1114), c. iv. Mansi, t. XXI, 100.

[32] See History of the First Commandment, *supra*.

fess and communicate at least three or four times a year, if they could not do so more frequently.[23]

The precept had thus gone further than human sloth was willing to follow. In spite of the general precept there were very few who did not violate the "rule" of the Church by simply confining themselves to one yearly confession. From the famous Alanus of Lille (1114–1203) we learn about the new disciplinary rule and the manner in which it was observed just a few years before the fourth Lateran Council.

"In the first place," he says, "all must go to the priest at Easter time, even if they are not conscious of any sin; and, though secret sins are remitted in the general confession, all are counselled to present themselves to the priest and tell him that they are not conscious of any sin, thereby avoiding even the appearance of transgressing the ecclesiastical discipline."[24]

What Alanus understands by *general* confession he explains in his *Summa de arte praedicatoria*, where he says: "There are two kinds of

[23] "Oportet tamen, addit [Otto], et vos ipsos ter vel quater in anno, si amplius fieri non potest, et confessionem facere atque ipsi sacramento communicare." *Vita Ottonis Bambergen. episcopi*, c. li. *P. L.*, t. CLXXIII, 1300.

[24] "Nullius peccati conscius, ad confessarium accedere debet in Paschate. . . . Et quamvis in generali confessione occulta peccata remittantur, tamen consilium est, ut ad sacerdotem accedat, ne *regulam ecclesiasticae institutionis* praetermittere videatur, dicens sacerdoti se nullius peccati conscium sibi esse." ALANI AB INSULIS, *Liber Poenitentialis*. Migne, *P. L.*, t. CCX, 299.

confession, a general one and a special one. The general one is that which is made every day at the morning Mass and the evening office, *i. e.* at Compline, for the venial and occult sins. The confession that is obligatory three times a year is the *special* confession. This has for its object mortal and public sins; the clerics are held to make it every Saturday, lay people three times a year, at Christmas, Easter, and Pentecost."[25]

How was this law observed in practice? Very poorly. Alanus acknowledges the fact with regret: "To-day things have come to the point that lay people and clerics hardly confess once a year, and when they do so, we have reason to fear that they do it rather through habit than from motives of contrition."[26]

Such a degree of laxity had been reached at the beginning of the eighteenth century, that there was every reason to fear that the decline had not reached its lowest ebb. It was time for a reaction.

[25] "Duplex est autem peccati confessio, quaedam generalis, quaedam specialis. Generalis, quae fit in dies, in sacrificio matutino et vespertino, id est in completorio, pro venialibus et occultis; specialis, quae fit pro mortalibus et manifestis: ad quam tenentur clerici singulis sabbatis, laici vero ter in anno tenentur specialiter confiteri: videlicet in Natali Domini, in Paschate et in Pentecoste." *Ib.*, 172-173.

[26] "Sed hodie invaluit ut vix laicus vel clericus semel confiteatur in anno, et dum confitetur, timendum est ne confiteatur potius ut satisfaciat consuetudini, quam ex contritione animi." *Ib.*

In order to render the reaction useful, an attempt was made to make the discipline uniform by imposing everywhere a minimum of obligation, but this minimum was henceforth to be more strictly exacted.

The Fourth Lateran Council.—The fourth Lateran Council (1215), in its twenty-first canon, *Omnis utriusque sexus,* laid down the famous rule which still governs ecclesiastical discipline on this point at present. The text of that canon may be found in the *Corpus Juris,* l. V, tit. xxxviii, and in the text-books of moral theology; we will simply analyze it.

The following are the obligations imposed for confession: (1) all the faithful who have arrived at the age of discretion must make a private confession of their sins at least once a year; (2) They must make it each to his own pastor, unless permission has been obtained from him to go to another priest; (3) Disobedience is punishable with a double penalty—exclusion from the Church during life and denial of Christian burial after death.

The first two points had been obligatory for a long time; we have seen in Chrodegang's rule that the Christian people had to confess to their pastors;[27] the sanction alone seems new. But if

[27] It has also been seen above what an important part the priest played in his parish in all that concerned the spiritual life of his parishioners.

the obligation itself was not an innovation, it was at least made uniform for all.

Few disciplinary canons have obtained a success equal to this one. During the whole course of the thirteenth century provincial councils and diocesan synods in turn renewed it and recalled its sanctions. The Constitutions of Richard of Sarum, after 1217; the councils of Toulouse (1229); of Rouen (1235); Canterbury (1236); Worcester (1240); Chichester (1246); Albi (1254); Sens (1269), and others constantly insisted on its observance.

Confession at Least Once a Year.—But no one believed that the Lateran decree had abrogated the more exacting diocesan laws or customs; and many bishops continued legislating on lines of greater severity. However, the necessary distinction between the two sources of obligation was well drawn; the privation of ecclesiastical communion, either during life or after death, was inflicted only on those who did not confess at least once a year, and omitted to communicate at Easter. Here is the decision of the Constitutions of Richard of Sarum: "All must confess three times a year, but those who will not do so at least once, shall incur the penalties inflicted by the decree of the Lateran." [28]

[28] "Confessiones tres in anno audiantur . . . quicumque autem semel in anno, ad minus, proprio non confessus fuerit sacerdoti, et ad minus ad Pascha Eucharistiae sacramentum non acceperit, nisi consilio sui sacerdotis duxerit abstinendum: et vivens, ab

In some dioceses the publication of the decree *Omnis* was deemed sufficient;[29] but in nearly all the documents left us, in addition to the obligations of this decree, the constitutions or particular customs then in vogue were retained, that is, the obligation of confessing three times a year before each of the three obligatory communions. Such is the case at Toulouse, in 1229, and the decree which recalls this obligation begins—is it an intentional coincidence?—with the same words as that of the Lateran: "The faithful of both sexes, who have attained the age of discretion, shall confess their sins three times a year, each to his own pastor, . . . in order to receive three times a year the sacrament of the Eucharist, confession always preced-

ingressu ecclesiae arceatur; et mortuus christiana careat sepultura." *Constitution. Ricardi, Episcop. Sarum* (1217-1228), c. xxv. MANSI, t. XXII, 1115; repeated word for word, in the *Constitution. S. Edmundi Cantuarien. Archiep.* (1236), c. xviii. MANSI, t. XXIII, 421; the same may be found, though not literally regarding the invitation to confess on the three principal feasts, in the *Synod. Wigornien.* (1240), c. xvi. MANSI, *ibid.*, 531; the same invitation is more vigorously renewed in 1287, *Synod. Exonien.*, c. v. MANSI, t. XXIV, 790.

[29] See in particular *Praecepta antiqua dioces. Rothomagen.* (1235), c. lxxxii. MANSI, t. XXIII, 387; *Statuta Ricardi Cicestrien.* (1246), de Poenitentia. MANSI, *ib.*, 705; *Concilium provinc. Moguntin.* (1261), c. xxvi, *ib.*, 1090; *Synod. Claromontan.* (1268), c. vii, *ib.*, 1193; *Concil. Senonen.* (1269), c. iv. MANSI, t. XXIV, 5; *Concil. Treviren.* (1277?), § 3, no. 6, *ib.*, 194; *Concil. apud Pontem Audomari* (1279), c. v, *ib.*, 222. *Synod. Colonien.* (1280), § 8, Item sacerdotes, *ib.*, 355; *Synod. Nemausen.* (1284) § 7, *ib.*, 535; *Concil. Bituricen.* (1286), c. xiv, *ib.*, 632; *Synodicon Constantien.* (1300), c. xxxiii. MANSI, t. XXV, 37-38, etc., etc.

ing communion."[30] Such is the case also at Albi.[31]

The Age at which Confession Becomes Obligatory.—The Lateran Council had declared that every faithful Catholic was held to confess and to communicate "postquam *ad annos discretionis* pervenerit," and then asked—and the question was well worth official consideration because of the penalty imposed for disobedience—at what age one attained the "annos discretionis."

To-day the common teaching of theologians is well determined. The age of discretion is reached when reason is sufficiently developed to distinguish good from evil; which means, on the average, seven years, and from the age of seven, children are therefore held to confess once each year. Everywhere the diocesan constitutions remind the priests in charge of souls of the obligation which they are under of hearing the confession of all children who have attained that age, even though they have not yet made their first communion.

Everyone did not reason thus at the time of the Lateran Council. While the canon *Omnis utriusque sexus* restricted itself to the class of vague

[30] "Omnes autem utriusque sexus, postquam ad annos discretionis advenerint, confessionem peccatorum faciant ter in anno proprio sacerdoti; . . . ter in anno . . . sacramentum Eucharistiae cum omni reverentia suscepturi; ita quod confessio communionem praecedat." *Conc. Tolosan.* (1229), c. xiii. MANSI, t. XXIII, 197.

[31] *Conc. Albien.* (1254), c. xxix, *ib.*, 840.

formulas we have cited and, according to its first commentators, for instance Hostiensis,[32] simply obliged children who had attained the age of discretion or reason, the texts of particular councils and diocesan synods are more precise, for they give a determined age, fourteen years. Such is the decision of a council of Narbonne, A. D. 1227,[33] one at Lucca,[34] another at Avignon,[35] another at Béziers.[36] At Tarragona a distinction between boys and girls was established as to when the age of obligation begins, fourteen for the former, and twelve for the latter.[37]

This diversity in explaining the Lateran canon would be of a nature to cause wonder if we could not ascertain its cause. If the councils of the thirteenth century delayed the obligation of annual confession to the age of twelve and fourteen, it was not because the children of that time were less developed than those of our own day, or that they

[32] *Summa* (Lyons edition of 1588); f. 335, v°. 1, and f. 342. r°. 2.

[33] "Illi vero qui confiteri contempserunt saltem semel in anno a quartodecimo anno supra, vivis, introitus Ecclesiae . . ." *Conc. Narbonen.* (1227), c. vii. MANSI, t. XXIII, 23. *Statuta Synodalia Eccles. Leodien.* (1287), c. xxiii, § 4, de Poenitentia. MANSI, t. XXIV, 893.

[34] *Synod. Lucana* (1308), c. lvii. Mansi, t. XXV, 189.

[35] *Statuta Avenionen.*, edita anno 1341, in Synodo S. Lucae, MARTÈNE, *Thesaurus Anecdotorum*, t. IV, 566.

[36] *Concil. Biterren.* (1351), c. xii. MANSI, t. XXVI, 250.

[37] "Ex quo ad annos discretionis, masculus videlicet ad XIV, foemina vero ad XII pervenerint, tenentur saltem semel in anno . . ." *Concil. Terraconen.* (1329), c. lxvii. MANSI, *ib.*, 870.

required a more advanced age to discern good from evil, but because the authorities wanted to delay the obligation of the law until puberty. Azor shows that such was the real motive; this opinion still had serious supporters at the end of the sixteenth century. To use the scholastic terminology, the obligations imposed by the canon were taken not *in sensu diviso* but *in sensu composito*. The whole of the text was considered not as a collection of various obligations, but as only one obligation, comprising at the same time the precept of confession, that of communion, and the punishment threatened by both. The precept and the penalty formed one whole. But, said the commentators, as the penalties of a positive law ordinarily do not affect children, it follows that children before the age of twelve or fourteen do not come under the Lateran penalty, and that consequently the precept is not binding on them. Others, without using this argument, explained according to the Gloss the words of the Council: "who have attained the age of discretion." The Gloss said that one had attained the age of discretion when one was "doli capax"; now that expression was susceptible of a double interpretation; one according to the common parlance and another in the technical language of the law. As there was question here of a legal obligation imposed by the Church, it was evidently in the juridical sense that

THE THIRD COMMANDMENT

the phrase "doli capax" was to be understood. In that sense confession is obligatory only at the approach of puberty. Such was the opinion of Peter of Ancharano, a famous professor of canon law at Padua and later at Bologna,[38] and of St. Antoninus, who was unfavorably inclined towards the opinion which submitted children to the precept from the age of seven.[39]

In spite of the opposition of this great theologian and archbishop of Florence, the opinion which he condemned was adopted. His adversaries simply showed, as did Azor later on, that the precept was to be taken *in sensu diviso,* that therefore the canon *Omnis utriusque* obliged all who had attained the age of discretion. That this age differed according to the acts commanded, mattered little, for all were held to accomplish each part of

[38] "Et dicitur doli capax, quando est proximus pubertati secundum quosdam: quam opinionem sequitur Petrus de Ancharano . . . et subdit . . . quod proximus pubertati dicitur, quum magis appropinquat futurae, quam praeteritae infantiae: quod contingit in masculo, quando habet decem annos et dimidium, et aliquantulum ultra, et in femina quando habet undecim annos et dimidium, et ultra aliquantulum." S. ANTONINUS, *Summa Theologica,* p. IX, tit. ii, c. viii, § 2. Verona, 1740, t. II, p. 989-990.

[39] "Temerarium ergo videtur asserere, et publice praedicare, quod immediate post septennium teneantur pueri ad istud praeceptum servandum: alias peccant mortaliter, et ipsi et parentes eorum, qui non faciunt eos confiteri. Sed bene laudabile est et pium, praedicare, et exhortari parentes parvulos suos septennes et quinquennes, ut faciant confiteri, ut sic assuefaciant se moribus christianorum, etiamsi nondum habent usum rationis, quamvis non teneantur." *Ibid.,* 990.

the precept in due time. For confession the age of discretion is that when children are capable of discerning good from evil, commonly about seven years, and at this age therefore the obligation binds them. That the ecclesiastical penalties should not affect children before the age of puberty, according to the axioms of the law, and that the child in case of disobedience should become subject to the legal penalties pronounced by the council only after the age of puberty, was not in the least an abnormal occurrence in law. When Azor wrote his *Institutiones Morales* this was the common opinion, and children did not await the age of twelve to go to confession.[40] To-day it is the unanimously received opinion.

The Season of the Year at Which Confession Was to be Made.—The question was not raised in what sense "year" was to be taken. Confession was established as a preparation for communion and, as communion was to be received at Easter, at Easter time was confession to be made. Hostiensis states this in few words without suspecting that there could be matter for dispute: One must confess once a year, and at least at Easter.[41] Therefore it was not from one first of January to the other, nor from one 25th of March to the other, that the year of confession was

[40] *Institution. Morales*, p. I, 1. vii, c. xxix, *sexto quaeritur*, in fine. Brescia, 1622, t. I., p. 898.

[41] *Summa* of HOSTIENSIS, fol. 342 v⁰, col. 1.

counted. The precept was to be fulfilled at Easter time; this was the common opinion, as set forth by the canons of diocesan constitutions, synods, and councils.

In Paris a special decree was made which ordered fathers and mothers to confess before Palm Sunday, otherwise they would suffer the penalty of having their fast prolonged until Quasimodo Sunday.[42] The same legislation existed at Clermont.[43] In Liège the period was still further extended, *viz.* from Candlemas to Palm Sunday, and under the same penalties.[44] Elsewhere the Lenten period was indicated simply as the time designated for confession.[45] The pastors had to instruct their parishioners about it from Septuagesima,[46]

---

[42] "Presbyteri suos parochianos moneant . . . quod omnes saltem patres familias et matres, ad confessionem veniant ante Pascha floridum: et qui hoc negligentes fuerint, in poenam, usque post octavam Paschae, ad confessionem non admittantur: sed usque ad illud tempus a carnibus jejunabunt, sicut in quadragesima." *Additiones Willelmi Parisien. episcopi* (1220-1223), *ad Constitution. Gallonis*, c. vii. MANSI, t. XXII, 767.

[43] *Synodus Claromontan.* (1268), c. vii. MANSI, t. XXIII, 119.

[44] *Statuta Synodal. Eccles. Leodien.* (1287), § 4, de Confessione et Poenitentia, c. xxiii. MANSI, t. XXIV, 893.

[45] *Concil. Arelaten.* (1275), c. xix. MANSI, t. XXIV, 152; *Concil. Aschaffenburgen.* (1292), c. xii. MANSI, *ib.*, 1087; *Synod. Exonien.* (1287), c. v. MANSI, *ib.*, 790; *Concil. provinc. Moguntinen.* (1261), c. xxvi. MANSI, t. XXIII, 1090; *Synod. Bajocen.* (about 1300), c. lxxx. MANSI, t. XXV, 74. *Constitut. S. Edmundi, Cantuarien. Archiep.*, c. xvii. MANSI, t. XXIII, 421; *Statuta Ricardi, ib.*, 705, etc.

[46] *Concil. Palentin.* (1322), c. xxvii. MANSI, t. XXV, 722.

or at least from the beginning of Lent.[47] The Lateran Council had ordered the frequent publication of this decree in the churches, so that no one could pretend to be ignorant of it.[47a] This order must have been obeyed, for later synodal constitutions did not merely repeat the precept given by the decree *Omnis,* but fixed the number of times and the different periods of the year when the publication of the decree was to be renewed.

The Appointed Priest.—The annual confession which was to be made at least once a year—and which the particular constitutions fixed at Easter—was to be made by each of the faithful to his pastor, unless permission had been obtained from him to go to another priest. There was no need to designate more definitely who was the proper priest; this had been done by the whole previous legislation. The judge of the penitential forum was primarily the bishop and then the pastor of the parish. To give only a passing mention to the ancient text of the synodal statutes, supposed to have been given to the Church of Rheims by Sonnatius, which decrees very explicitly that no one but the pastor should hear the confession of penitents dur-

---

[47] *Conc. Ravennat. II* (1311), c. xv. MANSI, t. XXV, 457; *Constitut. Eccles. Ferrarien.* (1332), MANSI, *ibid.*, 904; *Concil. Beneventan.* (1331), c. lxvi. MANSI, ib., 971; *Synod. Lucana* (1308), c. lvii, *ib.*, 189; *Concil, Pragen.* (1346), c. lvii. MANSI, t. XXVI, 101.

[47a] "Hoc salutare statutum frequenter in ecclesiis publicetur, ne quisquam ignorantiae caecitate velamen excusationis assumat."

ing Lent,[48] we know from a variety of other sources how vigorously each pastor endeavored not to abandon his jurisdiction even in the slightest degree. Ayton of Basle, in his capitulary, recommends to the faithful who start on pilgrimages "ad limina" to go to confession in their parish church before leaving, because their bishop or pastor alone has the right to absolve them.[49] It is to the proper priest, "sacerdoti suo," as we have seen, that the faithful laity, according to Chrodegang, must go to confession; the monks, to the bishop or their prior.[50] No bishop or pastor, according to Regino, was to admit to reconciliation a strange penitent without the consent of the latter's pastor.[51]

These dispositions, confirmed by the decree *Omnis,* were maintained in diocesan and provincial legislation, and met with no opposition until the spread of the Mendicant Orders in the thirteenth century.

As early as 1260, the Council of Arles complained of interference by the Penitentiaries who

[48] Mansi, t. X, 598.

[49] "Et hoc omnibus fidelibus denuntiandum: ut qui causa orationis ad limina beatorum Apostolorum peregre cupiunt, domi confiteantur peccata sua et sic proficiscantur: quia a proprio episcopo suo, aut sacerdote, ligandi aut exsolvendi sunt, non ab extraneo." Hetto, *Capitulare,* c. xviii. *P. L.,* t. CV, 766.

[50] *Regula canonicor.,* c. xxxii. *P. L.,* t. LXXXIX, 1072.

[51] Regino, *De Ecclesiastic. disciplin.,* l. I, c. cccix. Migne, *P. L.,* t. CXXXII, 253; cf. *ib.,* c. cclxxxviii, col. 245; Burchard, *Decret.,* l. XIX, c. 11. Migne, *P. L.,* t. CXL, 949.

were sent to the cities and villages during Lent.[52] This occurred in spite of the fact that the pastors insisted that no priest, even though vested with delegated authority, could hear confession in a parish without the pastor's express permission;[53] and in spite of the law which obliged any penitent who had obtained permission to go to confession to another priest or to some monk, to make nevertheless a full confession to his own pastor once a year.[54] The bishops themselves were recommended not to grant a general permission to absolve reserved cases to the Friars Preachers or the Friars Minor, but to give such faculty only to specially chosen men.[55] To admit the ordinary as-

[52] *Concil. Arelaten.*, c. xvi. MANSI, t. XXIII, 1010-1011. Note this interesting text: "inhibemus ne confessores hujusmodi qui mittuntur solummodo ad praedicta [it is a question of *oppida*], per villas et parochias dioecesis discurrentes generalibus parochianorum confessionibus audiendis se occupent, nisi de mandato praelati et licentia curati, generalibus confessionibus audiendis se duxerint occupandos; sed eos ad proprios remittant sacerdotes, et casibus pro quibus mittuntur poenitentes absolvant."

[53] *Conc. Treviren.* (1277?), § III, n. 6, Mansi, t. XXIV, 194 (it provides a penalty for the priests who administer the sacrament of penance without the permission of the pastor); *Conc. apud Pontem Audomari* (1279), c. v, *ib.*, 222.

[54] "Si quis tamen alieno sacerdoti, vel alicui religioso, justa de causa voluerit confiteri, licentiam primo postulet et obtineat a proprio sacerdote; ita tamen, quod semel ad minus in anno proprio sacerdoti plene et integre (ut dictum est) confiteatur." *Synod. Colonien.* (1280), § 8. MANSI, t. XXIV, 355.

[55] *Concil. Rothomagen.* (1299), c. vi. Mansi, t. XXIV, 1206, which imposes also the conditions decreed by the Council of Cologne, *supra*.

sistance of another priest it was necessary that either the pastor be seriously ill or that the confessions be too numerous for him to hear.[56] Confession to a priest other than the pastor was a mere toleration which the Church restricted at will by forbidding the monks under pain of excommunication to give communion or administer any other sacrament to the parishioners of others, especially to *Beghards* and *Beguins*.[57] Some time later, at Prague, the audacity of the monks gave cause for protest, for they ventured to hear the confessions of the faithful without having received permission from the bishop, nay without even having been introduced to him.[58]

It does not come within our province to narrate the many incidents of the struggle between the secular and the regular clergy; it lasted long and the popes had frequently to intervene. The *Extravagantes communes* are proof of this papal solicitude. Thus, for instance, the Constitution *Vices illius, de Treuga et Pace,* ordered the mendicants to cease preaching that parishioners are not obliged to go to confession to their pastors at Easter.

As to the priests placed at the head of the par-

[56] *Concil. Treviren.* (1310), c. lxxxix. MANSI, t. XXV, 270.

[57] *Concil. Moguntin.* (1310), De confessionibus audiendis. MANSI, t. XXV, 345. Cf. *Concil. Saltzburgen.* (1420), c. xxv. MANSI, t. XXVIII, 998.

[58] *Concil. Pragen.* (1346), c. lvii. MANSI, t. XXVI, 102.

ishes, a pastor was also found for them, to whom they had to confess their sins at least once a year. At Bayeaux, this was the bishop or his Penitentiaries, and while in case of necessity the pastor of the parish could address himself to other approved priests, he was obliged to go to confession to the bishop or to the Penitentiary at least once a year.[59] At Ferrara the archpriests and other prelates under the bishop's jurisdiction had to obtain his special permission to be allowed to go to confession to any other than himself or his Penitentiary.[60] And Hostiensis in answer to the question: To whom must the parish priest go to confession? replies, "He must confess his sins to his bishop or to some spiritual or temporal superior, or else these priests can go to confession to one another with the permission of the prelate."[61]

The disputes between the secular and the regular clergy did not concern the confessions of pastors,

[59] *Synod. Bajocen.* (about 1300), c. cviii. MANSI, t. XXV, 80. Item, *Synod. Pictavien.* (1280), c. iv. MANSI, t. XXIV, 383.

[60] *Constitution. Eccles. Ferrarien.* (1332), c. vii. MANSI, t. XXV, 904.

[61] *Summa* of HOSTIENSIS, *De Poenitent. et remission.*, n⁰ 34. Lyons, 1588, fol. 340 v⁰, col. 2. Cf. the text of the Council of Padua: "Statuimus, ut singuli plebani, Rectores, vicarii, et capellarii nostrae Diocesis de gravioribus seu majoribus suis peccatis confiteantur suo Decano: Decani nobis aut etiam Archidiacono, seu iis quos eis dederimus confessores. De minoribus autem et venialibus confiteantur aliis sacerdotibus, prout sibi viderint expedire, si suos commode accedere non possint confessores." *Synod. apud S. Hippolytum* (Patavien. dioecesis) (1284). MANSI, t. XXIV, 509.

but those of the faithful. The precept of confession gradually underwent the same modifications as that regarding assistance at Mass in one's parochial church. The regulars having become, by the fact of their direct and absolute dependence on Rome, the firmest upholders of pontifical power, received many privileges from the Holy See, particularly in the time of Sixtus IV, Paul III, Pius IV, Pius V, and Gregory XIII. And since the sovereign pontiff is by law pastor of the entire Church as the bishop is of his diocese, he could legitimately delegate his powers to the mendicants, who consequently had the same rights as the pastor on all the points included in their privileges. But it took a long time to come to an understanding. For many centuries the discussions continued between the secular clergy defending the rights of the pastors, and the monks defending their privileges. The Jesuits and other religious congregations were added to the mendicants later on. The Council of Trent simply stipulated that all confessors should first of all obtain the permission of the bishop.

In France, particularly, the struggle lasted for centuries. The Lateran decree obliged every Catholic who wished to go to confession to another priest, to obtain the permission of his pastor; the bishops sometimes added a new restriction by suspending the approbation which they had given to the regular confessors during the fortnight of Easter, and thus for a long time preserved the ancient jurisdiction of the pastors. But it could not be maintained indefinitely. Azor [62] protested in the name of the regulars, Busembaum affirmed their right to hear the confessions of the faithful even at Easter.[63] And the Congregation of Bishops being questioned on these episcopal ordinances answered that no one was obliged to observe them.[64]

The Penalties.—The third part of the decree *Omnis* determined the penalties for disobedience; they were: exclusion from church during life and after death: "alioquin et vivens ab ingressu ecclesiae arceatur, et moriens christiana careat sepultura."

All the councils or synods which followed that of the Lateran, faithfully renewed this provision. Moreover, the penalties affected not only those who violated both precepts, of annual confession and Easter communion, but also those who violated either one of the two.[65] Nevertheless, in spite of these penalties, and particularly that of

[62] *Institut. Moral.*, pars I, lib. XIII, c. ii.

[63] *Medulla theologiae moralis*, l. VI, tractat. IV, c. iii, dub. 2.

[64] ST. ALPHONSUS, *Theologia moralis*, l. VI, tract. IV, n. 564. See the exposition of these controversies in Benedict XIV, *Institution.* XVIII.

[65] Cf. the Council of Narbonne, of 1227, already quoted, which applies the double penalty of the decree of the Lateran Council to those who only omitted the annual confession.

refusal of ecclesiastical burial, which was perhaps the most dreaded of all, many never made their annual confession. It was deemed necessary to employ graver penalties against these delinquents. A German council refused ecclesiastical burial even if the deceased had confessed *in extremis*, unless serious reasons induced the archdeacon or the official to grant this privilege by way of exception.[66]

It was not thus everywhere. In France a more lenient policy was followed: the Council of Bourges, 1286, mentioning the privation of ecclesiastical burial inflicted on those who had not gone to confession during the year, adds the following by way of attenuation: unless however they have been so surprised by death that a legitimate excuse can be found for them, or have given evident signs of repentance.[67]

Indifferent Christians, who endeavoured to escape the precept of confession and at the same time to preserve the exterior advantages of obe-

[66] "Si quis ad minus semel in anno . . . suam confessionem . . . potestatem habenti non fecerit sacerdoti, huic, si illo anno decesserit, quamvis confessionem faciat in extremis, nihilominus, auctoritate hujus concilii, ecclesiastica denegabitur sepultura, nisi forte aliqua legitima causa suadente, locorum archidiaconi aut officiales diocesanorum sepulturam hujusmodi duxerint indulgendam; ut alii hac poena deterriti ad tam salubris sacramenti remedium ferventius studeant convolare." *Conc. Aschaffenburg.* (1292), c. xii. MANSI, t. XXIV, 1087.

[67] *Concil. Bituricen.* (1286), c. xiii. MANSI, *ib.*, 631-632.

dience, tried every means to elude the vigilance of the clergy. In order to secure the strict observance of the law, each pastor was obliged to keep a detailed roster of all those who had made their Easter confession, and the other priests or monks would communicate to him in writing the names of those who had made use of their ministry. Thus he could easily ascertain who of his parishioners had not fulfilled the precept, and their names would be communicated to the bishop in synod after Easter.[68]

But the Church was even more anxious to protect Christians against their negligence than to punish those who avoided the sacrament; consequently she ordered, sometimes under pain of excommunication,[69] priests and above all pastors, to obtain the text of the Lateran decree and publish it in the

[68] *Concil. Narbonnen.* (1227), c. vii: "Statuit praesens synodus, quod nomina illorum omnium qui peccata sua confessi fuerint, scribantur a capellanis, qui confessiones audiverunt eorundem." MANSI, t. XXIII, 23. Cf. *Concil. Arelaten.* (1275), c. xix. MANSI, t. XXIV, 152; item, *Concil. apud Pontem Audomar.* (1279), c. v, *ib.*, 282. The Council of Benevento of 1331, c. lxvii, Mansi, t. XXV, 971-972, prescribes the communication to the bishop of the names of those who have confessed. See also the *Statuta Avenionen. edita an.* 1341, *in Synodo S. Lucae*, c. ii. Martène, *Thesaurus Anecdotor.*, t. IV, 566; *Concil. Biterren.* (1351), c. xii. Mansi, t. XXVI, 250. In Spain it is simply prescribed that a register be kept with the names of those who are old enough to be subject to the precept. *Concil. Toletan.* (1339), c. v. MANSI, t. XXV, 1146.

[69] *Concil. Bituricen.* (1286), c. xiv. MANSI, t. XXIV, 632.

THE THIRD COMMANDMENT

vernacular. The councils sometimes reinforced the penalties of the spiritual order with a pecuniary fine, which affected all those, priests and faithful, who had not complied entirely with the precept of annual confession.[70]

All these accessory prescriptions are now obsolete, even the one concerning the exclusion from church during life, of all those who do not make their annual confession. The one that has survived longest is the refusal of ecclesiastical burial. This is still mentioned in the ritual but with a very notable attenuation; the guilty shall be punished only if they have not given any signs of contrition before dying.

For some time [71] the exclusion from church of those who had not gone to confession at the appointed time was observed with great strictness, for theologians held all those who passed more

[70] *Constitut. Ecclesiae Ferrarien. a Guidone* (1332), c. vii: "Qui vero offenderit aut fecerit contra praedicta, vel aliqua praedictorum pro qualibet vice quadraginta solidos ferrarienses persolvat." MANSI, t. XXV, 904. But there was still further severity. The Council of Benevento of 1331 fined priests who did not communicate to the episcopal curia the roster of those who had not satisfied the precept of annual confession and Easter communion. It was the same at Avignon, where the negligent priests had to pay a fine of five sous for each offense: "pro qualibet vice poenam quinque solidorum usualis monetae incurrat in usus pauperum et alios pios usus nostro arbitrio convertendam." *Statuta Avenionen.* (1341), *loc. cit.*

[71] *Concil. Toletan.* (1339), c. v. MANSI, t. XXV, 1146.

than a year without recourse to confession as suspect of heresy.[72] But in proportion as the number of the guilty increased, the application of the penalty became necessarily less rigorous; if the men who frequented church fulfilled their other Christian duties, they were not to be expelled even if they stayed away from confession through negligence or human respect, or for some other similar motive.

Summary.—It is very difficult to ascertain how many times in a year, or in a series of years, the faithful were obliged to go to confession during the first centuries. The custom of annual confession seems to have been introduced as a parallel to the rite of annual public penance, observed in Lent. This custom spread and became firmly established. Little by little it entered into the canons of synods and councils about the middle of the ninth century. Some of these canons prescribe that confession shall be made to one's pastor three or four times a year.

At the end of the twelfth century laxity has reduced the number of prescribed confessions to one. The Lateran Council of 1215 extends the obligation to the entire Church. This constitution scarcely introduced a novelty; the first and second parts resemble the older prescriptions; only the

[72] FAGNANI, in c. *Omnis, De Poenitent. et Remission.* nº 15, cites Hostiensis, Joannes Andreae, and Panormitanus.

third, which lays down the penalties for disobedience, is new. But as the decree of the Lateran did not alter human nature, it was necessary to struggle on as before to insure its observance. In spite of all these efforts complete success was not obtained.

The old practice, upheld by the decree, reserved to the pastor of each parish the right to hear the confessions of his parishioners. Against this exclusive right there was a reaction, of which the popes, more or less consciously at first, were the most active agents. As a result of the privileges granted to the Mendicants, and later to the Jesuits, and finally extended little by little to practically all other priests, both regular and secular, the obligation of making one's Easter confession to one's pastor was suppressed, in spite of strong and continued opposition on the part of the bishops and the parochial clergy, especially in France.

The sanctions laid down in the third part of the decree were as a rule not applied literally; for almost nowhere was ecclesiastical burial refused to those who had neglected to make their annual confession if they gave signs of contrition before dying. As to excluding them during life, this penalty was enforced only while the political influence of the Church throve in all its vigour.

Of the decree *Omnis* only the prescription contained in the first part, which is really the essential portion, still subsists in all its obligatory force. Its observance is no longer as general as it used to be, but the Church still maintains the obligation and there is no indication that she means to relax it.

CHAPTER VI

THE FOURTH COMMANDMENT

Ton Rédempteur tu recevras,
Au moins à Pâques saintement.

Thou shalt receive thy Redeemer,
Holily at least at Easter time.[1]

We do not intend to establish for the Fourth Commandment, any more than we have for the Third, a dogmatic or moral thesis, such as the dogma of the Real Presence, or an obligation, based on the divine law, of receiving communion a certain number of times during life. Our object is merely to trace the date of the ecclesiastical precept of Easter Communion, and to study its modifications and vicissitudes through the centuries.

The testimonies on this point are not very ancient.

Origin.—There is some reason to believe that, in the Infant Church, the more or less frequent Eucharistic gatherings, held in private houses,[2] ended with the communion of all present.

---

[1] This commandment is included in the Fourth Commandment in our Baltimore Catechism: "To receive the Holy Eucharist during the Easter time."

[2] *Acts*, II, 42, 46.

Some years later, the Didache implies that all the faithful had to eat and drink of the Eucharist, by remarking that the unbaptized must be excluded from the Sacrament.[3]

St. Justin states that on Sunday, after the consecration of the Eucharist, the deacons distributed to each of those present the consecrated bread, wine and water, and carried some to the absent.[4]

Tertullian describes it as a general custom that everybody takes part in the Communion on the days of assembly,[5] and that the faithful even take away with them small pieces of the Eucharist, so as to communicate on other days.[6]

St. Cyprian speaks of Communion as a daily practice,[7] to which, he says, all must remain faithful, especially at the approach of persecution, when the struggle is more imminent, more vivid, and more intense than ordinarily.[8]

In certain churches, the lukewarm who did not communicate, were excluded from the meetings of the faithful until they had done penance.[9]

[3] *Didache*, IX, 5.

[4] *Apol.*, LXV, 5; cf. *ib.*, LXVII, 3 et 5.

[5] "Similiter et stationum diebus non putant plerique sacrificiorum orationibus interveniendum quod statio solvenda sit, accepto Corpore Domini." *De Orat.*, c. xix. Migne, *P. L.*, t. I, 1181-1182.

[6] *Ibid.*, 1183. Cf. l. ii. *ad uxor.*, c. v; *ib.*, 1296.

[7] *De Orat. Dominica*, c. xviii. *P. L.*, t. IV, col. 531-532.

[8] *Epist.* LVI, i, *ibid.* 350.

[9] "Omnes qui in ecclesiam ingrediuntur et sacras scripturas audiunt, orationi autem cum populo non communicant, vel sanctam

This "excommunication" evidently indicates that there was already manifesting itself a tendency towards laxity. This tendency, however, in the early days, was weak, or at least very restricted, for documents contemporaneous with the synod *"In Encoeniis"* show the faithful communicating very frequently, even on days when Mass was not celebrated, so convinced were they of the truth announced by St. Basil at the head of his twenty-first moral rule, that "participation in the body and blood of Christ is necessary to obtain eternal life." [10] Christians, especially monks, were accustomed to take home several particles of the consecrated bread, in order that they might administer communion to themselves in the course of the week. St. Basil affirms that this was a common custom in Egypt even among the simple faithful.[11]

However, there was no general rule on this matter, each diocese, each church had its own usages, which, on the whole, were quite divergent.

Eucharistiae participationem propter aliquam insolentiam aversantur, eos ab Ecclesia expelli, donec postquam confessi fuerint, fructusque poenitentiae ostenderint, et imploraverint, veniam assequi possint." *Conc. in Encoeniis* (Antioch, 341), c. ii. MANSI, t. II, 1310. Cf. *Canones Apostolor.*, c. ix. BRUNS, *Canones*, t. I, 2.

[10] "Quod necessaria etiam ad vitam aeternam sit participatio corporis et sanguinis Christi." *Moralium Regulae*, XXI. Migne, *P. G.*, t. XXXI, 738.

[11] *Epist. XCIII, ad Caesariam patritiam.* Migne, *P. G.*, t. XXXII, 483.

Some scrupulous souls, afraid to receive the Eucharist so frequently, questioned those who appeared best informed regarding both the demands of piety and the ecclesiastical customs, whose diversity troubled them. One of these asked St. Jerome: "Is it necessary to communicate every day, as they do in Rome and in Spain?" The holy doctor answered: "The learned Hippolytus has treated this question, and so have other authors, who draw their inspiration from divers ecclesiastical writers; but please remember that in what concerns ecclesiastical traditions, especially those not contrary to the faith, the ancient tradition is to be followed, without believing that the traditions of one church are destroyed by those of another." [12]

St. Jerome, however, was not always so tolerant. Elsewhere in his writings he expresses astonishment at the fact that many dare to communicate after the conjugal act, and though he does not expressly condemn the Roman custom which allows it, it is evident that he does not approve it.[13]

[12] "Quod quaeris . . . de Eucharistia, an accipienda quotidie, quod Romana Ecclesia et Hispaniae observare perhibentur, scripsit quidem et Hyppolytus vir disertissimus; et carptim diversi scriptores e variis auctoribus edidere. Sed ego illud breviter te admonendum puto, traditiones ecclesiasticas (praesertim quae fidei non officiant) ita observandas, ut a majoribus traditae sunt, nec aliorum consuetudinem, aliorum contrario more subverti." *Ep. LXXI, ad Lucin.*, n. 6. Migne, *P. L.*, t. XXII, 672.

[13] *Epist. XLVIII, ad Pammach.*, n. 15, Migne, *P. L., ibid.*, 505-506.

In Africa St. Augustine was questioned whether one must communicate daily, or on certain days only. He answered, like St. Jerome, that customs vary according to countries; while in some daily communion is in vogue, others do not observe the practice. Unless one has committed grave faults, St. Augustine advises daily communion.[14]

Yet, even at this period, the frequency of communion does not seem to have been left entirely to the good-will of the faithful; they could communicate frequently if they wished, but on certain days or at certain periods they were obliged to do so, and this obligation was imposed either by custom or by a law or precept. In Antioch, at the end of the fourth century, St. John Chrysostom severely blames lukewarm Christians who are eager to communicate on certain days but unwilling to correct their faults. The periods in which communion is recognized as obligatory, according to Chrysostom, are Lent (or Easter) and Epiphany.[15]

[14] "Alii quotidie communicant corpori et sanguini Domini, alii certis diebus accipiunt. . . . Ceterum, peccata si tanta non sunt, ut excommunicandus quisque judicetur, non se debet a quotidiana medicina Dominici corporis separare." *Ep. LIV, ad Januar.* Migne, *P. L.*, t. XXXIII, 200-201.—"Eucharistia panis noster quotidianus est." *Sermon., LVII, in Matth. VI,* 9-13, c. vii. Migne, *P. L.*, t. XXXVIII, 389.—"Intelligitur etiam, hoc et valde bene, *Panem nostrum quotidianum da nobis hodie,* Eucharistiam tuam, quotidianum cibum. Norunt enim fideles quid accipiant, et bonum est eis accipere panem quotidianum huic tempori necessarium." *Serm., LVIII,* c. iv; *ib.,* 395.

[15] "Multos video qui Christi corporis sunt participes inconsider-

At the other end of the Christian world it seems the faithful were less eager to receive holy communion. According to Mansi, a synod held by St. Patrick, about 450-462, mentions the Easter Communion as absolutely necessary for all Christians. We must often communicate, it says, because we need it; but he who would not communicate on the night of Easter, would not be a faithful Christian.[16]

In Gaul, under the influence of Caesarius of Arles, the Council of Agde (506) showed itself more severe by treating those who did not communicate on the three great feasts of Christmas, Easter, and Pentecost, as apostates.[17] Caesarius himself insisted on this point in his homilies or discourses delivered at the approach of Christmas,[18]

ate et temere, et magis *ex consuetudine et praescripto*, quam ex cogitatione et consideratione. *Si advenerit*, inquit, *tempus sanctae quadragesimae*, qualiscumque fuerit quispiam, fit particeps sacramentorum, *si advenerit dies Epiphaniorum*. . . . In aliis quidem temporibus, cum ne mundi quidem saepe sitis, acceditis; *in Paschate* autem, etiamsi aliquod scelus a vobis sit admissum, acceditis." *In Epist. ad Ephes. Comment.*, Hom. III, n. 4. Migne, *P. G.*, t. LXII, 28.

[16] "Sumenda est [Eucharistia], maxime autem in nocte Paschae, in qua qui non communicat fidelis non est." MANSI, t. VI, 525.

[17] "Saeculares, qui Natale Domini, Pascha et Pentecoste non communicaverint, catholici non credantur, nec inter catholicos habeantur." *Conc. Agathen.*, c. xviii. BRUNS, *Canones*, t. II, 150.

[18] "In Natali domini, fratres carissimi, . . . cogitemus ad quale convivium invitati sumus. Invitati enim sumus ad mensam, ubi non invenitur cibus hominum, sed panis ponitur angelorum." *Inter opp.* S. AUGUST., *Sermon.*, 16, 2. Migne, *P. L.*, t. XXXIX, 1975-1976.

Easter,[19]—(I have not found any text for Pentecost), and other feasts, such as the dedication of a church or of an altar;[20] declaring at the same time that the necessary dispositions of purity, patience, and charity, can be obtained only by means of long and careful preparation.

The First Legislation.—The practice indicated by St. Caesarius was gradually imposed on all the faithful and became a law of the Church.

The decision of the Council of Agde was substantially repeated by a Council of Autun, about 670;[21] also in the *Excerptiones* of Egbert of York (732–766);[22] and in a council of Tours in the early part of the ninth century.[23] Later it was reproduced in identical terms by Atto of Verceil (924–960);[24] by the divers collections of the capitular-

[19] "Et cum sancta solemnitas Paschalis advenerit, . . . cum gaudio exsultationis mundo corde et casto corpore ad altare Domini possitis accedere, et corpus et sanguinem ejus unusquisque vestrum non ad judicium animae suae mereatur accipere." *Ibid., serm.* 10, col. 1760.

[20] This seems to be implied in nos. 2 and 5 of a sermon on dedication, *Inter Opp. S. Augustini,* serm. 229. Migne, *P. L.,* t. XXXIX, 2166-7, 2169.

[21] *Conc. Augustodunen.,* c. xiv. MANSI, t. XI, 126.

[22] *Excerpt.* 38. (ex synodo Agathen.) MANSI, t. XII, 417.

[23] "Ut, si non frequentius, vel ter laici homines in anno communicent, nisi forte quis majoribus quibuslibet criminibus impediatur." *Concil. Turonen.* III (813), c. i. *Mon. Germ., Concilia,* t. II, 293.

[24] *Capitul.,* c. lxxiii. MANSI, t. XIX, 257.

ies of Ansegise,[25] Regino,[26] Burchard,[27] Yves of Chatres [28] (who attributes it to Pope Fabian), and from there it passed into the Decree of Gratian,[29] and became, so to speak, a universal law.

It was the law of minimum requirement. Ordinarily, to comply with its letter was not held to be satisfactory, and the bishops tried every means to obtain more. Thus Theodore of Canterbury affirms in his Penitential that in the Greek Church all communicate every week, and that to stay away for three Sundays would expose one to excommunication; but, he adds, among the Romans every one does as he pleases and excommunication is less frequently inflicted.[30] A Bavarian Council affirms that the Greeks, Romans, and Franks generally communicate every Sunday and that weekly communion ought to be the rule.[31]

[25] *Capitul. Ansegis.*, l. II, c. xlv.

[26] *De Ecclesiastic. Disciplin.*, l. II, c. v. Migne, *P. L.*, t. CXXXII, 285; *ibid.*, 189.

[27] *Decretor.*, l. V, c. xvii. Migne, *P. L.*, t. CXL, 756.

[28] *Decret.*, pars IIa, c. xxvii. Migne, *P. L.*, t. CLXI, 167.

[29] C. xvi, Dist. II, *de Consecratione*.

[30] "Graeci omni dominico die communicant sive clerici, sive laici, et qui tribus dominicis non communicaverit, excommunicetur. Romani similiter communicant qui volunt, qui autem noluerint, non excommunicantur." *Capitul.* THEODOR. CANTUARIEN. *archiep.*, c. xii. SCHMITZ, *Die Bussbücher und die Bussdisciplin der Kirche*, t. I, 534.

[31] "Ut sanctum sacrificium sumere non tardent . . . et non sicut, pro dolor! a multis fieri solet ut aliquando spatium anni pertransit, quo non percipit suae sacramenta salutis qui numquam unam septimanam progredi debuit. Attamen ita vos ammone-

In spite of all invitations and admonitions, however, frequent communion did not strike root among the greater number of the faithful. In the very country where Theodore of Canterbury was laboring to introduce it, the Council of Cloveshow, giving up all hope of success, and seeing that many sorely lacked the necessary dispositions, turned to the children and the aged, and asked that at least young children in whom the passions were still dormant and old people who had ceased to sin be exhorted to receive the Eucharist more frequently.[32]

Alongside of this discipline, we find another, less exacting than that of weekly communion, but stricter than that of the Council of Agde, and an attempt is made to introduce this especially for the time of Lent. Theodulf of Orleans commands all except excommunicated persons, to receive the Eucharist every Sunday in Lent, on Holy Thursday, Good Friday, and Holy Saturday, on Easter and the days of the week following.[33] The same re-

mus, ut infra tertiam et quartam dominicam a vobis non neglegatur, cum etiam et Graeci et Romani seu et Franci omni dominico communicent." *Conc. Bajuwaric.* (740-750), c. vi. *Mon. Germ., Concilia*, t. II, 52.

[32] "Laici pueri similiter hortandi sunt, qui necdum videlicet lascivientis aetatis corruptela sint vitiati, ut saepius communicent: nec non et provectioris quoque aetatis, seu coelibes, seu etiam conjugati, qui peccare desinunt, ad hoc ipsum admonendi sint, quatenus frequentius communicent." *Conc. Cloveshov.* II (747), c. xxiii. MANSI, t. XII, 402.

[33] "Singulis diebus dominicis in Quadragesima, praeter hos qui

quirements are found in a *Capitulum* of Rodulf of Bourges and in the *leges ecclesiasticae* adopted by a synod of Anse.[34]

Pope Nicholas I invites, nay urgently exhorts the Bulgarians to communicate every day in Lent.[35]

All these regulations prove that there was no law in the proper sense, imposing a strict obligation. People were invited to communicate frequently, and those who did not receive at least three times a year were deemed poor Christians, but they were Christians nevertheless. A large number of them received the Eucharist only once a year. And this was not a new practice. At the end of the fourth century, the author of the treatise *De Sacramentis* testifies to the custom. He laments over it; he grants (he was better informed than Theodore of Canterbury) that many Greeks

excommunicati sunt, sacramenta corporis et sanguinis Christi sumenda sunt, et in Coena Domini, et in Parasceve, in vigilia Paschae et in die Resurrectionis Domini, penitus ab omnibus communicandum, et ipsi dies paschalis hebdomadae omnes aequali religione colendi sunt." THEODULF. AURELIANEN. *Capitular*. xli. MANSI, t. XIII, 1005.

[34] "*Capitul*. xxix. MANSI, t. XIV, 957. *Leges Ecclesiastic*., (Concil. Ansan.), c. xli. MANSI, t. XIX, 192.

[35] "Corpori et sanguini Dominico quotidie in quadragesima majori si deberetis communicare consulitis: quod ut fiat Dominum omnipotentem suppliciter exoramus, et vos omnes vehementissime exhortamur, si tamen mens in affectu peccandi non sit. . . . Interim tantum quadragesima, quam mos Ecclesiae majorem appellat, omni est die servato superiori tenore communicandum." *Ad consulta Bulgaror*., c. ix. Migne, *P. L.*, t. CXIX, 983, 984.

do likewise; but, living before the Council of Agde, he cites no law obliging one to do more, and merely tries to persuade his readers that the heavenly bread should be taken daily.[35a]

Amalarius of Metz (died about 850), being outside the sphere of influence exercised by the Council of Agde, knows of no positive law on this matter and leaves every one to the dictates of his piety and the judgment of his conscience.[36] Theodulf of Orleans supplies another very interesting text which enables us to estimate correctly the one already cited, *viz.*: as an exhortation rather than an absolute command. "Notify the people," he says, "that the body and blood of Christ are not to be received with indifference, nor to be forgone too long; likewise that, as it is dangerous to receive them without a pure soul, so it is dangerous, too, to remain away from them too long. A middle course is to be pursued between the excommunicated who are allowed to communicate only at certain stated periods, and the monks who lead a holy life and communicate nearly every day."[37]

[35a] "Si quotidianus est panis, cur *post annum* illum sumis, quemadmodum Graeci in Oriente facere consueverunt? Accipe quotidie quod quotidie tibi prosit." *De Sacrament.*, V, iv, 25. Migne, *P. L.*, t. XVI, 452.

[36] "Sunt autem intra sanctam Ecclesiam qui raro communicant, et qui quotidie. Faciat autem unusquisque quod secundum fidem suam pie credit esse faciendum." *De Ecclesiasticis Offic.*, l. III, c. xxxiv, de Eucharistia. Migne, *P. L.*, t. CV, 1153-1154.

[37] THEODULFI AURELIANEN. *Capitul.*, xliv. Migne, *P. L.*, t. CV, 205.

Yet, little by little, going to communion three times a year had become so deeply rooted a custom that the generality of the faithful complied with it; the negligence of the lukewarm manifested itself rather by insufficient preparation than by infrequent reception. Theodulf's successor, Jonas of Orleans, reproaches his diocesans, not with omitting to go to communion three times a year, but with going as a mere matter of routine rather than from a motive of devotion,[38] and with failure to realize that the soul, to live, needs spiritual just as the body needs material food.[39]

The Four Annual Communions.—The three Communions imposed by the Council of Agde soon increased to four. Every Christian was to communicate at Easter, Pentecost, and Christmas; but, according to Ratherius of Verona (died about 974), the Easter Communion was twofold, one to be received on Holy Thursday, the other on Easter Sunday.[40] This custom soon acquired the force of

[38] "Sunt item plerique . . . qui ab hoc sacramento partim incuria, partim desidia adeo se subtrahunt, ut vix in anno, nisi sub tribus tantum festis praeclaris ex consuetudine potius quam ex devotione faciant." JONAE AURELIANEN. *De Institution. Laical.*, l. II, c. xviii. *P. L.*, t. CVI, 202.

[39] JONAS AURELIANEN., *ibid.*, 202. Cf. *Concil. incerti loci et tempor. in Normann. celebrat.* post ann. 950, c. xii. MANSI, t. XVIII, 433.

[40] "Quater in anno, id est, Natali Domini, et Coena Domini, Pascha et Pentecoste, omnes fideles ad communionem corporis et sanguinis Domini accedere admonete." RATHER. VERONEN. *Epist. Synodica ad Presbyteros*, n. 10. Migne, *P. L.*, t. CXXXVI, 562.

an obligation. The omission of one of those communions, according to the formulary of Burchard, was a sin which had to be confessed.[41] St. Ulrich of Augsburg simply repeats Rathier's invitation,[42] and perhaps it is in the same sense that the recommendation of Otto of Bamberg is to be understood which we have quoted elsewhere.[43]

Still the surviving records generally mention but three communions on the great feasts.[44] Besides, an attentive reading of the conciliar and other documents shows that these three communions have neither the same importance nor the same degree of obligation. The most important was incontestably that of Easter, whether it was received on Holy Thursday or the following Sunday. Easter Communion is always insisted upon, whereas the special preparation to be made for the communion of Christmas or of Pentecost is less frequently mentioned. Caesarius of Arles speaks of the Christmas communion; but most writers mention only the Easter Communion, which is sometimes prepared for by the office of Good Fri-

[41] "Neglexisti ut non acciperes corpus et sanguinem Domini, istis quatuor temporibus, id est in Coena Domini, et in Pascha, et in Pentecoste, et in Natali Domini?" *Decretor.*, l. XIX, c. v. Migne, *P. L.*, t. CXL, 963.

[42] *Sermo Synodalis*, MANSI, t. XIX, 314.

[43] See above, p. 165.

[44] Cf. besides the texts already quoted, *Leges ecclesiast. Canuti regis*, c. xix. MANSI, t. XIX, 559; *Conc. Aenhamen.*, c. xx. MANSI, *ib.*, 308-309; *Conc. Strigonien.* (1114), c. iv. MANSI, t. XXI, 100; etc.

day, as a Council of Toledo [45] notes at length; sometimes fixed for Holy Thursday, on which the public penitents were reconciled; [46] or for Sunday, as is indicated by a Scottish council held about 1076, under the inspiration of the saintly Queen Margaret, and which seems to consider only Easter Communion as of absolute obligation.[47]

Summary of the Discipline in Vogue Before the Fourth Lateran Council.—The first stage of the discipline, previous to the Fourth Council of the Lateran, can be summed up as follows: Beginning with the Council of Agde, in most of the Western countries efforts were made to enforce at least three communions annually, *viz.*: at Christmas, Easter, and Pentecost. The Easter communion in certain dioceses was received twice, *viz.*: on Holy Thursday and Easter Sunday. Nearly everywhere

---

[45] *Conc. Toletan.* IV (633), c. vii. BRUNS, t. I, 224.

[46] "In Coena Domini a quibusdam perceptio Eucharistiae negligitur. Quae quoniam in eadem die ab omnibus fidelibus, exceptis his quibus pro gravibus criminibus inhibitum est, percipienda sit, ecclesiasticus usus demonstrat, cum etiam poenitentes eadem die ad percipienda corporis et sanguinis dominici sacramenta reconciliat." *Concil. Cabilonen.* II (813), c. xlvii. *Monum. Germ., Concilia,* t. II, 283.

[47] "Aliud quoque ponens regina jussit, ut ostenderent qua ratione die sanctae Paschae secundum morem sanctae et apostolicae Ecclesiae sacramenta corporis et sanguinis Christi sumere negligerent. In die resurrectionis Dominicae ad ejus mensam in catholica fide accedentes, carnem et sanguinem agni immaculati Jesu Christi, non ad judicium sed ad peccatorum sumimus remissionem." *Conc. Scotien.* (about 1076), sectio xv. MANSI, t. XX, 480.

the canon of the Council of Agde became a diocesan or provincial precept, or a law of custom. Some churches succeeded in inducing the faithful to receive communion every Sunday in Lent. But the main obligation, the minimum below which no one could fall without being cut off from Christian fellowship, was annual communion, which even the lukewarm practiced in the fourth century, which the author of *De Sacramentis* believes insufficient, and which a council of Scotland, held under the influence of the saintly Queen Margaret, requires absolutely.

We have so far spoken only of the laity; from clerics more frequent communion was required. This demand is mentioned particularly by a council of Gran in the twelfth century (1114),[48] and represented as very simple and quite natural by Robert Pulleyn about the same period (1146).[49]

The Fourth Lateran Council.—Such was the situation when the Fourth Lateran Council opened. A law imposing three communions a year, provincial in origin, had gradually extended its sphere

[48] "Ut omnis populus in Pascha et Pentecoste et Natali Domini poenitentiam agat et communicet; clerici vero in omnibus majoribus festis communicent." *Conc. Strigonien.*, c. iv. MANSI, t. XXI, 108.

[49] "Aliis saepius, aliis rarius mos est communicari. Statuta tamen Patrum sanciunt ter in anno communicandum, die Natalis, Paschae et Pentecostes. Sacerdotes tamen frequentius opus est confortari; laicos autem ter saltem." *Sentent.*, l. VIII, c. vii. Migne, *P. L.*, t. CLXXXVI, 968.

of action beyond the limits of France, but the laxity and negligence of a large number of Christians in course of time had suppressed in practice the two communions of Christmas and Pentecost. Then, outside the sphere of influence of the Council of Agde, the paschal communion alone remained obligatory.

The work of the Fourth Lateran Council (1215) was to render the discipline uniform by requiring nothing more than the minimum universally accepted. The council combined the prescriptions concerning confession and communion in its twenty-first canon, *Omnis utriusque sexus*. The obligations imposed are: first, every Christian of either sex who has attained the age of discretion, must receive the Eucharistic Communion at Easter; second, he or she can be exempted by the pastor only by way of exception and for reasonable motives; third, disobedience is punishable by a double penalty: exclusion from Church during life, (*"alioquin et vivens ab ingressu ecclesiae arceatur"*) and privation of Christian burial after death (*"et moriens christianâ careat sepulturâ"*).

Although the obligations concerning annual confession and paschal communion were united in one precept, there were notable differences between the two; the most important being that the pastor could, for a reasonable motive, permit his parish-

THE FOURTH COMMANDMENT

ioners to abstain temporarily from communion.[50]

Communion "ad minus in Pascha."—The Council ordained that the decree be frequently published in the churches.[51] This command was obeyed. During the entire thirteenth century and a part of the fourteenth, provincial councils and diocesan synods constantly recall it. Let us cite, for instance, Richard of Sarum's (about 1217) *Constitutions*,[52] the Councils of Sens, Treves, Pont-Audemer, Nîmes, Bourges,[53] and Coutances.[54] But official promulgation was not always sufficient to stir up the faithful, and hence councils held at Tarragona[55] and Salamanca[56] required that this precept be published four times each year, and one

[50] "Nisi forte de consilio proprii sacerdotis, ob aliquam rationabilem causam, ad tempus, ab ejus perceptione duxerit abstinendum." Can. *Omnis utriusque sexus*, xii, X, *de Poenitent. et Remissionibus*.

[51] "Hoc salutare statutum frequenter in ecclesiis publicetur." *can. cit.*

[52] *Constitutiones* . . ., c. xxv. MANSI, t. XXII, 1115.

[53] *Conc. Senonen.* (1269), c. iv. MANSI, t. XXIV, 5. *Conc. Treviren.* (about 1277), § III, n. 6. MANSI, *ib.*, 194; *Conc. Treviren.* (1310), c. xc. MANSI, t. XXV, 271; *Concil. apud Pontem Audomar.* (1279), c. v. MANSI, t. XXIV, 222; *Synod. Nemausen.* (1284), § 7. MANSI, *ib.*, 535; *Conc. Bituricen.* (1286), c. xiii. MANSI, *ib.*, 631.—Note in this council the following prescription: "Et quod nomina sic confitentium in scriptis redigant, quibus in festo Paschae viaticum dent."

[54] *Synodicon Constantien.* (1300), c. xxxiii. MANSI, t. XXV, 37-38.

[55] *Conc. Terraconen.* (1329), c. lxvii. MANSI, *ib.*, 870.

[56] *Concil. Salmanticen.* (1335), c. xvi, n. 41. MANSI, *ib.*, 1057.

held at Palencia that it be read every Sunday from Septuagesima to Easter.[57]

The decree *Omnis* had created a new legislation, but it did not make this new legislation irreconcilable with the old, and hence the particular enactments regarding communion were treated as those concerning communion had been treated. The decree on penance had not mentioned the previous particular legislation, and therefore had derogated or changed it only in as much as its dispositions were in contradiction with the ancient discipline. Similarly, the constitutions or synodal decrees which required a more frequent reception of the Eucharist were not abrogated by the Lateran decree. The diocesan law remained in force and as obligatory as before; to disobey it exposed one to the existing diocesan penalties; the Lateran law was only a minimum conceded to the negligent Christians, the final limit of tolerance: not to obey it exposed one inevitably to excommunication.

It was in this sense that the law was generally understood. It was interpreted thus by the Constitutions of Richard of Sarum already cited,[58]

---

[57] *Concil. Palentin.* (Valladolid, 1322), c. xxvii. MANSI, *ib.*, 722.

[58] "Ter communicare teneantur: in Pascha, in Pentecoste, et in Natali Domini ... quicumque autem semel in anno ... ad minus ad Pascha, Eucharistiae sacramentum non acceperit, nisi consilio sui sacerdotis duxerit abstinendum; et vivens ab ingressu Ecclesiae arceatur, et mortuus christiana careat sepultura." *Constitution. Ricardi ...*, c. xxv. MANSI, t. XXII, 1115.

and those of St. Edmund of Canterbury.[59] Elsewhere, at Albi for instance, an attempt was made at reconciling the ancient particular with the new general discipline. Confession was made obligatory at least once a year, but Communion was to be received three times, *viz:* at Christmas, Easter and Pentecost, unless there was a serious excuse, approved by the *proprius sacerdos*.[60] The Council of Albi added, at least as a counsel, that confession should precede communion: "Ita quod confessio communionem praecedat."

At Toulouse it seems the diocesan authorities tried to establish a singularly severe discipline for which the Lateran canon *"Omnis"* was to serve as a prop. A decree resembling the *Omnis* in tenor obliged all Christians to go to confession and communion three times a year under pain of being suspect of heresy. This particular discipline was so carefully couched in the phraseology of the general decree, that the inattentive reader might imagine, in reading it, that he had before him the Lateran canon.[61]

[59] He recalls the preceding Constitutions almost word for word. *Constitution. S. Edmundi Cantuar. Archiep.* (1236), c. xviii. MANSI, t. XXIII, 421.

[60] *Concil. Albien.* (1254), c. xxix. MANSI, *ib.*, 840.

[61] This proceeding can be realized in reading the exact text of Toulouse, only a part of which was given above: "Omnes autem utriusque sexus, postquam ad annos discretionis advenerint, confessionem peccatorum faciant ter in anno proprio sacerdoti, vel alii de voluntate ipsius, vel mandato, injunctam poenitentiam

Needless to say, it was difficult to maintain for any length of time a twofold legislation, a particular one (diocesan or provincial) and the universal legislation of the common law, both backed by a sanction, but the latter being practically the only one with a penalty sure of infliction everywhere. From the first half of the thirteenth century, some statutes admit only the Easter Communion as obligatory;[62] and little by little the constitutions of the diocesan synods or provincial councils mention none other. About the end of the thirteenth century an Avignon council, the records of which are somewhat uncertain, mentions communion at Easter and Pentecost;[63] but a council of Treves held a little later, counsels rather than commands,[64] and seems to threaten with excommuni-

et humiliter et pro viribus impleturi, *et ter* in anno, in Natali Domini, Pascha et Pentecoste, sacramentum Eucharistiae cum omni reverentia suscepturi; ita quod confessio communionem praecedat: nisi forte ob aliquam causam rationabilem, ad tempus, ab ejus participatione abstinuerint, de consilio proprii sacerdotis. Solliciti sint itaque presbyteri circa ista, ut ex nominum inspectione cognoscant, sicut superius est expressum, utrum sint aliqui qui communicare subterfugiant. Nam si quis a communione, nisi de consilio proprii sacerdotis, abstinuerit, suspectus de haeresi habeatur." *Concil. Tolosan.* (1229), c. xiii. MANSI, *ib.*, 197. The same decision is given *Concil. ap. Pontem Audomar.*, c. v. MANSI, t, XXIV, 222.

[62] *Statuta Cenomanen.* (1247). MANSI, t. XXIII, 746.—The same is given in *Synod. Claromontan.* (1268), c. vi. MANSI, *ib.*, 1192.

[63] *Concil. Avenionen.* (1282), c. v. MANSI, t. XXIV, 442.

[64] "Omnes fideles in tribus anni temporibus, videlicet in Natali, in Pascha, in Pentecoste, ad communionem corporis et sanguinis

THE FOURTH COMMANDMENT

cation those only who neglect the paschal communion.[65]

Shortly after a council of Toledo mentions three annual communions, but it does this to draw attention to the fact that they are an obligation of the clergy, whose piety should surpass that of the laity.[66]

In its practical application the Lateran decree naturally gave rise to many canonical questions. In what church was the Easter Communion to be received? Within what period was the obligation to be fulfilled and under what penalty was it enforced? At what age did the obligation begin? Who possessed the exclusive right of administering it?

Some of these questions were settled by the special decision of councils, others were left to the canonists, who based their decisions either on current discipline and custom, or on general principles, which they sometimes derived from the civil law.

Domini sint monendi." *Concil. Treviren.* (1310), c. lxxxix. MANSI, t. XXV, 270.

[65] It is only on those who omit the Paschal Communion that the 90th canon of the same council inflicts the penalties provided for by the Lateran decree: "Et saltem in Paschate Eucharistiam recipiant . . . alioquin a rectoribus et capellanis viventes ab ingresu Ecclesiae et sacramentis ecclesiasticis arceantur, morientibus ecclesiastica sepultura denegetur." *Ib.*, 271.

[66] "Alii vero clerici, ut ostendant se ad plus teneri quam laici, ad minus communicent ter in anno." *Concil. Toletan.* (1324), c. vii. MANSI, *ib.*, 734.

The Church in which Easter Communion was to be Received.—The text of the decree *Omnis* did not specify the church in which a Christian had to comply with his Easter duty. But the ancient discipline clearly pointed to the parish church. The parish in olden times formed an almost exclusive society, under somewhat of a feudal constitution, with the faithful as members and the pastor as lord. Christian life was centered around and emanated from the parochial church; but confession and communion are important parts of this life; therefore they could not be accomplished elsewhere. Consequently, we may apply to the paschal communion *a priori* what has been said of annual confession.

Another sign of the suzerainty of the pastor in this matter is the following: We have seen that the decree was to be published frequently in the churches (*i.e.* the parochial churches) (*"hoc salutare statutum frequenter in ecclesiis publicetur"*). We have likewise seen that it was the *"proprius sacerdos,"* that is, the rector of the parish, who in particular cases could permit a Christian to abstain for a time from participation in the Eucharist. It also belonged to the head of the parish to turn the negligent away from church and to refuse them ecclesiastical burial after death.

The Council of Avignon, already cited, commands the faithful to assist, on Sunday and holy days, at Mass *in their parish church,* and therein

THE FOURTH COMMANDMENT

to receive, with the required dispositions, especially at Easter, the Eucharist, which is the viaticum of our pilgrimage here below.[67] The councils of Treves (1310), Cologne (1310), Mayence (1310), Avignon (1337),[67a] all affirm the same in various ways, and especially when answering the following question:

To Whom Does the Right to Distribute the Paschal Communion Belong?—The only authorized minister of the paschal communion is the *"proprius sacerdos,"* that is, the pastor. The Lateran decree implies this, and subsequent councils clearly affirm it. The Council of Avignon, *e.g.*, says: "The parishioners shall receive the viaticum of the Eucharist from their own priest;"[68] that of Bourges points to the pastor as the only dispenser of the Eucharist at Easter, as he has been the only minister of confession;[68a] that of Cologne still more clearly declares that the faithful cannot, without a special and authentic privilege, receive the Eucharist from any other priest than the

[67] "Quilibet parochiani . . . venire ad *suas parochiales ecclesias* . . . tenentur, et *in eis*, inter missarum solemnia, Eucharistiae nostrae peregrinationis viaticum recipere." *Concil. Avenionen.* (1282), c. v. MANSI, t. XXVI, 442.

[67a] *Concil. Colonien.* (1310), c. xx. MANSI, t. XXV, 242; *Concil. Treviren.* (1310), c. xc, *ib.*, 271; *Concil. Moguntin.* (1310), *ib.*, 345; *Concil. Avenionen.* (1337), c. iv, *ib.*, 1089.

[68] *Loc. cit.*

[68a] "Et quod nomina sic confitentium in scriptis redigant, quibus in festo Paschae viaticum dent." *Concil. Bituricen.* (1286), c. xii. MANSI, *ib.*, 631.

pastor, under pain of temporary excommunication left to the latter's discretion.[69] Regulars, with the permission of the pastor, were sometimes allowed to hear confessions in a parish, but they were forbidden (by some councils under pain of excommunication *latae sententiae*) to administer the other sacraments, particularly the Eucharist, especially to Beghards, Beguins and other such persons.[70]

What Was the Precise Period for the Easter Communion?—That the Paschal Communion was to be received from the hands of the pastor is evident from the decisions given by another council of Avignon of the same period. This council, in order to render all fraud impossible, forbids pastors under pain of excommunication, incurred *ipso facto*, to allow their parishioners, within the fortnight of Easter, (from Palm Sunday to Quasi-

---

[69] "Statuimus item, ut nullus parochianus ab alio quam *a suo vero plebano*, communionem recipiat: nisi de hoc privilegiis authenticis sit munitus. Contrarium facientes a perceptione corporis Christi abstineant, quousque ipsi plebano satisfecerint de contemptu." *Concil. Colonien.* (1310), c. xx. MANSI, t. XXV, 442.

[70] "Quamvis Ecclesia toleret, quod cum conniventia proprii sacerdotis subditi plebanorum, pro maturiori consilio adipiscendo, religiosis quibusdam confiteantur interdum, nolumus tamen, immo sacri concilii auctoritate, sub poena excommunicationis jam latae sententiae, vetamus omnibus religiosis, ne subditos plebanorum, maxime autem beginas et beckardos aut inclusas ac alias personas hujusmodi communicent corpore Domini, aut alia porrigant ecclesiastica sacramenta parvulis, vel adultis." *Concil. Moguntin.* (1310). MANSI, *ib.*, 345. Cf. *Concil. Saltzburgen.* (1420), c. xxv. MANSI, t. XXVIII, 998.

modo), to receive Holy Communion outside of their parish church.

Even the bishops were forbidden to grant permissions of this kind.[71]

The Age at Which the Obligation of the Paschal Communion Began.—We have already seen[72] that a discussion arose among the canonists on the question at what age children became subject to the precept of annual confession. The Lateran decree said: "having attained the age of discretion"; but these words were susceptible of diverse interpretations. As the same text applied to pas-

---

[71] "Desiderantes, illud praeceptum generalis concilii . . . quod omnis utriusque sexus, postquam ad annos discretionis pervenerit, reverenter recipiat, ad minus in Paschate, Eucharistiae sacramentum, sic a Christi fidelibus sollicitudini nostrae commissis efficaciter observari, quod nullis quaesitis coloribus, et simulatis devotionibus, vel alias, dum ab aliis quam a propriis sacerdotibus recipere velle se asserunt Corpus Christi, fraudem quaerentes facere canoni, fraudent potius semetipsos: praesentis deliberatione concilii statuimus inhibendo quod curati nostrarum civitatum, dioecesum, et provinciarum, nulli parochiano cujuscumque conditionis vel sexus existat, in festo Paschae, nec in octo diebus immediate praecedentibus, nec in octo diebus immediate subsequentibus, concedant licentiam recipiendi, nisi ex causa infirmitatis, nec etiam alicui conferendi seu ministrandi sacramentum Eucharistiae extra ecclesias suas parochiales, vel alias ecclesias, ubi per ipsos curatos ministrari extitit consuetum. Si qui autem curati hujusmodi statuti fuerint trangressores auctoritate praesentis concilii excommunicationis incurrant sententiam, ipso facto. Praelati autem sic praesens statutum diligenter observent, ut alicui, nisi ex causa rationabili, recipiendi sacramentum praedictum, illo tempore, alibi quam in parochiali ecclesia, licentiam non concedant." *Concil. Avenionen.* (1337), c. iv. MANSI, t. XXV, 1089.

[72] Cf. above, p. 170 and following.

chal communion, it might have been expected that the same discussions would arise on this point. But such was not altogether the case. It naturally followed that communion would not be obligatory sooner than confession, and that the solutions given for the latter would serve as a basis to solve the former. When the most ancient conciliar decrees, which place the age of confession at fourteen, so interpret the Lateran text, as was done for instance by the Council of Narbonne (1227), the synods of Liège, Luca, Avignon,[73] they evidently suppose that the paschal communion is not obligatory before the age of discretion. A council of Spain expressly says that the "annus discretionis" of the Lateran decree signifies fourteen years for boys and twelve for girls.[74] This was in accord with jurisprudence and the common teaching of the great theological writers. The "postquam ad annos discretionis pervenerit" has never been understood as meaning the age of reason, but as signifying a more advanced age, *i.e.* from ten to fourteen. That was the opinion of St.

[73] *Concil. Narbonen.* (1227), c. vii. MANSI, t. XXIII, 23; *Statuta Synodalia Eccles. Leodien.* (1287), c. xxiii, § 4. MANSI, t. XXIV, 893; *Synod. Lucana* (1308), c. lvii. MANSI, t. XXV, 189; *Statuta Avenionen.* edita anno 1341, in synodo S. Lucae. MARTENE, *Thesaurus Anecdotorum*, t. IV, 566.

[74] "Praecipimus ecclesiarum rectoribus ... ut ... exponant parochianis suis, qualiter juxta statutum concilii generalis, quilibet, ex quo *ad annos discretionis, masculus* videlicet *ad XIV, femina vero ad XII* pervenerint, tenentur ..." *Concil. Terraconen.* (1329), c. lxvii. MANSI, t. XXV, 870.

THE FOURTH COMMANDMENT

Thomas.[74a] It was also that of the ablest among his successors, particularly St. Antoninus, who met with more success in this question than in that of confession. In his view the age for communion is about eleven or twelve, without any necessary relation to the age of puberty.[75] Parents and teachers could oblige children to go to confession, but it was the pastor's place alone to judge whether the child was capable of receiving holy communion.[76] If the child had the required understanding, his age and size, and even custom, had nothing to do with the question.[77]

Half a century later, Angelo de Clavasio gave the same solution. In reading his work we get the impression that he had to struggle against a more benign tendency, which without any consideration as to age, would leave the decision to the judgment of a prudent man. We are likely to interpret him rightly in concluding that the age of ten or twelve,

---

[74a] *In IV Sententiar.*, dist. IX, art. 4, ad 4um.

[75] We have said above, in studying the history of the third commandment, that, for St. Antoninus, the obligation of confession only became binding when the child had become, in the juridical sense of the word, "doli capax."

[76] "Parentes, quamvis ad confessionem debeant quodammodo regere, sicut et magistri scolarum: non autem sic ad communionem; sed debent bene eos hortari, si vident eos habere bonam discretionem vel dimittere in judicio confessorum suorum." *Summa Theologica*, pars IIa, tit. IX, c. ix. Verona, 1740, t. II, 996.

[77] "Retrahendo autem eos solum ex hoc, quia sunt parvi, et quia non est de more patriae, pueros quantumcumque habeant usum rationis, quod communicent, graviter peccant." *Ibid.*

thereafter decided upon and generally admitted,[78] is the very one indicated by him.

The interpretation of the "annus discretionis" has hardly changed since; and various motives, which we need not set forth here, in particular the distinctively French practice of solemn first communion, have given a greater, perhaps too great an importance to the question of age, for the admission of children to the first solemn reception of the Eucharist.[79]

Penalties.—The Lateran Council declared those who omit annual confession and Easter communion to be excluded from the Church during life, and refused them Christian burial after death. These penalties were not incurred before the legal age of puberty.[80] Nor could they be enforced except in cases where the delinquents were known. To find them out, synodal and provincial statutes directed the pastors to keep a roster of all persons subject to the precept. Such is the ruling of a council held at Toledo.[81] Another held at Benevento com-

---

[78] "Quando est aetas debita. R. Aureolus . . . quod relinquendum est arbitrio boni viri. Et ideo dico quod tunc est aetas debita quando queri habent usum rationis, quum possunt concipere devotionem hujus sacramenti et discernere et dijudicare corpus Christi: et revereri ab alio cibo saltem ex aliorum instructione, quod potest esse in decimo vel saltem in duodecimo anno." *Summa Angelica de Casibus Conscientie*, verbo *"Eucharistia,"* iiio, no 12.

[79] Cf. S. C. C. in Annecien. 21 July, 1888.

[80] Cf. *supra*, p. 173 sq.

[81] "Et *illos qui* sibi vel alteri potestatem habenti, de quo constet

mands pastors, under pain of a fine, to communicate to the bishop, at least once a year, the names of those who had fulfilled the duty of confession and communion, even outside the paschal season.[82] Elsewhere the keeping of such lists and their communication to the bishops had been obligatory a long time previously.[83]

Discussion of Details.—The discipline which had been inaugurated, or standardized, by the Fourth Lateran Council was thus settled and completed. This did not mean, however, that all discussion had been suppressed. Quibbling moralists managed to find many points for further debate. St. An-

ei, *confessi fuerint, consignet*, eosque ad recipiendum Eucharistiam excitet." *Conc. Toletan.* (1339), c. v. MANSI, t. XXV, 1146.

[82] "Item dictis parochialibus presbyteris nostrarum civitatis, dioecesis et Provinciae, statuendo praecipimus, et mandamus, quod nomina omnium suorum parochianorum eis in anno confitentium, et quibus in Pascha ad minus, vel alio tempore, sanctum Eucharistiae sacramentum dederint, in scriptis redigant, et nobis semel saltem in anno, et quoties poterunt, aut vicario nostro seu suffraganeis nostris, aut eorum vicariis in scriptis dare procurent. Alioquin non observantes hanc nostram constitutionem poenam unius Augustalis applicandam curiae nostrae, seu dictorum suffraganeorum nostrorum, incurrere volumus ipso facto." *Concil. Benevetan.* (1331), c. lxvii. MANSI, *ib.*, 971-972.

[83] Cf. *Concil. apud Pontem Audomari* (1279), c. v: "Adjicientes quod nomina talium, per suos presbyteros, ordinario eorum insinuentur." MANSI, t. XXIV, 222; *Concil. Bituricen.* (1286), c. xiii. Note that, according to the latter council, the pastor is to refuse communion even to those who have gone to confession, if they have made their confession to another than their pastor, or to some priest not provided with the permission of the pastor or the bishop. Mansi, *ib.*, 621.

toninus, for instance, minutely studied the question whether Paschal Communion was fixed for the day of Easter, or whether it was allowable to fulfill the precept on Holy Thursday or on one of the two days following Easter. In his opinion Communion was to be received on Easter Sunday or on one of the two following days, which he regarded as integral parts of the feast. Those who do not communicate on one of these three days can be excused only on the plea of having acted in good faith. Their ignorance he attributes to preachers who are very daring and claim to know more than they ought.[84] He is so anxious to attach the obligation to the day of Easter that he holds that the obligation ceases after that day, just as one is not held to fast on another day if he has neglected to do so on the day appointed; or as one is not held to hear mass on a week day if he has missed it on Sunday or a holy day of obligation.[85]

The views of St. Antoninus, however, did not prevail. Thus Angelo de Clavasio, whose authority was very great, flatly contradicts him; first, concerning the obligation being fixed on the day

[84] "Et qui hoc praedicant, scilicet alia die, quam in Pascha communicandum, plus sapiunt, quam oportet sapere." *Summa Theolog.*, loc. cit., t. II, p. 995

[85] It would take too much space to cite the text; we simply refer the reader to the summa of the holy bishop: *Summa Theolog.*, pars II^a, tit. IX, *de Acidia*, c. ix. Verona (1740), tom. cit., p. 998-999.

THE FOURTH COMMANDMENT

of Easter, regarding which he invokes a declaration of Eugene IV;[86] and secondly in interpreting the words "at least once a year," on which point he says: "Otherwise he who does not communicate at least once a year, must be excommunicated."[87]

Angelo's opinion prevailed. St. Alphonsus de' Liguori, in answer to the question: "Is one who has omitted the Easter Communion held to communicate as soon as possible?" replies: "The first opinion, which is the more common one, and to which I subscribe, absolutely affirms it."[88] This view was adopted by the majority of writers and determined the practice of the faithful. Moreover, in order to facilitate the fulfillment of this duty, the paschal time was gradually extended by diocesan statutes and by custom.

The primitive rigor was relaxed also on other points. While it is still generally held that the Paschal Communion should be received in one's parish church, it need not be received from the hands of the parish priest, and when there are serious reasons for receiving the Easter Commun-

[86] "Quod autem quidam voluerunt intelligere praecise de die Paschae non bene senserunt, cum papa Eugenius declaravit ad removendas ambiguitates quod sufficit in die jovis sancta et ulterius usque ad dominicam post Pascha immediate sequentem inclusive." *Summa Angelica*, loc. cit., n. 36.

[87] *Ibid.*, n. 37.

[88] *Theolog. Moral.*, l. VI, tr. III, de Eucharistia, n. 297.

ion in another church, it is agreed that the consent of one's pastor may be presumed. However, Bonacina's opinion that anyone could receive the Paschal Communion in the cathedral church of his diocese, was contradicted by Lugo and has not obtained the assent of theological writers.

Summary.—The Church has always held that the faithful are obliged by divine law to receive communion, and for many centuries Christians satisfactorily complied with this obligation. When the early fervor diminished, it was thought necessary to strengthen the moral obligation by a juridical one. It is difficult to indicate the precise date at which the precept was formulated, for the first conciliar decisions on this subject were perhaps of the nature of a counsel rather than a binding law; but it seems quite certain that the juridical value of a positive law was soon attributed to them.

The legal obligation varied in different countries. In a large number of dioceses it was obligatory to receive communion three or four times a year; in others, one communion at Easter was deemed sufficient.

However, even where the discipline of three annual communions (at Christmas, Easter, and Pentecost) was observed, that of Easter was considered more important than the other two.

When the Fourth Lateran Council decided to

check the increasing laxity, and to enforce a uniform discipline throughout Christendom, the Easter Communion naturally survived.

The decree *Omnis,* supported by diocesan laws, made the practical application more precise in detail; thus the Easter Communion was to be received in one's own parish church from the hands of the pastor, by all who had attained the age of discretion, under the double penalty of exclusion from the Church during life and the denial of Christian burial after death.

Various papal or conciliar decisions, and the discussions of the moralists, helped to elucidate certain points. Easter time was interpreted as meaning the fortnight from Palm Sunday to Quasimodo, and by means of an extension which was not clearly implied in the Lateran text, that is, by the application to communion of the incidental clause "at least once a year," which seemed to aim at confession only, all finally agreed that the precept continued to bind those who had not fulfilled it within the prescribed period. Then, too, the age of discretion was commonly agreed upon as lying somewhere around 12 or 14 years.

The rights of the pastor and of the parish church have been better maintained with regard to the Paschal Communion than with respect of annual confession; a decision of the Sacred Congregation of the Council, quoted by Fagnani, forbade those who had received communion from the hands of their pastor on Holy Thursday, to receive it from the monks on Easter Sunday.[89] The opinion which allowed the faithful to receive the Paschal Communion in the cathedral church of the diocese, was eventually rejected by the majority of theologians.

Unfortunately, in spite of all precautions, the relaxation did not cease. Different penalties, including the suspicion of heresy,[90] which exposed one to very serious inconveniences, did not affect men who excommunicated themselves with such indifference. The only penalty which still holds good, *i.e.* the refusal of Christian burial, has almost vanished in practice. The Roman Ritual indeed still enumerates among those to whom Christian burial must be refused, all who have omitted the Paschal Communion, but according to De Angelis, this applies only to those who have neglected their Easter duty "for many years," and as the Ritual adds, who have died without giving any sign of contrition.

Little, therefore, can be expected from the penalties, and we must rely more than ever on the strength of individual conviction.

Will the Church become still less exacting, as

[89] S. C. C., January 13, 1586. FAGNANI, in c. *Omnis*, n. 43.
[90] *Ibid.*, n. 15.

regards the Paschal Communion? We doubt it. The juridical obligation will continue as an authoritative confirmation of the moral obligation and of the divine threat: "Except you eat the flesh of the Son of man, and drink His blood, you shall not have life in you." (John VI, 54.)

CHAPTER VII

THE FIFTH COMMANDMENT

Quatre Temps, Vigiles jeûneras
et le Carême entièrement.

On Ember days thou shalt fast,
On Vigils and throughout Lent.[1]

This commandment embodies a very ancient discipline, determined for a far longer time than the precept of annual confession and Easter Communion. It was formerly even thought that the prescription concerning Ember Days, Vigils, and Lent, dated back to the Apostles. Historians, on the authority of the *Liber Pontificalis,* and canonists, following the chapter *Jejunium, Distinct. LXXVI,* attributed the institution of the Ember Days to Pope Callixtus. Baronius, basing his conclusions on divers documents of Christian antiquity, and on the lessons of the Roman Breviary for the feast of St. Callixtus, ascribed its origin to the Apostles. To-day we are less positive;

[1] The fifth and sixth commandments of the Church in the French catechisms form but one in our Baltimore Catechism:— *viz.*, the second, which says, To fast and abstain on the days appointed.

in fact we modestly admit that we do not know the precise date.

We must acknowledge, however, that the theory which attributes an Apostolic origin to the Ember Days, Vigils, and Lent, is not entirely wrong. For though the Apostles did not formally institute the discipline, they furnished the rudiments from which it developed.

In this chapter we will speak only of the fast, reserving the question of abstinence for the next chapter.

I. EMBER DAYS.—The origin of the Ember Days is differently explained by our two great authorities on liturgical lore, Mgsr. Duchesne and Dom Morin.

According to Duchesne, the Ember Days are of Roman origin, a remnant of the primitive week with its Wednesday and Friday fast, substituted for the Jewish fast of Monday and Thursday. His opinion is that "the arrangement of the services in Ember weeks still preserves some features of the early religious weekly observances as practiced by the Church at Rome." The fast of the Ember Days appears to Duchesne "to be none other than the weekly fast, as observed at the beginning, but made specially severe, as well by the retention of the Wednesday, which had disappeared early from the weekly Roman use, as by the substitution of a real fast for the semi-fast of the ordinary Stations."[2]

Such is not exactly the opinion of Dom Morin. Our Ember Days, according to him, have not so ancient an origin, but were instituted by the Church to compete with the pagan holidays.[3]

Perhaps the truth can be arrived at by combining the two theories. It would seem that the Ember Days were indeed instituted for the purpose mentioned by Dom Morin, and that they were fixed on Wednesday and Friday because of the part these two days played in the primitive Christian week.[4] Were the reason of the institution of the Ember Days that indicated by Msgr. Duchesne, it would be hard to understand why the fast of the Ember Days, succeeding the primitive weekly fast, is found only in Rome. For, when history first points out their existence,—not earlier than the fifth century—Rome[5] alone seems to know of them.

[2] *Christian Worship*, London, 1903, p. 232 sq.

[3] *L'Origine des Quatre-Temps*, Rev. Bénédictine, 1897, p. 337 sqq. Each year, towards the beginning of summer, autumn, and winter, Rome invoked the protection of the gods for the harvests, vintage and sowing; these were the feasts that the popes changed into three stations with fast, celebrated in June, September, and December. On the other hand, as Msgr. Duchesne has already remarked, the liturgical prayers of these Ember Days referred to the crops of wheat, grapes, and olives. Cf. *Liber Pontificalis*, t. I, 141, note 4. To these three stations was later joined that of spring, which falls in Lent.

[4] Cf. *Didache*, viii, 1.

[5] It is from Rome that the Ember Days were introduced into

THE FIFTH COMMANDMENT

From that time we can follow their history. The most ancient documents which show us the Ember Days as already fully organized are the sermons of St. Leo. Their institution evidently must date farther back. St. Leo traces their origin to the Old Testament, affirming that this fast partakes of the permanency of certain other precepts, such as this: *Thou shalt adore the Lord thy God, and thou shalt serve no one but Him,* and adding that their definite institution must be attributed to the Apostles.[6] At the time when this holy Pontiff wrote, the discipline of the Ember Days was complete, and the religious meaning attached to them is given by him as well as their dates. Ember Days occur four times a year, at each of the four seasons, for various symbolical reasons.[7] Each of

England, Germany, and France. Spain did not become acquainted with them till later, and the Church of Milan later still.

[6] "Jejuniorum vero utilitatem Novi Testamenti gratia non removit: quoniam sicut permanet apud intelligentiam christianam: *Dominum tuum adorabis et illi soli servies* . . . et caetera talium mandatorum; ita quod in eisdem libris de jejuniorum sanctificatione et curatione praeceptum est, nulla interpretatione vacuatur." (*Serm.* 15, *De jej. decimi mensis,* c. ii. Migne, *P. L.,* t. LIV, 175.) Cf. an extract from a sermon on the seventh month's fast: "Cui medicinae, dilectissimi, licet tempus omne sit congruum, hoc tamen habemus aptissimum, quod *et apostolicis et legalibus institutis* videmus electum." (*Serm.* 93, c. iii, *ib.,* 457.)

[7] "Ita per totius anni circulum distributa sunt, ut lex abstinentiae omnibus sit ascripta temporibus. Siquidem jejunium vernum in quadragesima, aestivum in Pentecoste, autumnale in mense septimo, hiemale autem in hoc, qui est decimus, celebramus, intelligentes divinis nihil vacuum esse praeceptis, et verbo Dei ad eruditionem nostram omnia elementa servire; dum per ipsius

the four series had, in addition, its particular meaning. The Ember Days of the tenth month, for instance, had for their special object the offering of thanks to God for the harvest, and for their spiritual fruit the invitation to give alms.[8] Since the time of Leo, too, the formula by which Ember Days were announced can be said to be stereotyped. "Let us fast on Wednesday and Friday; and on Saturday let us celebrate the Vigil of the Apostle St. Peter."[9]

According to St. Leo, the fast of the Ember Days was the revived fast of the Jews, but it did not involve, as the Jewish fast did, obligatory abstention from work.[10]

Each of the four seasons had its Ember Days. But at what time in the season was each series fixed? We learn this, as noted above, from the sermons of St. Leo: the fast of spring fell in Lent, that of summer at Pentecost, the other two in September and December. As to the part of the month on which the fast fell, it is difficult to de-

mundi cardines, quasi per quatuor evangelia, incessabiliter discimus quod et praedicemus et agamus." *Serm.* 19, *De jej. decimi mensis*, c. ii. Migne, *P. L.*, t. LIV, 186.

[8] "Ut omnium fructuum collectione conclusa . . . circa pauperes esset effusior." *Serm.* 16, c. ii, *ib.*, 177.

[9] "Quarta igitur et sexta feria jejunemus; sabbato autem apud beatissimum Petrum apostolum vigilias celebremus."

[10] St. Leo opposes the "nec a justis et necessariis operibus abstinentes" of the Christians to the "otiosa jejunia" of the Jews. Cf. *Serm.* 89, 1. Migne, *P. L.*, t. LIV, 344.

THE FIFTH COMMANDMENT

termine for the time of St. Leo and the period immediately following. "The attempt was made early," writes Dom Morin, "to affix the Ember Days to determined weeks of the liturgical cycle, but with no immediate success. For a long time afterwards there was a certain indetermination."

Moreover, as has been remarked,[11] the passage of the *Liber Pontificalis* concerning Pope Callixtus mentions only three Ember periods and not four, implicitly excluding the Ember Days of Lent, and the same omission appears in the formulas of indiction contained in the Sacramentaries. Although the fast of the first month, often falling in Lent, is known at an early period, it is none the less interesting to note that the oldest record to be found of the observance of Ember Days in England mentions only three series of fasts, *viz.* in the fourth, seventh, and tenth months. It is of even greater interest to note that the necessity of conforming with the Roman custom is insisted upon. It seems, moreover, from the decree, that the Ember Days were not favored or accepted without great reluctance in Great Britain; hence it was required that they be faithfully announced to the people before the opening of each week of Ember Days, and that the people be notified that they must put themselves in accord on this point with the whole Church.[12]

[11] *Revue Bénédictine, loc. cit.,* p. 343.

[12] "Decimo octavo statutum est mandato, ut jejuniorum tem-

However, about the same time, Egbert of York in his book *De Institutione Catholica,* gives a well established discipline, based on an already venerable tradition, which dates back, he declares, through St. Augustine of Canterbury to Pope St. Gregory.[13] This discipline places the fast of the first month in the first week of Lent, the second fast in the week after Pentecost, the third in the week before the September equinox, without considering whether it be the third week of the month or not, and the fourth in the week before Christmas.[14] It must be acknowledged, however, that some liberty was taken on this point, and that the Council of Enham, when deciding that St. Gregory's prescriptions should be followed in England, admitted that the discipline was different in other countries.[15]

Perhaps it was from England, through the inter-

pora, id est quarti, septimi et decimi mensis, nullus negligere praesumat: sed ante horum initia per singulos annos admoneatur plebs, quatenus legitima universalis Ecclesiae sciat atque observet jejunia, concorditerque universi id faciant, nec ullatenus in ejusmodi discrepent observatione, sed secundum exemplar, quod juxta ritum Romanae Ecclesiae descriptum est, studeant celebrare.'' *Conc. Cloveshov.* II (747), c. xviii. MANSI, t. XII, 401.

[13] "Ut noster didascalus beatus Gregorius, in suo Antiphonario et Missali libro per paedagogum nostrum beatum Augustinum transmisit ordinatum et rescriptum.'' EGBERT., *de Instit. Cathol.,* c. xviii, *de Jejunio quatuor Temporum.* Migne, *P. L.,* t. LXXXIX, 441.

[14] *Ib.* 441 and 442.

[15] "Jejunia vero Quatuor Temporum nos observare oportet, ut sanctus Gregorius nobis constituit; quamvis aliae gentes aliter

mediary of the British missionaries, that Germany received the Ember Days, although the mention made there of ordinations conferred at the same time, rather recalls the Roman custom. The decrees of the Council of Estinnes (743) contain its oldest mention. The Ember Days are affixed to the months of March, June, September, and December, and the priests are directed to instruct the people confided to their care in the observance of these days.[16] A capitulary of Charlemagne, 769, reminded the clergy of the observance of the Ember Days and their obligation of announcing them to the people.[17] But the most important decree on this subject is undoubtedly that of the Council of Mayence, of 813. It is the most precise and detailed ordinance of its kind that we know of, for it fixes not only the weeks of the month for fasting, but also the hour on which the fast ends. The weeks are the first week of March, the second of June, the third of September, and the

exercuerunt." *Conc. Aenhamen.* (1009), c. xvi. MANSI, t. XIX, 308.

[16] "Doceant etiam presbyteri populum quatuor legitima temporum jejunia observare, hoc est in mense Martio, Junio, Septembrio et Decembrio, quando sacri Ordines juxta statuta canonum aguntur." *Statuta S. Bonifacii in Conc. Leptinen.* (743), *ut videtur, promulgata,* c. xxx. Migne, *P. L.,* t. LXXXIX, 823. The text is not a decree of the council but a decision of St. Boniface, probably communicated to his clergy during the council or on the occasion of its meeting.

[17] "Ut jejunium Quatuor Temporum et ipsi sacerdotes observent et plebi denuntient observandum." BORETIUS, t. I, 46.

last full week before Christmas in December. The fast is to be observed until the hour of None, and entails abstinence from flesh meat.[18]

Henceforth the discipline was uniform in the whole empire under Carolingian rule. The Mayence prescriptions were renewed as a rule, or merely alluded to, as, for instance, by Herard of Tours in his *Capitula*.[19]

Regino and Burchard cite the text of the Council with variants;[20] the bishops by asking questions in their synods, watched over its observance.[21] The confessors were obliged to speak of it in the examination of conscience which they

[18] "Constituimus, ut quatuor tempora anni ab omnibus cum jejunio observentur, id est, in martio mense ebdomada prima, feria iv et vi et sabbato veniant omnes ad ecclesiam hora nona, cum laetaniis, ad missarum solemnia; similiter in mense Junio, ebdomada secunda, feria iv et vi et sabbato jejunetur usque ad horam nonam, et a carne ab omnibus abstineatur; similiter in mense Septembrio, ebdomada tertia et in mense Decembrio ebdomada quae fuerit plena ante vigiliam nativitatis Domini, sicut est in Romana Ecclesia traditum." *Concil. Mogunt.* (813), c. xxxiv. *Monum. Germ., Concilia*, t. II, 269.

[19] "De jejuniis quatuor temporum et aliis pro diversis necessitatibus constitutis, ut non solvantur nisi certis infirmitatibus." *Capitul.*, c. x. MANSI, t. XVI (appendix), 678.

[20] REGINO, *De Eccles. disciplin.*, l. i, c. cclxxvii. Migne, *P. L.*, t. CXXXII, 243. BURCHARD, *Decret.*, l. XIII, c. ii. Migne, *P. L.*, t. CXL, 885. It is cited in an abridged form by Gratian, c. ii, dist. LXXXI.

[21] "Si aliquis jejunium quadragesimale non observat, vel quatuor Temporum." REGIN., l. II, c. v, n⁰ 49. Migne, *P. L., t. cit.*, 284; BURCHARD, *Decret.*, l. I, c. xciv, interrogat. 48. *P. L., t. cit.*, 576.

THE FIFTH COMMANDMENT

made for their penitents, and to punish its transgression by a severe penance.[22]

In Northern Italy there had been some difficulty, it seems, in establishing the observance of the Ember Days; one of the few witnesses in this region who mentions it, Ratherius of Verona, asks his priests to insist with all possible vigor upon its observance, as well as on that of the Rogation Days and the Major Litany.[23]

Such, then, was the number of fasts observed about the eleventh century: four series of fast-days in the months of March, June, September, and December, in a great number of countries; in others, England for example,[24] the March series is replaced by that of the first week of Lent; and elsewhere perhaps other local customs prevailed.

This diversity of custom induced the Fathers of the Council of Seligenstadt to frame a decree for the purpose of securing uniformity. This decree

[22] "Solvisti jejunium Quatuor Temporum et non custodisti illud cum caeteris Christianis? XL dies in pane et aqua poeniteas." BURCHARD, *Decret.*, l. XIX, c. v. Migne, *P. L., t. cit.*, 962.

[23] "Jejunium Quatuor Temporum et Rogationum et litaniae majoris plebibus vestris omnimodis insinuate." *Synodica ad presbyteros.* Migne, *P. L.*, t. CXXXVI, 562.

[24] "Quod jejunium sancti Patres in prima hebdomada mensis primi statuerunt quarta et sexta feria et sabbato, exceptis diebus quadragesimalibus. Nos autem, in Ecclesia Anglorum, idem primi mensis jejunium . . . indifferenter de prima hebdomada quadragesimae servamus." EGBERT, *De Instit. cathol.*, c. xvi. *De jejun. Quat. Tempor.* Migne, *P. L.*, t. LXXXIX, 441.

decided that when the month of March began on Thursday, the Ember Days should be held over to the following week; if the June fast fell on the week before Pentecost, it also should be postponed to the following week; if the month of September began on a Thursday, the fast should be transferred to the fourth week; and in December the fast should occur in the week preceding the vigil of Christmas.[25]

Uniformity was indeed obtained, but not by reason of this decree nor in conformity with it, for half a century later a council at Rouen ordained that, according to divine institution (*secundum divinam institutionem*), the Ember days were to be observed in the first week of March, the second of June, and the third of September and December.[26]

To establish uniformity Pope Gregory VII assigned the Ember Days, not to the first week of March and the second week of June, but to the first week of Lent and the week of Pentecost.[27] The decision was published in Germany by the Council of Quedlinburg,[28] and at the Council of

[25] The decree of the Council of Seligenstadt can be found in Gratian, Dist. LXXVI, c. iii.

[26] *Conc. Rothomagen.* (1072), c. ix. Mansi, t. XX, 37.

[27] *Neues Archiv*, t. XIV, p. 620-622. Cf. *Micrologus*, XXIV. Migne, *P. L.*, t. CLI, 995.

[28] "Item ut vernum jejunium in prima hebdomada quadragesimae, aestivum in Pentecoste semper celebretur." *Conc. Quintiliniburgen.* (1085), c. vi. MANSI, t. XX, 608.

THE FIFTH COMMANDMENT

Plaisance, in 1095, Urban II confirmed the decree of his predecessor, Gregory VII.[29] Since that time the discipline has remained substantially unchanged to the present day.

However, it would be a mistake to believe that it was immediately observed everywhere. Such was not the general rule at that period with disciplinary decisions. Almost half a century later, Geoffrey of Vendôme asked Hildebert of Lavardin in what week of June [30] the fast must be observed, and a century later, in 1222, a council at Oxford, legislating on the fast days of obligation, Vigils, and Ember Days, again assigned the first series of Ember Days to the first week of March, and for the second admitted the existence of an indefinite discipline varying according to locality.[31]

But these texts are the last witnesses of a custom already on the wane. From this time onward, throughout the greater part of the Latin Church, the most complete uniformity reigned, thanks to the decree of Gregory VII. Spain received this

---

[29] C. *Statuimus*, iv, Dist. LXXVI.

[30] "In qua hebdomada junii jejunia sitis celebraturus, nobis notificare curetis." GODEFRIDI VINDOCINEN. *Epistol.*, lib. III, *ep.* xxiii. Migne, *P. L.*, t. CLVII, 126.

[31] *Jejunia Quatuor Temporum in totius anni temporibus.* "In martio prima hebdomada jejunandum est feria IV et VI et sabbato. In junio, in secunda, quod dupliciter observatur a pluribus: in prima hebdomada post litanias, aut in hebdomada Pentecostes." *Conc. Oxonien.*, c. viii. MANSI, t. XXII, 1154.

discipline together with the Roman liturgy; in Milan it was established by St. Charles Borromeo.

II. THE VIGILS.—The liturgical observance of vigils antedates that of the Ember Days. Originally this word signified a watch or nocturnal assembly preceding the Sunday liturgy. At the time of Pliny the Younger, who mentions it as the ordinary gathering of Christians, the vigil was passed in singing the praises of Christ, and it probably constituted the particular meeting which the early converts from Judaism held after the assemblies of the Sabbath, which were common to all Christians.[32] But there was not yet any special fast.

The obligation of fasting only began later on. It would be difficult to give the precise date of its origin. Perhaps the linking of the fast with the vigil is an extension of the ancient fast by which the faithful prepared themselves for Easter.

Fasting was always considered as a necessary preparation for the infusion of grace. According to the Didache, the catechumen to be baptized, the baptizing bishop or priest, "and all other persons who are able," had to fast before Baptism.[33]

---

[32] Cf. *supra*, Ch. I.

[33] *Didache*, viii, 4: "Let the baptizer, the one baptized, and other persons who are able, fast before baptism; at least order the person baptized to fast on one or two days before." Likewise St. Justin: "Then we teach them to pray and ask God,

THE FIFTH COMMANDMENT

Fasting also played an important part in the religious practices of Judaism. For these reasons it was imposed on the eve of Easter, both as a token of mourning because of the painful memories of the Passion, and as a preparation for Baptism.

Easter was anciently regarded as the model feast, the pattern after which all the other feasts must be fashioned. Every Sunday is, as it were, a reproduction, yes, we may say, a repetition of Easter; so likewise, after a fashion, are the feasts of the martyrs. It is becoming, therefore, that they should all be preceded by a vigil. In fact this was the case from remote antiquity. The feast of Easter was always preceded by a vigil on which fasting was prescribed, and it was this vigil which developed into our Lent. Its existence and necessity have never been controverted. In the midst of the discussions which disturbed the Church during the dispute with the Quartodecimans, the debate never touched on the existence of the preparatory fast. The difficulty concerning the fast was simply this: for some the fast ended on the fourteenth of Nisan, while for the others it continued until the Sunday on which they celebrated the Resurrection, but all fasted before Easter and regarded the fast as a preparation

while fasting, for the remission of their sins, and we ourselves pray and fast with them." *Apolog.* I, c. lxi, n. 2.

for that feast. The fast of the Paschal Vigil being an indisputable discipline, it was becoming that a vigil should also precede the "weekly Easter."

Another reason is this: Some concluded from the Apology of St. Justin that in his time (*i.e.*, in the second half of the second century) there was as yet no stated season for the conferring of Baptism. From the description which the apologist gives of this ceremony, it may simply be inferred that the first communion of the neophytes took place at the Mass following Baptism, and that the day selected for this ceremony must have been one of the great liturgical assemblies, or some solemn feast. Later on the administration of Baptism was restricted to the feasts of Easter, Pentecost, and Epiphany. For this reason, too, one is justified in believing that Sundays and the other great liturgical days of assembly were preceded by a vigil, on which fasting was prescribed for the catechumens, for those who were about to baptize them, and "for all other persons able to fast." We do not wish to attach too much importance to these deductions. But they appear to us to be well founded and to indicate in what sense the fervent Christians of the early age can be said to have kept vigils.

We have more positive testimonies scattered through primitive Christian literature, particularly the writings of Tertullian, in regard to the existence of vigils in the sense of nocturnal assemblies without fasting.

After peace had been established, the development of ecclesiastical discipline can be more easily traced. In regard to the fast of the vigil, one of the oldest testimonies is that of Philastrius of Brescia. This learned bishop declares that the churches observe four days of fast, which he naturally finds fore-shadowed in the Old Testament, by Zachary who says: "Thus saith the Lord of hosts: The fast of the fourth month, and the fast of the fifth, and the fast of the seventh, and the fast of the tenth month, shall be to the house of Juda, joy, and gladness, and great solemnities." (viii, 19.) And adds: "The Prophet in speaking of four fasts, means four days of fast, and that is what we have in the Church, at Christmas, at Easter, at the Ascension, at Pentecost, for on those four days fasting is obligatory." [34]

The testimony of the Apostolic Constitutions (of about the same date) is less comprehensive than that of Philastrius, but it is more detailed and more precise. It shows the Christians spending in prayer the night of Holy Saturday until the

[34] The text is not quite as clear as it would seem from this translation; it reads: "Sed cum dicit quatuor jejunia, veluti dies quatuor jejunandos decernit. . . . Nam per annum quatuor jejunia in Ecclesia celebrantur: in Natali primum, deinde in Pascha, tertium in Epiphania, quartum in Pentecoste." *De Haeresibus*, c. cxlix. Migne, *P. L.*, t. XII, 1285.

following morning. They listen to readings and instructions concerning salvation and pray for Jews and Pagans; then follow the liturgical oblation and the dismissing of the assembly, which ends the fast.

According to these documents the vigil is simply a night of prayer, passed in common and accompanied by the fast necessary for prayer and for the reception of the Eucharist. It comprises the time of the "watch," from night till morning. We can easily understand why, under these conditions, the fast is not expressly mentioned:— it was not the direct object of the precept but a simple, though normal, accompaniment of the gathering held in the churches.

When the watch was kept outside the churches, in private houses, those assisting, being no longer bound by the respect due to the holy place or the intention of communicating, sometimes abandoned themselves to unbecoming conduct, which drew upon them the censure of writers and councils. Such mishaps were not unheard of even in churches; it was the scandal caused by some reckless individuals that furnished Vigilantius with his strongest arguments against the vigils. These abuses proved nothing against the vigils held in churches where the authority of bishops or priests was able to maintain order, if necessary by force;

but the vigils held in private houses had to be suppressed by the bishops.[35]

There is reason to believe, however, that the watches held in private houses were not the only ones affected by those prohibitory decrees, but that, incidentally, many of the vigils in churches suffered the same fate or, at least, fell into desuetude. For this very reason the authorities became more anxious to preserve the Vigil of Easter in all the splendor of its primitive institution. That night, says the Council of Auxerre, the people shall not be sent away before the second hour of the night, and no drink shall be taken after midnight— evidently to enable people to receive the holy Eucharist at Mass,—and it shall be the same on the night of Christmas and on the vigils of other solemnities.[36]

Both the discipline of the watch and the motive of the fast are indicated in this Auxerre decree. The principal object of the Vigil is a prayer in preparation of the approaching feast; the fast its

[35] This was decided in particular by the Synod of Auxerre, held in the last third of the sixth century: "Non licet compensus in domibus propriis nec pervigilias in festivitates sanctorum facere." c. iii. Cf. c. v.: "Ominino inter supradictis conditionibus previgilias, quos in honore domini Martini observant, omnimodis prohibite." MAASSEN, *Concilia Aevi Merovingici*, p. 179, 180.

[36] C. xi: "Non licet vigilia Paschae ante ora secunda noctis vigilias perexpedire, quia ipsa nocte non licet post media nocte bibere, nec Natale Domini nec reliquas sollemnitates." MAASSEN, *ib.*, p. 180.

necessary accompaniment, so to speak. The fast is observed because the watch is kept in church and to enable the faithful to communicate at Mass.

Evidently, the Vigil could not be practised by the whole populace; it directly affected only clerics and pious persons; above all those clerics who voluntarily celebrated the nocturns of the Matins in holy places and at fixed hours, ascetics, confessors, pious women, virgins, and all such persons as the pilgrim lady Etheria met at Jerusalem at the night offices.

It is customary in the Church first to advise the faithful to imitate the practices of pious persons, then to recommend these practices more insistently, and finally to impose them upon the people at large and gradually embody them in the laws. Such was the case of the vigil. St. Boniface, in the statutes which he communicated to the clergy at the Council of Estinnes, literally reproduced the eleventh canon of the Council of Auxerre;[37] and added that pastors must notify their people that on the Saturday of Pentecost, as on Holy Saturday, all are bound to fast and to gather in church at the ninth hour.[38] Evidently the fast at

[37] *Statuta S. Bonifacii*, c. xxiv. Migne, *P. L.*, t. LXXXIX, 822.

[38] "Et hoc notum facient presbyteri omni populo, ut sabbato Pentecostes, sicut sabbato sancto Paschae, omnes jejunent, et ad ecclesiam hora nona conveniant, quando, sicut vesperascente sabbato sancto Paschae, celebrafur: et ipsum diem Pentecostes similiter celeberrimum habeant, ut sanctum Paschae." *Statuta S. Bonifacii*, c. xxxiv, *ib.*, 823.

this time occupies a more prominent place in the vigil, which it maintained and extended by certain decisions attributed to the famous Council of Compiègne (757).[39] Burchard quotes this text twice in his collection,[40] which proves that it was current discipline. The penalty for breaking the fast on vigils, according to the Penitential books, was a twenty-day black-fast on bread and water.[41] Hence at this time, in France, the fast of the vigils was no longer merely a pious practice, but a legal obligation.

From the Watch to the Vigil.—At first, as we have said, the vigil-watch or nocturnal assembly of the faithful was held in church. How and under what conditions did it develop into the vigil we know? How did the fast of the night become a day of fasting? This happened in consequence of the modifications introduced into the celebration of the liturgical office. In the first centuries, up to the eighth, as has just been seen, the liturgical office was begun on Saturday night before Easter and Pentecost, and on the eve of the other solemn feasts with vigils. During the night of Holy Sat-

[39] "Item cum presbyteri sacras festivitates populo annuntiant, etiam jejunium vigiliarum, ubi esse debet, eos omnimodis servare moneant." Cf. REGINO, *De Eccles. Disciplin.*, l. I, c. ccxliv and cclxxviii.

[40] *Decretor.*, l. II, c. lxxviii et l. XIII, c. xvi. Migne, *P. L.*, t. CXL, 640 and 887.

[41] "Si non observasti jejunium . . . vigiliarum sanctorum, XX dies in pane et aqua poeniteas." *Decretor.*, l. XIX, c. v, *ib.*, 962.

urday the people were instructed in Sacred Scripture by the reading of long passages, extracts from which are preserved in the prophecies of Holy Saturday and of the Vigil of Pentecost—the latter more brief, because the night was shorter. At day-break on these two principal vigils, after the baptism of the catechumens, Mass was celebrated. This enables us to understand the peculiar significance of the *Alleluia* which the deacon sang on Easter morning to the faithful, tired out, perhaps, by the long night but joyful at heart. That the ceremonial was similar for the other vigils is evidenced by the office of the two Ember Saturdays of Advent and Lent. In the Mass of both these days the Gospel is identical with that of the following Sunday; both remain as mute witnesses of the existence of an office which was originally one but eventually came to be divided into two.

Little by little the hour for the office and the Mass was advanced. Ordinations, which had been conferred during the long night office, gradually began to be held a little earlier, first in the evening of Saturday and finally in the morning of the same day, as the discipline survives to-day. Mass, then, did not end the vigil. Fasting, which was one of the elements of the vigil, had to be observed until the very day of the feast, and, what was called the fast of the vigil, instead of beginning in the evening before the feast and being kept up until after Mass, began on the morning which preceded the Mass of the vigil. It thus became a fast of an entire day. In the ninth century it is an accomplished fact. The proof comes especially from the answer of Pope Nicholas I *Ad consulta Bulgarorum*. The Pope prescribes fast and abstinence from meat on all the vigils of great feasts. We could see no reason for that prescription if the vigil was still a part of the watch. Consequently, before the year 867, the date of the letter to the Bulgarians, the old vigil-fast had become the fast of the vigil with which we are familiar; and since the night-watch had disappeared from the practice of the faithful, more insistence was placed on the fast itself, which had been changed from an accessory to a principal part and constituted almost the sole exterior preparation for the celebration of great feasts.

In the twelfth century the separation of the watch from the fast had been so long established that its history was but a vague memory. The word "Vigilia" had lost its meaning of "watch" and had only preserved that of a fast preparatory for feasts. Honorius of Autun explains the change as follows: Formerly, the people who came in crowds to the feast, spent the whole night in singing the praises of God. But wicked libertines turned holy things into ridicule and desecrated the watches by shameful songs, dances, drunkenness, and still more criminal deeds. From that time on watches were forbidden and the days consecrated to fast alone retained the name of vigil.[42] The explanation became classical; for it is given in almost identical terms by John Beleth, in his *Divinorum Officiorum Explicatio*, on the occasion of the vigil of St. John the Baptist,[43] and was consecrated, as it were, by Durand of Mende, in his *Rationale Divinorum Officiorum*.[44] Later on, it is true, liturgists like Stephen Durant[45] challenged the historical correctness of this explanation, but they did not deny the fact that the vigils, understood as watches, had fallen into disuse and nothing remained of them but the name.

Which Were the Feasts With Vigils?—Easter and Christmas must be placed first, as we have seen before; then Pentecost, which did not become generally established except by dint of some controversy. In the ninth century, probably, the As-

[42] "Populus, qui ad festum confluxerat, tota nocte in laudibus vigilare solebat. Postquam vero illusores bonum in ludibrium permutaverunt, et turpibus cantilenis ac saltationibus, potationibus et fornicationibus operam dederunt, vigiliae interdictae et dies jejunii dedicati sunt, et vigiliarum nomen retinuerunt." *Gemma Animae*, l. III, c. vi. Migne, *P. L.*, t. CLXXII, 644.

[43] "Ideo factum est ut vigiliae mutarentur in jejunia, unde etiam nunc antiquitatis nomen retinuit, vocatur enim vigilia." c. cxxxvii. I am quoting an edition of Naples, 1860. Migne gives the work of John Beleth in his Latin Patrology, t. CCII.

[44] L. VI, c. vii, n. 8.

[45] *De Ritibus Ecclesiae Catholicae*, l. III, c. iv.

THE FIFTH COMMANDMENT 247

sumption was added, and little by little, in the various countries, as popular devotion would have them, but at dates difficult to determine, the larger number of the feasts of the Apostles. These vigils became obligatory everywhere.

Besides these, there were other, diocesan or provincial vigils, imposed by custom or episcopal constitutions, as for example, the constitution by which St. Perpetuus established a calendar of vigils at Tours.[46] It is likely that everywhere the feast of the patron saint was preceded by a vigil. These diversities of discipline became so solidly established that the popes (*e. g.* Innocent III) recognized their obligatory force.[47] To the feasts of the Apostles were ultimately added those of St. Lawrence, St. John the Baptist, and in the Frankish countries, that of St. Martin.

For a long time the tendency was rather to diminish the number of vigils on which fasting was obligatory. In France, the only vigils on which fasting was enjoined, were those of Christmas, Pentecost, the feast of SS. Peter and Paul, the Assumption and All Saints.[47a]

[46] St. Gregory of Tours, *Histor. Francor.*, 1. X, c. xxxi, 6. Migne, *P. L.*, t. LXXI, 566.

[47] C. *Consilium*, X, *de Observat. jejuniorum*.

[47a] In the United States only four vigils are observed with fasting: the vigils of Christmas, Pentecost, Assumption, and All Saints. *Cath. Encyl.*, Vol. v, art. "Eve of Feasts," p. 647.

The Feast of St. Mark and the Rogation Days.
—Besides Ember Days and vigils the ancient discipline also recognized as days of fasting the day of the Major Litany with the procession known as St. Mark's, and the three Rogation Days.

The most ancient of these vigils are those of the Rogation Days. They were, at a certain period, celebrated so solemnly that abstention from servile labor was imposed. The Rogation Days are one of the few examples of a general disciplinary institution originating outside of Rome. It is to St. Mamertus, bishop of Vienne, that we owe their institution (about 470). Before his time the dioceses of Gaul already practiced more or less periodical "Litanies" whose celebration was rather uncertain; but those instituted by Mamertus in the painful circumstances which St. Avitus, his second successor, has narrated for us, (circumstances which were not altogether peculiar to Vienne), immediately obtained great vogue. Four or five years later, they were observed, according to Apollinaris Sidonius, in Visigothic Gaul, and were rapidly spreading from place to place. The Council of Orleans, A. D. 511, made their celebration obligatory throughout Frankish Gaul by the following decree: "It has pleased the council that in all the churches the Rogations, that is, the days of the Litanies before the Ascension, be celebrated in such manner that this three-day fast may end on the feast of the Ascension of Our Lord. During those three days let servants be released from all work in order to facilitate the gathering together of the entire people. During those three days all shall observe abstinence and shall use only the foods permitted in Lent."[48] This practice was immediately accepted and survived for years. Half a century later, a canon of the Council of Lyons (567-570), establishing Litanies for the first week of November, offered as a model to be followed in their observance the Litanies before Ascension.[49] At the same period, the Council of Tours, A. D. 567, mentioned the observance of the Rogation days in regard to the point which was most difficult in the existing discipline, *viz.* fasting,[50] which seems to have been forbidden during the whole paschal season until Pentecost. How-

[48] "Rogationes, id est, laetanias, ante Ascensionem Domini ab omnibus ecclesiis placuit observari, ita ut praemissum triduanum jejunium in Dominicae ascensionis festivitate solvatur; per quod triduum servi et ancellae ab omni opere relaxentur, quo magis plebs universa conveniat. Quo triduo omnis absteneant et quadraginsimalibus cibis utantur." *Concil. Aurelian.* (511), c. xxvii. MAASSEN, p. 8.

[49] "Placuit etiam universis fratribus, ut in prima hebdomada noni mensis, hoc est ante diem dominicam, quae prima in ipso mense illuxerit, litaniae, sicut ante ascensionem Domini sancti patres fieri decreverunt, deinceps ab omnibus ecclesiis seu parochiis celebrentur." *Conc. Lugdunen.* (567 or 570), c. vi, ib., p. 140.

[50] "De jejuniis antiqua a monachis instituta conserventur, ut de Pascha usque quinquagessima excepto rogationes omne die fratribus prandium praeparetur." can. xviii, *ib.*, 126.

ever, their success for a long time did not extend beyond the frontiers of Gaul. Spain, which practiced other three-day Litanies in the autumn and spring,[51] (not to mention those she introduced later on for every month of the year),[52] received the Rogation days much later; England imposed them in the eighth century at the same time with the Major Litany;[53] and Rome adopted them towards the year 800, about the time that she gave to France, as it were in return, the Major Litany or St. Mark's procession.

This latter had been instituted at Rome as a substitute for a pagan ceremony, to which it seems the Roman people were much attached. Each year, on the 25th of April, the pagan population celebrated the *Robigalia,* a feast which consisted of a long procession, at the end of which, in a small grove consecrated to him, Robigo, the god of frost, was invoked with petitions to preserve the young plants from frost and to procure the protection of the gods for the harvest. The Popes did not deem it advisable to suppress this ceremony, but, instead, altered its character and, by the invocation of the true God and the saints, transformed it into a Christian celebration. In-

[51] The Council of Gerona mentions two triduums of litanies, from Thursday to Saturday after Pentecost, and in the first week of November. c. ii and iii, Bruns, t. II, p. 18 and 19.

[52] *Conc. Toletan.* XVII (694) c. vi, *ib.,* t. I, 388.

[53] Cf. *Conc. Cloveshov.* II (747), c. xvi. MANSI, t. XII, 400.

stead of going to the grove of Robigo, the procession, after arriving at the Milvian bridge, turned towards the Vatican and came to an end at St. Peter's with the "station mass." When the 25th of April was assigned for the feast of St. Mark, the procession became known as the procession of St. Mark, although it was independent of the feast, as it still continues to be.

Since this Litany and the Procession were acts of penance, the day on which they took place was a day of penance, a fast-day in some churches, in others one of simple abstinence.

It was the council of Mayence, A. D. 813, which imposed its observance for three days in all the states of Charlemagne.[54] But the procession, on account of its length and owing to the spring season, soon assumed a festival aspect; people followed it on horse-back garbed in beautiful clothes. The Church protested; variants of the text just cited, taken from twelfth-century manuscripts, prescribe that except in case of sickness the faithful should assist in penitential garb, bare-footed and in hair-cloth.[55]

Like that of the Rogations or *Minor Litanies,* the observance of the *Major Litany,* too, became

[54] "Placuit nobis, ut laetania major observanda sit a cunctis Christianis diebus tribus." *Conc. Moguntin.,* c. xxxiii. *Monum. Germ., Concilia,* t. II, 269.

[55] "Non equitando, nec preciosis vestibus induti, sed discalciati, cinere et cilicio induti, nisi infirmitas impedierit." *Ib.*

firmly established. It took its place with Lent, the Ember Days, and the Vigils, among the juridically specified duties of the Christian. The bishop in synod would ask his pastors: Is there anyone in your parishes who does not observe the fast of Lent, of the Ember Days, of the Major Litany, or of the Rogation days?[56] And the confessor notified his penitents in the confessional that the infraction of this precept entailed a penance of twenty days on bread and water, instead of forty days as for the Ember Days.[57]

When Burchard's collection appeared, in the twelfth century, the observance of the Major Litany and of the Rogation days had reached the extreme of its rigor. Not long after, its observance was enforced with less severity, first in one country, then in another; gradually the obligation of the fast disappeared and only that of abstinence remained. While Durand of Mende (about 1290) speaks of the fast of the Major Litany and of the

[56] "Si aliquis jejunium quadragesimale non observat, vel Quatuor-Temporum, sive Letaniam majorem vel Rogationum." REGINO, *De Eccles. Discipl.*, l. II, c. v, n. 49. Migne, *P. L.*, t. CXXXII, 284. BURCHARD, *Decretor.*, l. I, c. xciv, interrog. 48. Migne, *P. L.*, t. CXL, 576. Cf. l. XIII, c. vi et vii. *ib.*, 886.

[57] "Solvisti jejunium Quatuor Temporum, et non custodisti illud cum caeteris christianis? XL dies in pane et aqua poeniteas. Si non observasti jejunium Litaniae majoris et dierum Rogationum . . . ? XX dies in pane et aqua poeniteas." BURCHARD, *Decretor.*, l. XIX, c. v, *ib.*, 962. Cf. *Conc. Engilenheim.* (948), c. vii. MANSI, t. XVIII, 421.

Rogation days as universally observed,[58] and the synods or synodal constitutions of Bayeux and of Coutances (about 1300) mention it as obligatory for all the faithful who have attained the required age;[59] the statutes of the dioceses of Rodez, Tulle, and Cahors (about 1288) only prescribe abstinence during the Rogation days (the Wednesday being a fast day in addition because it was the vigil of the Ascension). The last named constitutions counsel the clerics in sacred orders, and especially priests, to fast on those days, adducing the same reason as for Advent and the two days which follow Quinquagesima Sunday.[60]

This decline constantly increased. Perhaps in some places the Christian spirit resisted longer, but in the seventeenth century, the exacting and severe Fagnani acknowledged that to fast on Rogation days was not obligatory by common law;[61] in the eighteenth, Ferraris and Billuart denied that it had ever been obligatory.

[58] *Rationale divinor. officior.*, l. VI, c. cii, n. 4.

[59] *Synodicon Constantiense*, c. liii. MANSI, t. XXV, 46; *Synod. Bajocen.*, c. lxvi, *ib.*, 71.

[60] "Honestum est et pium, ut clerici in sacris ordinibus constituti, et maxime sacerdotes in diebus adventus Domini, et in diebus lunae et martis ante Cineres, et in diebus lunae et martis ante Ascensionem Domini jejunarent. . . . Diebus autem lunae et martis et mercurii ante festum Ascensionis Domini est generaliter ab usu carnium abstinendum." *Synodal. statuta Cadurcen. Ruthenen. et Tutelen. Ecclesiar.*, c. xxxi. MANSI, t. XXIV, 1054-1055.

[61] In c. *Consilium, X, de Observatione jejunior.*, n. 25.

Abstinence was better maintained, at least in France. Nevertheless for some forty years back the indults periodically renewed by the Holy See have practically suppressed it there, as had already been done in nearly all the other countries of the Latin Church.[62]

III. LENT.—The origin of Lent and the vicissitudes of its discipline are much better known. A brief exposition will therefore suffice.

Its Origin.—The oldest record regarding the quadragesimal fast is a text of St. Irenaeus (130–202), transmitted to us by Eusebius. Allusion was made to it above. The disagreement between Pope Victor and the bishops of Asia, says the learned Bishop of Lyons, bore not only on the day on which Easter was to be celebrated but also on the manner of fasting; some thought that the fast should last one whole day; others upheld a two-day fast; still others maintained that it should cover forty consecutive hours.[63] This text of St. Irenaeus takes us back to the year 154 or 155.

A little later, in the time of Tertullian (about the year 200) in Africa, the faithful fasted without intermission on Good Friday and Holy Saturday, the two days when according to the Biblical language "the Spouse had been taken away."

---

[62] Cf. the indult of July 6, 1899, for Latin America, and the decree of September 7, 1906, for Italy.

[63] Eusebius, *Hist. Eccles.*, l. V, c. ii.

THE FIFTH COMMANDMENT

Outside these two days some of the faithful observed additional fasts, more or less frequently; but these two days were the only ones on which the fast was obligatory. The Montanists, who wished to appear more fervent, fasted two weeks a year, from which, however, Saturday and Sunday must be deducted.[64]

Half a century later a letter of St. Dionysius of Alexandria to Basilides mentions the week before Easter as a week of fast. All do not fast without intermission; some fast two days in succession; others three; some four; and others do not even fast one whole day; many esteem themselves fervent although they only observe two consecutive days of fast, *viz.* Good Friday and Holy Saturday.[65]

About the same period, towards the year 270, the Syriac *Didascalia* also speaks of a six-days' fast: "You shall therefore fast, says the Lord, six complete days from Monday to the night which follows Saturday, and this will be accounted unto you for a week."[66] And, further on, it indicates the manner in which the fast is to be observed in these terms: "Also from the tenth day, which is Monday, during the days of Easter, you shall fast, and you shall take only bread, salt, and water, at the

[64] *De jejunio*, passim. Migne, *P. L.*, t. II, 955-974.
[65] Migne, *P. G.*, t. X, 1277.
[66] *Didascalia*, c. xxi. Cfr. *Le Canoniste Contemporain*, 1902, p. 18.

ninth hour, until Thursday. On Friday and Saturday you shall maintain a strict fast and not taste anything . . . at three o'clock of the night which follows Saturday, you will end your fast."[67]

The Lenten fast, therefore, at the end of the third century, may be described as follows: the Catholics fasted during the week before Easter, but there was a certain diversity of custom; the Montanists, who affected more severe mortification, fasted two weeks with the exception of Saturdays and Sundays.

At the Council of Nicea (325) the expression "Quarantine" appears for the first time. The fifth canon, referring to the two synods to be held annually by the bishops of each province, decrees that "these councils shall be held, one before the Quarantine."[68] Everyone understood what was meant by Quarantine, for it was known that the Quarantine before Easter was a time of prayer, penance, and fasting. But it must not be concluded from this that the faithful fasted during the entire Quarantine. Lent was simply a period in which fasting was observed more than at other times. The paschal letters of St. Athanasius prove this. In the most ancient of these letters,

[67] *Ib.*, p. 22. Cf. *Constitut. Apostol.*, l. V, c. xviii. Migne, *P. G.*, t. I, 890

[68] "Αἱ δὲ σύνοδοι γινέσθωσαν, μία μὲν πρὸ τῆς τεσσαρακοστῆς." BRUNS, t. I, p. 15.

that of 329, the fast starts on Monday, as in the Syriac *Didascalia.* The following year, while fasting figures among the penitential practices of Lent, the only fast of obligation is that of the Holy Week. The discipline was more severe in Rome, and soon complaints arose against the laxity of the Egyptians who had but one week of fast. In other churches the faithful fasted two or three weeks, which were probably distributed through the Quarantine. Little by little the Quarantine came to be entirely given over to this manner of doing penance.

However, Sunday was always excepted, and in many regions, Saturday also. Such was the case, *e.g.*, in Milan during the episcopate of St. Ambrose. Such was generally the case in the East also, where the fast of the Quarantine was distinct from that of Holy Week, except for some time in Jerusalem and Alexandria, where Lent extended over seven weeks, but the days of fast did not exceed thirty-six, the number soon received everywhere in the West. All manner of good reasons were found in support of this number, *e.g.*, that it was the tithe of the year, and Lent thus appeared to be analogous to the tribute required by God from His people in the Old Testament.

Logical minds were not satisfied with this. The holy Quarantine, as it came to be called, was not complete when embracing only thirty-six days.

Besides, some (perhaps without attaching too much importance to the mystical reasons which seemed to consecrate this tithe of the year) exceeded the number of thirty-six. It seems that a fast of forty complete days was observed in Jerusalem at the time when the pilgrim lady Etheria made her visit to the holy places there (end of the fourth century). In the West the total of forty was finally attained in the seventh century. One of the Popes—his name is not known—added to the six weeks during which the fast was commonly observed, four days more, before the first Sunday of Lent, and thus "the sacramental number" was attained and fervent souls were satisfied. An attempt had been made in Gaul, in the sixth century, to make Lent a real Quarantine; but these efforts had met with vigorous opposition at the Council of Orleans, A. D. 541,[69] and eventually came to nought.

But, though not without toil and trouble, the fast of Saturday had been established in Gaul. The Council of Agde (506) had made it of strict obligation,[70] and the Council of Orleans of 541 confirmed this decision.[71]

[69] C. ii. MAASSEN, p. 87-88.

[70] "Placuit etiam ut omnes ecclesiae filii, exceptis diebus dominicis, in quadragesima, etiam die sabbato, sacerdotali ordinatione et districtionis comminatione jejunent." c. xii. BRUNS, t. II, 149.

[71] "Sed neque per sabbata absque infirmitate quisquis absolvat

THE FIFTH COMMANDMENT

In the seventh century, therefore, Lent appears definitively established. For a long time previously Pope St. Leo, and before him St. Jerome, had affirmed that it was of Apostolic institution; respect for ancient custom forbade any part of its observance to be changed. St. Isidore of Seville confirmed these declarations by his authority and thus completed the process of rendering them sacred.

But not all were satisfied. Many attempted to qualify and attenuate those traditional affirmations. Thus the compiler of the *Liber Pontificalis* (in the sixth century) attributed the institution of a seven-weeks' Lent to Pope Telesphorus.[72] This shows that at the time when he wrote the longer Lent was observed at least by some. Perhaps those seven weeks were meant simply to legitimate the total of thirty-six days commonly observed, for the same *Liber Pontificalis* attributes to Pope Melchiades (311–314) a prohibition of fasting on Thursdays,[73] which is supposed to have been suppressed by Pope Gregory II (715–731).[74] How-

quadragesimale jejunium, nisi tantum die dominico prandeat." c. ii, *loc. cit.*

[72] "Hic constituit ut septem ebdomadas ante Pascha jejunium celebraretur." DUCHESNE, *Le Liber Pontificalis*, t. I, 129. Cf. *Decr. Grat.*, c. *Statuimus*, iv, Dist. IV.

[73] "Hic constituit nulla ratione dominico aut quinta feria jejunium quis de fidelibus agere." *Ib.*, 168. Cf. c. *Jejunium*, xiv, Dist. III *de Consecratione*.

[74] Cf. *ib.*, p. 402, 412.

ever, these novelties had no effect on the general discipline. But they exercised some influence on the particular discipline of the clerics upon whom the obligation was imposed of beginning the fast on Quinquagesima Sunday. Another apocryphal document, under the name of Gregory the Great, made this fast obligatory for clerics in order to show the people that they were superior to the laity by their mortification as well as by the dignity of their consecration.[75]

This increase of penance affected not only the clergy, but in some places even the laity. Such was the case *e.g.* in Provence. "We, the inhabitants of Provence," writes Durand of Mende, "begin Lent on the Monday before Ash Wednesday, and thus fast more than the other nations." He adds an explanation which shows that he did not know the original motive for this particular discipline: "We observe this fast not only for virtue's sake, in order to purify ourselves to begin Lent on Ash-Wednesday, but because the Quarantine ends on Holy Thursday, and the last two days are fast-days because of their sanctity." "The clerics also are held to begin their fast on Quinquagesima Sunday," he says elsewhere, "the monks on Septuagesima Sunday."[76] This is one of the last testimonies we know of in support of

[75] *Ib.*, p. 129 and 130.
[76] *Rationale Divinor. Officior.*, l. VI, c. xxviii, 5 and xxiv, 6.

that custom. In the fourteenth century it fell into desuetude; Lent came to be equally observed by all, and its duration was never again changed.

Wherein Fasting Consisted.—What characterized the observance of Lent, therefore, was the fast. The complete fast, even as early as the time of Tertullian, distinguished the short Lent, such as they had it then, from the weekly stations, on which only a half-fast was obligatory.

What was the essential character of the fast? Under the ancient discipline, the fast seems to have had two essential characteristics: the partaking of only one meal a day, and the late hour at which it was taken. In reality, however, the only essential characteristic, according to the teaching of the Church, was and is the former: to take but one meal a day. However, the modifications introduced regarding the hour at which that meal was to be taken, have had considerable influence on the fast itself.

As has been observed above, the more fervent Christians of the first centuries went even further—they passed forty consecutive hours without eating anything. But such rigor was beyond the common reach. In the third century the *Didascalia* indicates very clearly the hour at which every fast-day ends; *viz.* the ninth hour, *i.e.* about three in the afternoon. This was undoubtedly the minimum, for the Greek fathers, SS. Basil, John

Chrysostom, and Epiphanius, indicate that the fast ended with the day. The Church historian Socrates gives the same decision as the *Didascalia,* but the Apostolic Constitutions make a difference between the great fasts (*i.e.* those of Holy Week) and the ordinary fasts; for the former the meal hour is at Vespers, for the others, at None. Outside of this meal no food was allowed.

At the end of the eighth century the hour of the meal is always after None. The fast continues until after mass, and it is at the hour of None that the mass of the feast is celebrated [77] on Ash Wednesday. On this point the authorities insisted with the greatest severity. Even when the rigors of abstinence began to be notably mitigated, the late hour of the meal was retained. Theodulf of Orleans, in the ninth century, maintained that those do not fast who hasten to take their meal at the hour of None; they do not satisfy the precept if they eat before the evening office is ended. Not until after mass, after the evening office, and after the offerings have been made to the poor, is one allowed to take food.[78] Gratian, in the twelfth

[77] "Ut feria IV ante initium quadragesime, quam Romani caput jejunii nuncupant, sollemniter celebretur cum laetania et missa post horam nonam." *Concil. Salisburg.* (800), c. x. *Monum. Germ., Concilia,* t. II, 212.

[78] C. *Solent,* Dist. 1, *de Consecratione.* Cf. a text of the *Leges ecclesiasticae* of the tenth century, given by Mansi, t. XIX, 191, which does not allow the breaking of the Lenten fast before the fourth hour of the night.

century, embodied this text in his compilation and himself confirmed the discipline which it enforces.

Nevertheless it was only with difficulty that this discipline could be maintained. A strong current of opinion followed the decisions of the *Didascalia*, and the fast was broken without scruple at None. In the tenth century Rathier of Verona finds no fault with this practice, and we know that Charlemagne anticipated vespers in Lent in order to give his servants a chance to eat something before the hour of None. In the beginning of the thirteenth century, Alexander of Hales taught that the Church had indicated this hour for the end of the fast. He adduced highly mystical reasons in its support; for instance, that since Christ had given up the ghost and ceased suffering at the ninth hour, None was the proper hour to end the mortification of the fast.

St. Thomas justified that choice by other reasons. Those who objected that in the Old Testament the fast lasted till night and that nothing less should be exacted under the New Law, which is more perfect than the Old, he answered with the text of St. Paul: night came first, but now day is drawing close; night was the Old Law in which fasting was to last until night; since the day has come with Our Lord, the fast may end in the day time.[79] There was no need of arguing this detail

[79] II^a II^{ae}, qu. cxlvii, vii, 1.

so scrupulously; it was sufficient to know that the fast ended about the hour of None; it was not necessary to have an astrolabe to determine the exact moment. Nay, in case there was danger in awaiting that hour, it could be somewhat advanced. Indeed, since the hour indicated by nature for dinner was noon, penance simply required that the fast be protracted somewhat beyond this hour.

These reasons did not however suffice to settle the practice for good. The Schoolmen were continually reasoning and seeking to discover the essence of things, and they soon realized that the essence of the fast was the taking of but one meal; the rest were only more or less indifferent and accessory modalities, which could be sacrificed if necessary. Besides, the custom of taking the meal at the hour of Sext, *i.e.* at noon, was being introduced. Obstacles to the custom were leveled by the above quoted arguments. In the fourteenth century the practice was so well established that the guardians of ecclesiastical discipline unanimously adopted it; popes, cardinals, even monks, who were specially given over to the practice of penance, took their Lenten meal at noon. In the fifteenth century it became the common teaching of theologians.

It was believed that, by sacrificing the accessory, the essence of the fast would be saved; but

THE FIFTH COMMANDMENT

this proved a miscalculation: with the growth of laxity, the essence soon joined the accessory.

To allow the meal to be taken at noon, was to render it possible to work harder in the afternoon; but then the fatigued body required some refreshment at night. A little liquid to quench the thirst was at first permitted, for it was held that liquids did not break the fast. The Church refrains from forbidding liquids because their primary function is to relieve thirst and aid digestion, rather than to nourish, although, as St. Thomas admits, liquids do give some nourishment.[80] However, the liquids in common use, water and wine, do not always suffice; they are not even an aid to digestion for everybody. Since there are other liquids more beneficial to digestion, and better able to quench thirst, *e.g.* the *electuaria, viz.* more or less liquid jellies, preserves, candied fruit; could not these *electuaria* replace water and wine? St. Thomas thought that it was just as lawful to take them as to take any other medicine, provided only that they be not taken in large quantities, or as a food. The permissible quantity was not specified and it devolved upon custom to determine it. Quantity like custom naturally varied in different localities. In the monasteries, where everything was better regulated, this little lunch, consisting of fruit, herbs, bread, water, or wine was taken in com-

[80] IIa IIae, qu. cxlvii, art. vi, ad 2um.

mon, while the *Collationes* of Cassian were read; hence the name *collation* was given it and an effort was made so to limit the repast that it might never be equivalent to a full meal. Thus the essence of the fast was saved.

The collation was for the night. But in the morning also the weakened stomach felt the need of some relief. Since liquid did not break the fast, it could not be forbidden. Neither did the *electuaria* break the fast, as we have seen above, provided they were not taken in too great a quantity, or *per modum cibi;* hence they were likewise permitted. Water, wine, coffee, were simple liquids; hot chocolate without milk was placed in the class of the *electuaria:* all were tolerated. A little bread is sometimes necessary with wine or coffee, *ne potus noceat,* so as not to inconvenience delicate stomachs; hence it likewise was permitted, and thus originated the morsel of food commonly called *frustulum*. So it was still true that only a single meal was taken.

The Age at Which Fasting Becomes of Obligation.—After the essence of the fast had been determined, the age at which fasting became obligatory needed to be fixed.

For many centuries the answer was practical rather than theoretical; one began to fast as soon as one felt able. The most ancient texts, as for example that of a Council of Toledo (A. D. 653, c.

THE FIFTH COMMANDMENT

IX), do not speak of the age at which fasting becomes obligatory, but only of the motives of abstinence.[81]

The council of 633 spoke only of Good Friday in its eighth canon, where it declared that on that day everyone, except little children, the aged, and the sick, must fast until after sunset at night, under pain of not being admitted to the Easter Communion.[82] But this indication was retained. In the ninth century Rodulf of Bourges excused from fasting only invalids and children.[83]

The twelfth century was reached without any further precision, at least in theory. *In praxi*, some fasted at the age of fifteen, others at twenty-one. Alexander of Hales chose the middle course, and for canonical and biological reasons fixed the beginning of the obligation of fasting at the age of eighteen, which was the age designated by the Church for admission into the religious life. But his arguments did not satisfy St. Thomas. That great Doctor fixes the juridical obligation of fasting at the age of twenty-one, because at this age, the end of the third septenary, as a rule bodily

---

[81] See Bruns, t. I, 282.

[82] "Quicumque in eo [die dominicae passionis] jejunium praeter parvulos, senes et languidos, ante peractas indulgentiae preces resolverit, a paschali gaudio depelletur, nec in eo sacramentum corporis et sanguinis domini percipiat." *Ib.*, p. 225.

[83] "In hoc [tempore] vero, praeter infirmos aut parvulos, quisquis non jejunat, poenam sibi adquirit." *Capitul.* xxix. MANSI, t. XIV, 957.

growth and the special need of food ends.[84] The question of age was thus definitely settled.

Beginning with twenty-one years, the law of fasting obliges indefinitely, except in case of illness, and binds all men, except those who are unable to comply with the law on account of sickness, travel, work or poverty.

The excuse of sickness served to settle a term in favor of the aged. Old age, by itself, does not exempt from fasting. Yet an opinion, mentioned (though not adopted) by Angelo de Clavasio (about 1486), affirmed that one was exempt from fasting from the age of fifty-five.[85] In the middle of the seventeenth century, at the time of Busembaum, sexagenarians were held exempt, unless they were evidently able to fast without danger; gradually, theologians came to excuse women above fifty, at least if they suffered from some infirmity or were of a delicate constitution.[86]

The case of workingmen was examined earlier and more closely. It was an early tradition in the Church that less was to be exacted, as regards fasting, from bondmen and servants than from the rich.[87] In the thirteenth century those who

---

[84] IIa IIae, qu. cxlvii art. iv, ad 2um. However, a Council of Prague, held about 1346, obliges all who have attained the age of twenty to fast. *Conc. Pragen.*, c. xli. Mansi, t. XXVI, 92.

[85] *Summa Angelica de Casibus Conscientie*, Verbo *Jejunium*, n. 15.

[86] See Marc, Haine, etc.

[87] "Sed et hoc sciendum est, ut cum venerint servi vel ancille ad

could not work whilst fasting were obliged to stay away from work. But St. Thomas admits that the necessity of travelling for whole days in succession, or of working at hard labor to support the material or spiritual life, exempts one from fasting if one cannot work and fast at the same time.[88] This solution was adopted by Gerson and Angelo de Clavasio. But even before the time of the latter a declaration of Pope Eugene IV is believed to have exempted from fasting artisans living in country districts, who, whether rich or poor, were engaged in laborious pursuits.[89] On this basis an attempt was made later on to determine just what these occupations were. And it is for the same reason of fatigue that those performing certain intellectual labors, often more exhausting than bodily work, were likewise exempted from fasting.

As for the poor, it was agreed from the first that those who beg from door to door, and have not the necessaries of life at home, are exempted from the obligation.

Penalties.—As has been seen above, the obligation of fasting, particularly in Lent, was not with-

penitentiam, ne eos cogatis jejunare tantum, quantum divites: quia non sunt in sua potestate; ideoque medietatem eis imponite." *Sacramentarium Fulden.* SCHMITZ, *Die Bussbücher*, t. II, p. 59, note 6.

[88] *Loc. cit.*, ad 3um.

[89] Cf. S. LIGUORI, *Theol. moral.*, l. IV, tract. VI, c. iii, d. 2, n. 1042.

out sanction; the penalty for non-compliance was, according to the Council of Toledo, exclusion from the Easter Communion. In England the penalties imposed were of a more material order, such as fines or blows.[90] Elsewhere the discipline was milder. Repeated omission of the Lenten fast rendered one liable to a year's penance; if the offense was frequently repeated, to the extent of becoming a habit, the penalty was excommunication.[91]

Dispensations.—The laws of fasting and abstinence were the first from which the ecclesiastical authorities granted dispensations. The bishops at an early date reserved to themselves the power of dispensation in order to counteract the laxity which began to be introduced towards the end of the fourth century, by Christians pretending to dispense themselves.[92] The question of dispensation from the fast often recurs in the correspondence of the Fathers and in their discourses. But it was not until much later that it became part of the

[90] "Si liber homo justum jejunium dissolvat, solvat mulctam, vel legis violatae poenam. Si servus hoc fecerit, vapulet, vel verbera redimat." *Leges Ecclesiasticae Eduardi Senior. Rg. Angliae*, c. viii. MANSI, t. XVIII, 239.

[91] "Si quis contempserit indictum jejunium . . . si in quadragesima, annum poeniteat. Si frequenter fecerit et in consuetudine erit ei, exterminabitur ab omni ecclesia Dei." *Poenitentiale Cummeani*, xii, 9 et 10. SCHMITZ, *Die Bussbücher und die Bussdisciplin*, t. I, 640, 641. Cf. *Pœnitent. Vallicellan.*, Ium, c. cvi, *ib.* 324.

[92] Cf. the Council of Gangres, c. xix. Bruns, t. I, 109.

THE FIFTH COMMANDMENT

ordinary practice of the Church. In the thirteenth century it is firmly established. St. Thomas teaches that if the reason excusing one from fasting is evident, the interested party can decide for himself, but if the motive be doubtful, he must consult a competent superior. Who was the competent superior? This was decided according to well-established juridical principles. It was not a simple priest, but the bishop, unless recourse to him could not be had without danger. It was added, however, that this was understood of a real dispensation, not merely of a common-sense decision, pronouncing that in given circumstances such or such a cause was sufficient to exempt one from fasting.

In course of time greater importance came to be attached to dispensation as an excuse from fasting. St. Thomas merely mentions it in passing. Angelo de Clavasio lays a little more stress on it. Busembaum gives to dispensation the first place over all other excuses, whether derived from work, sickness or necessity. At the same time the faculties of inferiors are extended. Not only when recourse to the bishop involves danger, but at all times can the pastor give a dispensation. Sanchez says that he can do so even when the bishop is present.

These dispensations are useful to reassure the consciences of those whose reasons for exemption are not sufficiently evident. They are moreover a proof that the precept remains in force; whoever does not come under one of the various categories of dispensed persons is obliged to fast under pain of sin. In the sixth century St. Caesarius said: Not to fast in Lent is a sin; our moralists say the same and thereby go back to the original tradition.

Is there any probability that the Church will return to that tradition by shortening Lent? A return to the Holy Quarantine of a six-days' fast, as observed in the third century, is most unlikely. But the Church, while preserving the liturgical Quarantine, could make the fast obligatory only on certain days; in fact, she has already done this for certain regions. An indult of May 6, 1899, for instance, grants to the bishops of Latin America for ten years the following powers which they have the right to delegate to pastors and confessors: to dispense the faithful, upon request, from fast and abstinence, on condition, however, that they fast on the Wednesdays and Fridays of Lent, on Holy Thursday, and on the Fridays of Advent. Is the Church likely to extend this privilege to other countries? There is no reason at present to believe so. In the unification of the indults on fast and abstinence which the Holy See has recently made for Italy,[93] the fasts of Lent, of the Ember

[93] Decree of September 7, 1906.

Days, and of the five principal vigils, have been entirely maintained.

The Fast of Advent.—The decree just cited imposes fasting on the Fridays and Saturdays of Advent. This discipline, which at the present day is observed by Italy alone among the nations of the West, is the last vestige of a very ancient fast, the fast of Advent.

On the antiquity of this institution the same views were formerly held as on that of Lent and of the Ember Days. Durand de Mende affirms that St. Peter decreed that the feast of Christmas was to be preceded by a preparatory period of three whole weeks.[94] But the fast of Advent does not go back to St. Peter, nor to the first century, though it is an institution of venerable antiquity. About the end of the fourth century, a council of Saragossa prescribed a preparation of twenty-one days for the feast then called Epiphany, which as a matter of fact embraced the two feasts of Christmas and the Epiphany. The preparation, to be made from the 17th of December to the 6th of January, consisted in assiduously frequenting the church.[95] Did it also comprise fasting? We have no document of that period which gives us ground for either affirmation or denial. From the following century on our information is more abundant

[94] *Rationale Divinor. Officior.* l. XI, c. ii, n. 2.
[95] *Conc. Caesaraugustanum* (380), c. iv. BRUNS, t. II, 13.

and precise. Among the institutions of St. Perpetuus, bishop of Tours (+ about 490), one of his successors, St. Gregory, remarks the establishment of a forty-day period extending from the 11th of November to Christmas, during which the faithful had to fast on Mondays, Wednesdays, and Fridays.[96] The "Lent of St. Martin" seems to have been gradually introduced in the neighboring dioceses, until the Council of Mâcon of 583 extended it to the whole kingdom of Burgundy,[97] with the avowed intention of imitating Lent in everything, even in the liturgy.

From Gaul this pre-Christmas Lent passed to England and Germany, as witnessed by St. Bede and Rhabanus Maurus, who originated a thesis which canonists and theologians repeated for a long time: *viz.* that this practice was of divine origin or based on Scripture (Jer. xxxvi), instituted by the Church, and explained that in Advent only three days of the week are fast-days, whereas in Lent every day is a fast-day.[98]

Outside of the countries mentioned it does not seem that the fast of Advent ever became obligatory. Nicholas I in his letter to the Bulgarians

---

[96] *Historia Francor.*, l. X, c. xxxi. Migne, *P. L.*, t. LXXI, 566.

[97] "Ut a feria sancti Martini usque natale Domini secunda, quarta et sexta Sabbati jejunetur et sacrificia quadragesimali debeant ordine caelebrari." *Conc. Matiscon.* (583), c. ix. MAASSEN, p. 157.

[98] *De Institutione Clericorum*, l. II, c. xxii. Migne, *P. L.*, t. CVII, 336.

presents the observance of Advent rather under the form of abstinence, as a practice of penance to be recommended to great sinners.[99]

Thus even before reaching full vogue the Advent fast was on the decline. At the end of the twelfth century it was nearly abolished. The Council of Avranches, A. D. 1172, made not only fasting but even abstinence in Advent a matter of simple counsel, especially addressed to clerics and soldiers.[100] In Rome, the observance still existed, but in Portugal it was not known whether it carried with it any obligation, for the Archbishop of Braga questioned Pope Innocent III on this point, and the Pope, instead of insisting that there is an obligation, simply states that in Rome the fast is observed.[101] No very clear information is to be obtained from Durand de Mende; if an Advent fast existed at his time, Durand does not speak of the way it was observed.[102] In England, it was obligatory only for monks, like the daily fast imposed by the Council

[99] C. iv. *P. L.*, t. CXIX, 981.

[100] "In adventu Domini, omnibus qui poterunt, maxime autem clericis et militibus, jejunium et abstinentia carnium indicatur." *Conc. Abrincen.* (1172), c. xi. MANSI, t. XXII, 140.

[101] C. *Consilium*, X, *de Observat. jejuniorum.*—This is the résumé which Innocent III gives in the *partes decisae* to the question asked: "Utrum etiam jejunandum sit in Adventu, quum inde sentiant diversi diversa, quibusdam dicentibus, sed paucioribus, jejunandum esse tunc temporis, pluribus vero se ad hoc asserentibus non teneri. . . . Jejunium apud nos in Adventu Domini agitur . . ."

[102] *Loc. supra citat.*

of Tours for the month of December up to Christmas;[103] in other countries it was regarded merely as a penitential work of supererogation and pure devotion. In the eighteenth century Ferraris cites as obsolete the precept by which Urban V imposed the abstinence of Advent on his whole court, clerics and lay people alike. To-day, says Ferraris, this observance is confined to the religious orders; and he is borne out in this statement by Benedict XIV, in his Institutions.

But it is only with regret that the Church permits her institutions to disappear. She wishes to retain at least a vestige of them as a witness to a former stage of development. This is what she has done for Italy by the decree of September 7, 1906.

[103] C. xviii. MAASSEN, 126.

CHAPTER VIII

THE SIXTH COMMANDMENT

Vendredi, chair ne mangeras,
Ni le samedi mêmement.

On Friday from flesh thou shalt abstain,
And likewise on Saturday.[1]

This precept is the last of the list in the French catechisms. It is, as it were, but a continuation of the preceding one. Its requirements, compared with those of the first centuries, are very modest; its observance is still easier; for practice has long since ceased to be in accordance with the injunctions of the law, if indeed it ever was generally observed.

Strangely enough the history of this precept is merely the record of its mutilations. While the other precepts developed little by little and became definitively fixed once they had attained their complete development, this one, very comprehensive at first, has undergone so many restrictions and reductions that it remains but a shadow of what it was in the beginning.

[1] This is the latter part of the second commandment according to our Baltimore Catechism, which reads as follows: To fast and abstain on days appointed.

The Wednesday Abstinence.—Before investigating the history of the Friday abstinence, let us cast a passing glance at the vicissitudes of Wednesday abstinence, so widely observed in the first centuries but now almost a dead letter. To-day, when mention is made of the weekly abstinence, we think of Friday and Saturday; formerly however it would have meant Wednesday and Friday.

The reader is already acquainted with the passage of the *Didache* in which the fast of the Monday and Thursday observed by the "impious" is opposed to that of the Christians on Wednesday and Friday.[2] Monastic chronicles of a later date tell us "that St. Pachomius saw the angels of Wednesday and Friday accompany the casket of a man who had fasted on these two days."[3] In Rome, while Pope Innocent I does not speak of the observance of Wednesday, it is observed for several centuries more. The ninth canon of the Council of Mâcon (583) associates Wednesday with Friday and Monday as a day of penance during the particular Lent lasting from St. Martin's day to Christmas;[4] in the Penitentials it occupies a place of honor along with Friday among the days spe-

---

[2] *Didache*, viii, 1.

[3] F. NAU, *Revue de l'Orient Chrétien*, 1907, p. 229; cf. *Const. Apost.*, l. V, c. xv. Migne, *P. G.*, t. I, 880.

[4] MAASSEN, *Concilia aevi merovingici*, p. 157; cf. *Concil. Bajuwaricum* (740-750), c. viii, which says purely and simply: "Ut jejunia per feriam IVam et VIam in usum adsumant." *Monum. Germ., Concilia*, t. II, 53.

THE SIXTH COMMANDMENT

cially designated for fast and penance, now as taking precedence of Saturday, now on a par with it.[5] At a much later date, Pope Leo IV (*De esu carnium*)[6] mentions it as a day of abstinence; his successor, Nicholas I, in a letter to the Bulgarians, sets it apart as a day of mourning along with Friday, without however imposing any obligation of abstinence.[7] Regino, on the contrary, speaks of it as a day of strict fast except in case of great necessity.[8]

But we soon perceive signs of a modification. In 990, the Council of Anse declares that Wednesday is a day of abstinence (no longer of fasting) for the laity;[9] and Peter the Venerable, a century and a half later, affirms that many lay persons do indeed abstain on that day;[10] the glossators speak of it in their commentaries on the chapter *De esu carnium* or other texts inserted in the *Corpus Juris*, but its observance had so fallen off that the austere Fagnani invokes the glossators themselves to substantiate the affirmation that the ab-

[5] Cf. *Poenitentiale Theodori*, I, xiv, 2; *Poenit. Cummean.*, III, no 19, 20, SCHMITZ, *Die Bussbücher und die Bussdisciplin der Kirche*, t. I, p. 535, 624.

[6] C. xi, Dist. III, *de Consecratione*.

[7] *Ad Consult. Bulgar. resp.*, c. v. P. L., t. CXIX, 981.

[8] *De Eccles. Discipl.*, *Appendix* 1a, c. xvii. Migne, P. L., t. CXXXII, 372.

[9] *Conc. Ansan.*, c. viii. MANSI, t. XIX, 102.

[10] "Abstinent plerique laicorum omni quarta [feria]." *Epistolar.*, l. VI, ep. xv. Migne, P. L., t. CLXXXIX, 419.

stinence of Wednesday is merely a matter of counsel.[11]

Undoubtedly it was thus considered for a long time, since from the end of the eighth century, statutes of the Church of Germany appear to have imposed it as a special obligation upon clerics;[12] and in the East, a *Didascalia of Our Lord Jesus Christ* (edited by Nau), promises particular blessings to those who fast on Wednesday and Friday.[13]

Of that discipline there remains to-day, besides the fast attached to the Wednesdays of the Ember week, only one witness, *viz.* the obligation, still maintained in certain of the most recent Lenten indults in France, to abstain, during that season, on Wednesday as well as on Friday.[13a]

The Friday Abstinence.—But the observance of Friday remained, at least with regard to abstinence.

Formerly there had been more severity. It was of fasting that the *Didache* and the ancient tradition spoke. In his well known letter to Decentius,

[11] In c. *Consilium, X, de Observ. jejun.*, n. 22.

[12] "Item placuit sancto Concilio, *quarta* et sexta feria a carne et vino cuncto clero abstinendum." *Statuta Rhispacen. Frising. et Salisburg.* (799-800), c. v. *Capitular.* (BORETIUS), t. I, 227.

[13] "Blessed is the man who fasts and prays with a pure heart on the fourth and sixth day" (c. vii). This *Didascalia* probably belongs to the eighth or ninth century. *Rev. de l'Or. Chrétien*, 1907, p. 245, 246.

[13a] This is the general practice in the United States.

bishop of Eugubium, Pope Innocent I mentions the Friday fast as an obligation known and accepted by all, and which met with no opposition.[14] The correspondence of St. Ambrose, that of St. Jerome, and that of St. Augustine [15] refer to Friday as a day of fast. It was so observed in Spain, according to St. Isidore of Seville, though, perhaps rather as a pious custom than a real obligation.[16] In Germany, it seems never to have been observed strictly. The Bavarian Council (740–750), cited above, imposes the obligation of putting it into practice. It may be inferred from a letter of Pope Adrian I to the bishop of Egila, about the end of the eighth century, that the latter was not very well informed regarding this discipline.[17] In fact, in those regions, the Friday fast existed only under the attenuated form of a simple abstinence imposed on the clergy, as may be judged from the text of the Council of Rhispach quoted above. The insertion of St. Isidore's text into one of the Capitularies does not seem

---

[14] "Sicut sexta feria propter passionem Domini jejunamus. . . . Non ergo nos negamus sexta feria jejunandum . . ." *Epist. ad Decentium*, c. iv, n. 7. Migne, *P. L.*, t. XX, 555, 556.

[15] Cf. in particular the latter's *Epist.* XXXVI, *ad Casulanum*, c. xiii. Migne, *P. L.*, t. XXXIII, 150.

[16] "Omnis sexta feria propter passionem Domini a quibusdam jejunatur." *De Eccles. Officiis*, l. I, c. xliii. Migne, *P. L.*, t. LXXXIII, 775.

[17] "Porro in ipsis referebatur apicibus tuis, qualiter vobis nimis intentio est de sexta feria et sabbato, quod istos duos dies dicimus jejunio mancipandos." Migne, *P. L.*, t. XCVI, 335.

to have resulted in enforcing the fast. Fasting in the Carolingian empire was but a work of supererogation, performed by men of good will, and was observed only by those who cared to do it, as the monk Ratramnus of Corbie writes.[18]

Rome, however, was stricter. In his letter to the Bulgarians, Pope Nicholas I refers twice to the observance of Friday and insists on the obligation of fasting and abstinence.[19] Regino goes even further; he inserts in his collection a text of Rufinus, quoted later on by Gratian, and which proved somewhat puzzling to the commentators. "The fasts imposed by the law, *i.e.* those of Wednesday and Friday, must not be dispensed with except in case of grave necessity. Wednesday, because it is the day on which Judas decided to betray Our Lord; Friday, because it is the day on which the Saviour was crucified. He therefore who on these days shall without necessity neglect to fast, appears to make himself the accomplice either of the traitor or of the executioners." [20]

[18] "Nec tamen hoc jejunium, quod quarta sive sexta sabbati celebratur, ab omnibus Ecclesiis vel orientalibus vel occidentalibus peragitur; sed a quibusdam quibus id placuit observare." *Contra Graecor. Opposita*, l. IV, c. iii. Migne, *P. L.*, t. CXXI, 315.

[19] "In sexta vero feria omnis hebdomadae . . . a carnium esu cessandum et jejuniis incumbendum." *Ad Consulta Bulgar.*, c. iv. Migne, *P. L.*, t. CXIX, 981.

[20] "Jejunia sane legitima, id est quarta et sexta feria, non sunt solvenda, nisi grandis aliqua necessitas fuerit, quia quarta feria Judas traditionem Domini cogitavit, et sexta feria crucifixus est Salvator. Videbitur ergo, qui in his diebus sine necessitate

But these efforts were of no avail. About the end of the tenth century, an attempt was made, by reducing the Wednesday fast to mere abstinence, to insure at least the Friday fast for persons who could bear it.[21] I do not know whether this attempt succeeded, for the councils always recur to this matter with remarkable insistence. In England, however, the Council of Enham admits an exception for feast days.[22] In Spain a synod of Coyac seems to consider it rather as a half fast, which was not completely to interfere with the daily work.[23] From that period on we have practically only two isolated testimonies in favor of the Friday fast, *viz.*: the synodal constitutions of a bishop of Paris, Eudes de Sully, in the thirteenth century, which appear to rank the fast of Friday with those of Lent, the Ember Days, and Vigils; [24]

solverit statuta jejunia, vel cum tradente tradere Salvatorem, vel cum crucifigentibus crucifigere." *De Ecclesiast. Disciplin.*, Append. I, c. xvii. Migne, *P. L.*, t. CXXXII, 372.

[21] "Laici omnes feria quarta a carne abstineant, et sexta feria jejunent, si ita possunt perficere." *Conc. Ansanum* (990), c. viii. MANSI, t. XIX, 102.

[22] "Sextae etenim jejunia feriae ab omnibus magnopere per singulas hebdomadas exercenda sunt; si tamen in eadem die aliqua festivitas non evenerit." *Concil. Aenhamen.* (1009), c. xvii. MANSI, *ib.*, 308.

[23] "Mandamus, ut Christiani per omnes sextas ferias jejunent, et hora congrua cibo reficiantur, et faciant labores suos." *Conc. Coyacen.* (1050), c. xi. MANSI, *ib.*, 789.

[24] "Omnes praecipiant jejunia instituta servari, ut jejunium quadragesimae, Quatuor Temporum, Vigiliarum, nisi ex magna et rationabili causa contra fiat, et sextae feriae; ex debito enim

and the sharp remonstrance of a council of Mayence, about the middle of the same century, against those who put off the Friday fast to another day, according to their caprice.[25]

We get the impression that for many years these laws had been disregarded by the mass of the faithful. Of the primitive fast only abstinence remained. We have already quoted Ratramnus' statement that only those fast on Friday who wish to do so. Raoul Glaber, in his narrative of the terrors of the year 1000, mentions as one of the reforms adopted by converted sinners, abstinence from wine on Friday and from flesh-meat on Saturday, but he does not say a word about fasting.[26] Otto of Bamberg, on leaving his Pomeranians, does not impose on them any other obligation for Friday than that of abstinence, which, he says, binds

tenentur facere talia jejunia." *Odonis de Soliaco Synodicae Constitutiones*, c. vi, de Confessione. Migne, *P. L.*, t. CCXII, 62.

[25] "Pravam quorumdam consuetudinem reprobamus, qui sextam feriam violant, sabbato vel alia die in hebdomada jejunantes: quod de cetero fieri hujus sacri auctoritate concilii firmiter prohibemus." *Conc. Provinciale Moguntinen.* (1261), c. xxvi. MANSI, t. XXIII, 1090. This text was taken over word for word by a provincial council of Magdeburg, in the last third of the following century, c. xxx. MANSI, t. XXVI, 583.

[26] "Plurima autem in eisdem conciliis statuta sunt, quae perlongum duximus referre. Illud sane memorandum, quod omnibus in commune placuit, qualiter omnibus hebdomadibus, sanctione perpetua, sexta die abstineretur a vino, et carnibus septima, nisi forte gravis infirmitas compelleret aut celeberrima solemnitas interveniret." *Histor.*, l. V. Migne, *P. L.*, t. CXLII, 678.

all Christians.[27] It is also simply from the point of view of abstinence that Robert Pulleyn seems to liken Friday to the fast days.[28] It is because abstinence is practiced by all, even children and invalids that, according to Peter the Venerable, abstinence from the use of fat on Friday is imposed upon the monks of Cluny.[29] St. Thomas Aquinas [30] and John Beleth,[31] treating of fasting, do not speak of the ordinary Fridays.

We have even better testimony. The glossators, when they came to comment on the chapter *Jejunia* (D. III, *De Consecrat.*), which Gratian had borrowed from Regino and which prescribes fasting on Wednesdays and Fridays, confess that they do not understand the prescription. Fasting

[27] "Deinde juxta sanctorum Patrum instituta haec eos servare docuit, scilicet ut sexta feria abstineant a carne et lacte more christianorum." *Narratio de S. Ottonis Bamberg. apostolatu in Pomerania.* Migne, *P. L.*, t. CLXXIII, 1337.

[28] "Sed quod carnem non comedis, usum sequeris, sicut sexta feria, cum jejunii diebus, carnes edere minime jam licet, quoniam id abstinentia Ecclesiae prohibet." *Sentent.*, pars VIIIa, c. x. Migne, *P. L.*, t. CLXXXVI, 975.

[29] "Statutum est, ut universi frates Cluniacenses, omni sexta feria, praeter Nativitatem Domini, si eadem die occurrerit, ab adipe abstineant. Causa instituti hujus fuit inconveniens non parvum, quod non solum clerici, non solum laici, sed et ipsi pueri et infirmi totius Latinae Ecclesiae ab omni esu carnis, et solidae vel attritae et liquefactae pro more jam antiquo, ea die, ob reverentiam passionis dominicae abstinebant." *Statuta Congreg. Cluniacen.* Migne, *P. L.*, t. CLXXXIX, 1028.

[30] IIa IIae, qu. cxlvii.

[31] Cf. *Rationale Divinor. Officior.*, c. viii-xi.

on Friday, according to H(uguccio) and G(andolf) is obligatory only for those who have made a vow, or received it as a penance. Though it may have been commanded in the Primitive Church, to-day, they say, it is only of counsel.[32]

The decline was complete and irrevocable. The few later canonists who treat of the matter at all, follow the teaching of the Gloss. Fagnani, following the teaching of Innocent IV and of Abbas, affirms that, according to the common opinion, the Friday fast is merely of counsel, not of precept, just as the abstinence from flesh-meat on Wednesday.[33]

This stage marked the end of the development. Abstinence from flesh-meat on Friday remains a practice strictly kept by good Christians all over the world.[34] It sometimes gives occasion to mortifications which appear to be heroic professions of the faith and will no doubt be duly rewarded.

[32] Cf. Gloss *s. v. Slovenda*. "Ab his qui ad hoc voto vel poenitentia sunt adstricti. Vel dic quod hoc fuit in primitiva Ecclesia necessitatis: hodie vero consilii." H. et G.

[33] "An autem sexta feria non solum abstinentia a carnibus, sed etiam jejunium sit in praecepto, Doctores non conveniunt, sed communiter tenetur jejunium non esse ex praecepto, sed ex consilio tantum, prout de communi testatur Abb . . . et notat Innoc." In c. *Consilium, de Observat, Jejunior.*, n. 23.

[34] Cf., however, the indult of May 6, 1899, for the countries of Latin America, the indults conceded for the dioceses of North America, for the negroes, and the special concessions periodically renewed for Spain by the bull of the Crusade, by which abstinence is compulsory only on fifteen days each year.

THE SIXTH COMMANDMENT

The Saturday Fast.—The discipline of Saturday abstinence is less ancient. Long continued efforts were needed before it was accepted by the faithful. It gave rise to many discussions; and when the popes believed that they had obtained success, it was only ephemeral. The reason is that the observance of Saturday, instead of originating from the bed-rock of primitive discipline at a time when the Eastern and Western Churches were still one, began much later in the West and appeared from the very beginning to be in opposition to a much older Eastern custom which pretended to go back directly to the Apostles.

The so-called *Canons of the Apostles* threatened with deposition any cleric, and with excommunication any layman, bold enough to fast on Saturday excepting once a year.[35] The *Apostolic Constitutions* declare in express terms that on no Saturday excepting Holy Saturday, should there ever be any fast, even in Lent.[36]

This tradition was not confined to the East, for we know that it was in vogue at Milan in the time

---

[35] "Εἴ τις κληρικὸς εὑρεθῇ τὴν κυριακὴν ἡμέραν νηστεύων ἢ τὸ σάββατον πλὴν τοῦ ἑνὸς μόνου, καταιρείσθω· εἰ δὲ λαϊκὸς, ἀφοριζέσθω." c. lxv. Bruns, t. I, 10.

[36] "Mandavit autem ... per ipsum sabbatum (Holy Saturday) jejunare; non quod jejunandum sit sabbato, die quo a creatione est cessatum, sed quod illo solo jejunari oporteat, in quo scilicet creator adhuc sub terra erat." *Const. Apost.*, l. V, c. xv. Migne, *P. L.*, t. I, 879-880.

of St. Ambrose.[37] But in the East, and in the countries liturgically related thereto, Saturday was solemnized as a feast-day, though attempts were made to take from it the special character of the Jewish Sabbath; during Lent, it was to this day and to Sunday that the celebration of the anniversaries of the martyrs was reserved.[38]

While in the East Saturday rather shared in the character of Sunday, in the West, on the contrary, it partook of that of Friday. The Friday fast was there extended to Saturday, and that practice became a general observance with which many councils, *e.g.* that of Elvira,[39] concerned themselves.

The decision of the Council of Elvira perhaps created some uniformity in Spain and Gaul; elsewhere, about the end of the fourth century and the beginning of the fifth, the discussions were very lively. The Christians of the East and those of Rome accused each other of heresy and schism; the former charged Rome with corrupting the Apostolic tradition, the latter reproached the Ori-

[37] "Quadragesima totis praeter sabbatum et dominicum jejunatur diebus." *De Elia et Jejunio*, c. x. Migne, *P. L.*, t. XIV, 708.—This peculiarity must be attributed to the partly eastern origin of that church.

[38] Cf. *Conc. Laodicen.* (about 380), c. LI. Bruns, t. I, 78.

[39] Did the Council of Elvira (c. xxvi. Bruns, t. ii., 5) forbid the addition of the Friday to the Saturday fast, as Msgr. Duchesne thinks; or did the council prescribe it, as Dom Leclerq believes? I do not know. In any case, a fast was kept on Saturday in Spain.

THE SIXTH COMMANDMENT

entals with not obeying the directions of the Supreme Pontiff.

We know from the correspondence of SS. Jerome and Augustine how the faithful were troubled by these discussions and the diversity of discipline. These great doctors were kept busy answering the anxious inquiries of people and priests who feared that, by not conforming to the customs of some portion of the Church, they would jeopardize their own salvation or that of the souls confided to their care. St. Jerome who, in his travels, had met with many different customs, became rather tolerant on this point. A certain Lucinus asked him: Must we fast on Saturday? He answered: "Keep the traditions of the Church, *i.e.*, those which do not contravene the faith, as you have received them from the ancients, and do not allow them to clash with the contrary traditions. Would to God that we could always fast! But since we cannot, let us permit each province to use its own judgment, and to observe as Apostolic laws the precepts of the ancients." [40]

St. Augustine was equally prudent. He reminds

---

[40] "De Sabbato quod quaeris, utrum jejunandum sit. . . . Ego illud breviter te admonendum puto, traditiones ecclesiasticas (praesertim quae fidei non officiant) ita observandas, ut a majoribus traditae sunt: nec aliorum consuetudinem aliorum contrario more subverti. Atque utinam omni tempore jejunare possimus . . . sed unaquaeque provincia abundet in sensu suo, et praecepta majorum, leges apostolicas arbitretur." *Epist. ad Lucinum*, 6. Migne, *P. L.*, t. XXII, 672.

Januarius, who questioned him on the subject, of the answer which he himself had received from St. Ambrose when he confided to him the scruples of his pious mother. St. Monica, arriving at Milan, was astonished at finding that Saturday was no fast-day there (which would indicate that the African discipline was in conformity with that of Rome on this point). What was she to do? Not daring to go herself to consult the bishop, she sent her son. Ambrose answered that he had no particular teaching to impose, and that if he had known a better custom than that of Milan, he would have followed it. When Augustine did not appear satisfied, Ambrose added: When I go to Rome, I observe the fast; when I am at Milan, I conform myself to the custom of Milan; do likewise if you wish to avoid giving scandal; follow the custom of the country in which you live, without judging or condemning others.[41]

In his answer to another correspondent, Augustine gives free rein to his wit. Casulanus ingenuously asked him whether it was permitted to fast on Saturday. He answers that it was, because otherwise Christ could not have fasted forty days in succession. As to the existence of an obligation, he says that a Roman, whom he designates by the nickname of Urbicus, tried to prove it, but

[41] *Epist.* LIV, *ad Inquisit. Januarii,* c. ii. Migne, *P. L.,* t. XXXIII, 200-201.

as he could not find the necessary arguments either in Scripture or Tradition, had recourse to billingsgate against the gluttonous and sensuous instincts of those who do not fast on that day. Poor man! he did not understand that insults are not proofs and that they could be turned against himself for the days on which the Church of Rome does not imitate the others and does not fast. On matters on which Holy Writ has decided nothing, it is not right to oppose tradition to tradition. The peace of the world would be uselessly disturbed by such a proceeding; the disputes would last forever and charity would suffer. Let everyone follow his bishop, the custom of his own church, and of the country in which he lives.[42]

These utterances indicate how much certain souls suffered from the endless discussions resulting from the existing diversity of discipline.

When he wrote in these rather caustic terms against Urbicus, St. Augustine had no intention of blaming or condemning the Saturday fast; on the contrary, he wished to see each church keep its particular customs, even though they were some-

[42] "Quid ergo me consulis, utrum liceat sabbato jejunare? Respondeo, si nullo modo liceret, profecto quadraginta continuos dies nec Moyses et nec Elias, nec ipse Dominus jejunasset. . . . In his rebus, de quibus nihil certi statuit Scriptura divina, mos populi Dei vel instituta majorum pro lege tenenda sunt. De quibus si disputare voluerimus, et ex aliorum consuetudine alios improbare, orietur interminata luctatio . . ." *Epist.* LXXXVI, *ad Casulanum*, c. xiii. Migne, *P. L.*, t. XXXIII, 150.

times opposed to those of other churches; he admired in them, as he tells Casulanus,[43] the Queen (which is the Catholic Church) *circumdata varietate,* as the psalmist says. What he opposed and condemned was the violent language of the intolerant and extremist defenders of a cause in itself legitimate. Provided the East and the churches dependent on it, were allowed to retain their ancient customs, he was willing that Rome should seek to spread her discipline everywhere.

It was this that Innocent I tried to obtain from Decentius of Eugubium. In a letter to this bishop, the Pope strongly insisted on the obligation of fasting on Saturday as well as on Friday. Friday and Sunday, he says, are days on which we recall, each week, the memory of the Passion; Sunday is the Easter of the resurrection, Friday the day of the Passion; it is to preserve these memories that we celebrate both days. Now Saturday recalls the sadness of the Apostles and their grief while they hid for fear of the Jews. Why not then fast on Saturday?[44]

[43] *Ibid.,* no 31.

[44] "Sabbato vero jejunandum esse, ratio evidentissima demonstrat. Nam, si diem dominicam ob venerabilem resurrectionem Domini nostri Jesu Christi non solum in Pascha celebramus verum etiam per singulas hebdomadas ipsius diei imaginem frequentamus, ac sicut sexta feria propter passionem Domini jejunamus, sabbatum praetermittere non debemus, quoniam inter tristitiam et laetitiam temporis illius videtur inclusum. Nam utique constat, Apostolos biduo isto et in moerore fuisse, et propter metum Ju-

This argument was improved later on by the famous monk Cassian, who found that the Roman discipline regarding the Saturday fast rests on the solid basis of a true Roman tradition; St. Peter himself was supposed to have instituted it for Rome, in memory of the Saturday when he fasted to invoke the help of God in his struggle against Simon the Magician.[45]

Whether Pope Innocent I carried his point, and whether Saturday became a day of fast in Italy, we do not know; but in Gaul the Council of Agde commanded a fast on the Saturdays of Lent, and the Council of Orleans (541) imposed the same law.[46] In Spain, in the seventh century, according to St. Isidore of Seville, there was fasting

daeorum se occuluisse. Quod utique non dubium est in tantum eos jejunasse biduo memorato, ut traditio Ecclesiae habeat isto biduo sacramenta penitus non celebrari. Quae etiam forma per singulas tenenda est hebdomadas propter id, quod commemoratio diei illius semper est celebranda. Quod si putant semel atque uno sabbato jejunandum, ergo et dominica, et sexta feria semel in Pascha erit utique celebranda." *Epist.* XXV, *ad Decent. Eugubin.*, c. iv. Migne, *P. L.*, t. XX, 555.

[45] "Cujus moderaminis causam nonnulli in quibusdam Occidentalibus civitatibus ignorantes, et maxime in Urbe, idcirco putant absolutionem sabbati minime debere praesumi, quod apostolum Petrum eadem die contra Simonem conflictaturum asserant jejunasse. Ex quo magis apparet hoc eum non consuetudine canonica fecisse, sed praesentis potius necessitate conflictus. Siquidem et ibi pro hac eadem re non generale, sed speciale videtur Petrus discipulis suis jejunium induxisse; quod utique non fecisset, si scisset illud canonica consuetudine solere servari." *Institut.*, l. III, c. x. Migne, *P. L.*, t. XLIX, 147.

[46] See above, p. 258.

on Saturdays for motives identical with those mentioned in the letter to Decentius.[47]

Another proof that the Roman custom was spreading more and more is that the Greeks were becoming jealous of it. In the Council *in Trullo* they feigned to be scandalized at the Saturday fast, and, assuming haughty airs, recalled the Roman Church to the obedience due to the sixty-fifth canon of the Apostles.[48] This conduct merely served to embitter the relations between Rome and Constantinople. In the West the same discipline continued to be observed. A century after the council, Pope Adrian I, in writing to the bishop of Egila, quoted his predecessors Sylvester and Innocent, as well as SS. Jerome and Isidore,[49] in support of the obligation of fasting on Saturday.

Away from Rome the Saturday fast never became deeply implanted. In the Frankish empire particularly (if we except the insertion of St. Isidore's text in a collection of capitularies) Saturday does not appear as a day of fast, or even of abstinence, in the decree of the Council of Rhis-

[47] "Omnis sexta feria propter passionem Domini a quibusdam jejunatur, sed et Sabbati dies a plerisque, propter quod in eo Christus jacuit in sepulcro jejunio consecratus habetur, scilicet ne Judaeis exsultando praestetur quod Christus sustulit moriendo." *De Officiis Ecclesiastic.*, l. I, c. xliii. Migne, *P. L.*, t. LXXXIII, 775.

[48] *Concil. Quinisextum*, c. lv. BRUNS, t. I, 53.

[49] "Sabbato jejunare, firmiter atque procul dubio tenens tua non desinat sanctitas . . ." Migne, *P. L.*, t. XCVI, 345.

pach. Neither is it described as a day of penance in the Capitularies, though these expressly mention the Wednesday fast. It occupies no place in the Penitentials. The *Vallicellanum I^{um}*, in its instructions to confessors, expressly excludes Saturday from the weekly fast.⁵⁰ The Penitential of Arundel alone admits it as a day of abstinence imposed on certain great sinners, just as Monday and Wednesday were.⁵¹ Pope Nicholas I, in his letter to the Bulgarians, mentions it neither as a fast-day nor as a day of abstinence;⁵² and Regino is satisfied with inserting the decretal of Innocent I in his appendix.⁵³ Ratramnus affirms that Rome alone, and a few among the Western churches, fast on Saturday, but that the majority do not.⁵⁴ The monk of Corbie may be biased by his controversy with the Greeks; but there are other testimonies that give his statement weight. Then, also, the Council of Anse, which

⁵⁰ "Qui ergo tota septimana jejunat pro peccatis, *sabbato* et dominica die manducet et bibat quicquid ei aptum fuerit." SCHMITZ, *op. cit.*, t. I, 242.

⁵¹ *Poenitent. Arundel.*, c. xxxii et lxiv, *ib.*, p. 446 et 454.

⁵² *Loco supra cit.*, c. iv. Migne, *P. L.*, t. CXIX, 981.

⁵³ *De Eccles. Discipl.*, c. xiv. Migne, *P. L.*, t. CXXXII, 372.

⁵⁴ "Culpant [Graeci] Romanos et Occidentales quod sabbato jejunent; quando quidem ipsi Orientales omni sabbato prandeant, nescientes, ut credimus, quod non omnes Occidentales Ecclesiae hac consuetudine teneantur, sed Romana, vel aliae quaedam Occidentales ecclesiae; siquidem major numerus Occidentalium in sabbato non jejunat." *Contra Graecor. Opposit.*, l. IV, c. iii. Migne, *P. L.*, t. CXXI, 311.

speaks of the Wednesday abstinence and the fast of Friday,[55] does not even mention Saturday, and the case is the same with the Council of Enham.[56] Rodulphus Glaber makes it a simple day of abstinence from flesh-meat.[57] Peter de Honestis in his *Regula Clericorum* speaks of it as a day given over to abstinence, but only at certain periods of the year, *viz.* from the nativity of St. John the Baptist to the autumnal equinox.[58]

Rome alone, and those who followed her closely, faithfully observed the Saturday fast. Cardinal Humbert[59] and St. Peter Damian[60] are among its last witnesses. As early as 1078, a council held in Rome recorded, as it were, the defeat that had been suffered by reducing the Saturday fast to a mere abstinence from flesh-meat.[61]

[55] Cf. *supra*, p. 283.

[56] *Ibid.*

[57] *Supra*, p. 284.

[58] "Carnis et sanguinis usum quarta et sexta feria ac sabbato interclusistis." c. iv. Migne, *P. L.*, t. CLXIII, 721. Cf. c. v, *ibid.*

[59] "Sabbatum . . . nullo convivio aut otio honoratur apud nos . . . sed oneratur jejunio et labore." *Adversus Graecor. Calumnias.* Migne, *P. L.*, t. CXLIII, 963.

[60] *Opuscul.* LIV, *de Jejunio Sabbati.* Migne, *P. L.*, t. CXLV, 795 sqq.

[61] "Quia dies sabbati apud sanctos Patres nostros in abstinentia celebris est habitus, nos eorumdem auctoritatem sequentes salubriter admonemus, ut quicumque Christianae religionis participem se esse desiderat, ab esu carnium eadem die (nisi majori festivitate interveniente, vel infirmitate impediente) abstineat." *Conc. Roman.* (1078), c. vii. Mansi, t. XX, 510.

THE SIXTH COMMANDMENT

In the Western Church, therefore, as a whole, Saturday observance was a very uncertain discipline. In one place the fast was observed, but little by little degenerated into simple abstinence; in another, abstinence was observed more or less faithfully by the laity; elsewhere it was imposed only on clerics. In the face of these facts we may well question whether there was not some rhetorical liberty in the exhortations of Peter the Venerable to the monks of Cluny, when he tells them that the clowns and valets abstain from meat on Saturday, while they (the monks) observe only the Friday abstinence.[62] Half a century later, Eudes de Sully, who mentions the Friday fast, does not speak of Saturday. At the same time (in the beginning of the thirteenth century) Innocent III recognizes the Saturday abstinence as a local custom to be faithfully maintained where it exists; but he does not indicate that it should be introduced where it does not already exist.[63]

[62] "Abstinent causa Dei ipsi mimi vel lixae a carnibus omni sabbato. . . . At, fratres nostri, sancti Ordinis, coelestis propositi, monachi, et hoc Cluniacenses, spreto Deo, abjecto pudore, totum, ut dicitur, annum, nulla, praeter sextam, excepta feria, in absumendis carnibus continuant . . ." *Epist.* XV. Migne, *P. L.*, t. CLXXXIX, 418.

[63] C. *Consilium, X, de Observ. Jejuniorum:* "Item, de illis, qui propter debilitatem, quam in se sentiunt, in sabbato juxta terrarum consuetudinem aliarum carnes sumunt, quod in partibus tuis nullatenus fieri consuevit, . . . respondemus, quod super hoc consuetudinem tuae regionis facias observari."

The canonists, perplexed by the decretal *Sabbato* of Innocent I, at times did not know how to reconcile the divergent texts. Guido de Baysio (about 1280) solved the difficulty by saying that the abstinence of Saturday was, for the Church at large, *de honesto*, not *de praecepto;* but the majority followed the principles of Innocent III and decided, with Abbas and Silvester, that it was merely a matter of counsel wherever custom did not impose it. Fagnani [64] approved of this view and drew the same practical conclusion, *viz.* that abstinence on Saturday is a local custom, obliging neither the French in Catalonia, nor the Greeks in their country.

It was difficult to maintain the Saturday abstinence even in Italy. The synodal constitutions of Lucca, which affirm its existence as a "laudable custom," decree severe penalties against those who fail to observe it, and the authorities evidently had to struggle against a widespread relaxation, since they imposed a fine of twenty-five pounds on clerics and one of ten pounds (to say nothing of other arbitrary penalties) on lay people, who neglected the observance of the Saturday abstinence, even where there was no scandal.[65] In Provence a

[64] In c. *Consilium*, n. 16 sqq.

[65] "Qui sine causa necessaria aliqua die sabbati in civitate vel dioecesi Lucana publice vel occulte carnes comederit, si fuerit clericus vel persona ecclesiastica XXV librarum, si vero laicus X librarum lucensium poenam ipso facto incurrat, alia poena spirit-

THE SIXTH COMMANDMENT

special decree was necessary to impose the obligation of abstinence upon clerics who either held benefices or were in major orders. Moreover, as the ancient tradition regarding the origin of the penitential practice in question had likely been forgotten, a new motive for its observance was adduced: the Saturday abstinence was proclaimed to be in honor of the Blessed Virgin. Dispensation, for reasons, was left to the individual conscience, but disobedience without sufficient cause was punished with a month's interdict.[66] This legislation was endorsed by the Council of Béziers of 1351 [67] and that of Lavaur of 1368; [68] and it is in the same form that this abstinence appears in modern times.

We thus see how little truth there is in the words of Thomassin: "Until the year 1400, Saturday abstinence was voluntarily observed rather than strictly enforced among the laity, though

uali nostro arbitrio imponenda." *Constitutiones Ecclesiae Lucanae* (1351), c. lxviii. MANSI, t. XXVI, 281.

[66] "Statuimus quod clerici beneficiati, aut in sacris ordinibus constituti, ab inde in antea semper in diebus sabbati, pro honore B. Mariae, carnibus abstineant: nisi ex causa necessitatis; de qua comedentis conscientiae relinquatur, vel nisi festum Natalis Domini in die sabbati contigerit evenire. Alioquin contrarium facientes, pro quolibet die sabbati, quo carnes comedere attentaverint, per unum mensem ipso facto ab ingressu Ecclesiae sint suspensi." *Conc. Avenionen.* (1337), c. v. MANSI, t. XXV, 1089.

[67] C. vii. MANSI, t. XXVI, 245.

[68] *Conc. Vauren.* (1368), c. xc, *ib.*, 522.

it was common enough among them."[69]

In the beginning of the sixteenth century, the synodal statutes of Stephen Poncher, in Paris, confine themselves to a mere exhortation to observe the fast, or at least abstinence, on Wednesdays, Fridays, and Saturdays.[70]

Nevertheless the abstinence of Saturday remained a law up to recent times, the Holy See preferring to dispense from it by temporary indults rather than to abrogate it. In 1840 a request of the bishops of the United States for a perpetual dispensation from the Saturday abstinence was answered by an indult granting this favor for twenty years. In France, for some forty years past, indefinitely renewed indults have made the suppression of abstinence regular in practice. In Italy, the bishop of Concordia, in a *Postulatum* presented to the Vatican Council, asked for the abrogation of the law;[71] but the *Postulatum* did not come up for discussion. The decree of September 7, 1906, made no modification for Italy; but the indult of May 9, 1899, for Latin America, gave permission to omit the Saturday abstinence for ten years. Will the precept itself

[69] *Les Jeûnes de l'Église*, IIe part., ch. xv.

[70] "Hortamur diebus praedictis jejunium non solvere, et ad minus ab esu carnium abstinere." c. *de Jejuniis*. *Synodicon Ecclesiae Parisiensis* (1777), p. 154.

[71] *Collectio Lacensis*, t. VII, 882.

be eventually abrogated? The future alone can tell.

The Precept of Abstinence.—What the Church now imposes on Friday, and used to impose on Saturday, is abstinence from flesh-meat. Formerly she was more exacting. To abstain from flesh-meat was not considered sufficient; other abstinences, which notably restricted the choice of foods, were added.

Abstinence was not considered simply as a mortification; it had been deemed, of old, one of the most suitable means of purifying the soul and keeping it pure, and we know that great importance has ever been attached to abstinence from certain kinds of food in the East. Flesh and wine were considered impure; their absolute exclusion from the human diet constituted one of the fundamental articles of the Gnostic or Manichean asceticism which the Church combated at the end of the third century. The second canon of the Apostles decreed deposition against any bishop, priest or deacon who would refuse to use flesh or wine on feast days merely because he considered them impure, and not simply as a manner of religious purification.[72] The fourteenth canon of Ancyra (314), confirming this discipline, says that many even refused to eat vegetables cooked with meat.[73]

[72] Bruns, t. I, 8. [73] *Ib.*, p. 68.

This condemnation of excesses did not, however, affect the legitimate abstinence recommended by St. Paul: "It is good not to eat flesh and not to drink wine." [74] In conformity with this counsel, abstinence from wine and flesh was made the basis and an essential part of fasting. In the fourth century St. Cyril of Jerusalem [75] and the *Apostolic Constitutions* say: "On the days of the Pasch, from Monday to Saturday, you should fast, and, during those six days, use only bread, salt, vegetables and water; abstain during that time from wine and flesh, for these are days of mourning and not of rejoicing; on Friday and Saturday those who are strong enough shall fast until the crow of the cock on Easter day." [76] Abstinence in the sense here under discussion appears, therefore, well established by the common law. The *Didascalia,* composed about the second half of the third century, imposes still severer regulations. "From Monday on, during the days of the Pasch, you shall fast, and eat nothing but bread, salt, and water. . . . On Friday and Saturday you shall fast absolutely and taste nothing." [77]

Manifestly there is question here not of a voluntary penance but of an abstinence imposed, if not

---

[74] *Rom.* xiv, 21.

[75] *Cateches.* IV, c. xxvii. Migne, *P. G.*, t. XXXIII, 489.

[76] *Const. Apost.*, l. V, c. xviii. Migne, *P. G.*, t. I, 890.

[77] C. xxii. *Canoniste Contemporain,* 1902, p. 22.

THE SIXTH COMMANDMENT

by a positive law, at least by a custom dating back to the very origin of the Church.

In order to proceed with greater order and clearness, we shall explain one by one the different prohibitions which entered into the law of abstinence.

Abstinence from Meat.—This is such an essential part of abstinence that it is always included in the term. There is no need of citing the innumerable texts which have come down to us. The use of flesh-meat on days of abstinence was forbidden at all times from the very beginning of ecclesiastical discipline.

But flesh-meat did not necessarily mean the meat of all animals. St. Epiphanius says that some abstain from the flesh of quadrupeds and birds, others from that of quadrupeds only.[78] And the historian Socrates gives the same information.[79] In course of time this anomaly ceased; whatever is simply called flesh-meat (the meat itself, blood, grease, juice) was forbidden. Many are the texts which forbid the use of blood for food, in fact it may be said that the prohibition of flesh and that of blood have always gone hand in hand. Grease is mentioned in the capitularies of Charlemagne as a food prohibited to monks on every Friday, on certain days before Christmas,

[78] *Expos. Fidei*, c. xxiii. Migne, *P. G.*, t. XLII, 828.
[79] *Hist. Eccles.*, l. V, c. xxii.

and from Quinquagesima until Lent.[80] As to meat juice, there can be no doubt that it was comprehended in the prohibition of flesh. Yet, on this point, as on the preceding one, the Church gradually introduced slight mitigations into her discipline. For many centuries, flesh-meat and its by-products, juice, lard, and grease, have been differently treated. Many are the minute discussions of theologians on this matter; the most divergent opinions appealed to custom, until at last the Church restored peace and calm of conscience by many gracious indults. Every year, the Lenten Pastorals mention these indults, which allow the use of such seasonings as lard and grease for every day except Good Friday.

To these mitigations we have added others which would have caused our ancestors some surprise. The Council of Laodicea recommended total abstinence from flesh-meat and all its by-products during the whole of Lent.[81] The ancient discipline prohibited the use of flesh in Lent, even on Sundays, and the Archbishop of Braga wrote Pope Innocent III to ascertain what penance was to be inflicted upon certain of his diocesans who, in a time of terrible famine, had found themselves

[80] "Ut habeant monachi . . . pinguedinem ad esum excepto sexta feria et viginti diebus ante nativitatem Domini et septimana illa quae ante Quadragesimam vocatur Quinquagesima." *Capitulare Monasticum*, c. xxii. BORETIUS, t. I, 345.

[81] C. 1, quoted in Gratian, c. viii. D. III, *de Consecratione*.

constrained to eat meat in Lent. The Pope's answer was the common-sense one: Those unfortunates deserve no penance, because necessity excused them from sin.[82] But the fact that the Archbishop believed himself obliged to ask the question shows how rigorously the use of meat was prohibited in Lent.

How much we have changed since then! The use of meat on Sundays was at first tolerated, then expressly permitted, for the greater part of Lent. Old people still remember the time when its use was completely forbidden in France from the Friday of Passion Week to Easter. Later, new dispensations allowed the gradual extension of the Sunday privilege to Tuesday and Thursday of each week, up to the Thursday before Palm Sunday. About the beginning of the pontificate of Pius IX, Monday was added to the days on which abstinence need not be observed;[83] a few years later the use of meat on those four days began to be permitted up to Wednesday of Holy Week. Lastly the Saturdays, except Ember Saturday and Holy Saturday, were included in the dispensations.

[82] "Quum autem quaesieris, quae sit illis poenitentia injungenda, qui diebus quadragesimalibus quo tempore tantae famis inedia ingruebat, quod magna pars populi propter inopiam annonae periret, carnes comedere sunt coacti, tibi breviter repondemus quod in tali articulo illos non credimus puniendos, quos tam urgens necessitas excusavit . . ." c. *Consilium*, X, *de Observ. Jejuniorum*, in Freiberg, *Corpus Juris*, t. II, who gives the complete text.

[83] See the Lenten Pastoral of the Archbishop of Tours, 1847.

Outside of France the indults granted are even more liberal.

Abstinence from Milk and Eggs.—As we have seen from the decree of Laodicea, abstinence at first comprised all foodstuffs endowed with or productive of life. This naturally included eggs and milk. The *Apostolic Constitutions* and the *Didascalia* allow only bread, salt, vegetables, and water during Holy Week. The fourth Council of Toledo permits fish.[84] St. Isidore couples two counsels of St. Paul, *viz.* to abstain from flesh and wine and to eat herbs (Rom. xiv, 2).[85]

In the East the Council *in Trullo* severely rebuked the Armenians and other Christians for using eggs and cheese on Saturdays and Sundays in Lent.[86]

In the West eggs and milk, with their by-products, were also excluded from the foods of Lent (*cibi quadragesimales*). However, in the ninth century, a very sensible relaxation was made. We have seen that Theodulf of Orleans did not attribute very great importance to the question of food, so long as an attempt was made to observe the fast. Probably, if he had been pressed he would have conceded the use of meat to those who

---

[84] "In quibus etiam praeter piscem et olus, sicut in illis quadraginta diebus, ceteris carnibus abstinetur . . ." *Conc. Tolet.* (633), c. xi. BRUNS, t. I, 226.

[85] *De Eccles. Officiis*, l. I, c. xlv. Migne, *P. L.*, t. LXXXIII, 777.

[86] BRUNS, t. I, 54.

could not fast without it. *A fortiori* does he allow the use of milk and eggs: "He who can abstain from eggs, cheese, fish and wine, gives proof of great virtue, he says; as for him who cannot abstain from them, let him use them. The essential point is to observe the fast till night and to drink no more wine than is necessary to keep one's strength. To abstain from milk, butter, and eggs, and not to fast, is foolish."[87]

This text, together with a passage of St. Bede, which antedates it by half a century, shows that the severity in matters of abstinence was lessening in the West. Jonas, the successor of Theodulf, seems to attach still less importance to the choice of food, for he says that there is more true penance in taking delicate meats in small quantities than in gorging oneself with permitted foods.[88]

The practice of the people corresponded to the theories of Theodulf and Jonas; Eneas of Paris admits this in his discussion with the Greeks, and

[87] "Qui vero ovis, caseo, piscibus et vino abstinere potest, magnae virtutis est; qui autem his, aut infirmitate interveniente, aut quolibet opere, abstinere non potest, utatur. Tantum ut jejunium usque ad vesperum solemniter celebret; et vinum non ad ebrietatem, sed ad refectionem corporis sui sumat. A caseo vero, lacte, butyro et ovis abstinere, et non jejunare, dementissimum est, et omni ratione semotum. Vini enim ebrietas et luxuria prohibita sunt, non lac et ova. Non enim ait Apostolus: *Nolite comedere lac et ova*, sed: *Nolite inebriari vino, in quo est luxuria.*" THEODULPH'S *Capitula*, c. xl. Migne, *P. L.*, t. CV, 204.

[88] *De Institut. Laicali*, l. I, c. x. Migne, *P. L.*, t. CVI, 139 sqq.

even pleads extenuating circumstances. "In one part of Italy," he says, "there is abstinence from cooked foods three times a week, and all are satisfied with vegetables and the fruit of trees which abound in that country; but another diet must be allowed the inhabitants of countries which do not possess such abundant resources. The Germans in general do not abstain from milk, butter, cheese, and eggs during Lent, except some who voluntarily do so."[89] The Council of Quedlinburg, two hundred years later, passed a special decree to forbid the use of eggs and cheese in Lent.[90] In Italy the rule of Peter de Honestis, made for clerics only, prescribes abstinence from eggs and milk only during certain periods of the year, and never on "feasts of nine lessons."[91] The rule forbidding eggs and milk was thus observed with difficulty, although it always existed, as is proven by the instruction given by St. Otto of Bamberg to his Pomeranian neophytes.[92]

In France, says Robert Pulleyn, the faithful would have been scandalized by the use of butter on Fridays and fast-days,[93] and a council of

[89] *Contra Graecos*, obj. iii, c. clxxv. Migne, *P. L.*, CXXI, 741.
[90] "Item ne quis caseum et ova comedat in Quadragesima." *Conc. Quintiliniburg.* (1085), c. vii. MANSI, t. XX, 608.
[91] *De Regula Clericorum*, l. II, c. viii, *De usu ovorum et casei*. Migne, *P. L.*, t. CLXIII, 722.
[92] *Ottonis Vita*, c. 1. Migne, *P. L.*, t. CLXXIII, 1298.
[93] *Sentent.*, pars VIIIa, c. x. Migne, *P. L.*, t. CLXXXVI, 975.

… Cognac forbade the use of eggs and milk on all fast-days, except in the week of Pentecost.[94] The synodal statutes of Liège prohibited their use on all vigils.[95] A century later, a council of Angers tolerates the use of milk and butter in regions where fish and oil cannot be easily obtained.[96]

The same council mentions an Apostolic privilege permitting the use of milk. There were, therefore, at that date already privileges of this kind. A sharp distinction must be drawn between a personal dispensation, which is transitory and often granted on an insufficient excuse, and a privilege, which, being an act of the legislator himself, is always, if not an abrogation of, at least a derogation from the law for a whole class of the faithful. Henceforth, the great bulk of Christians still continued to observe more or less faithfully the prescribed abstinence from eggs and milk, at least in Lent;[97] but means were found to obtain legitimate exemption for many. From the fif-

[94] "Exceptis jejuniis quae sunt in septimana Pentecostes, quibus possunt comedi ova et casei, ratione dignitatis festi . . ." *Conc. Copriniacen.* (about 1260), c. xix. Mansi, t. XXIII, 870.

[95] *Statuta Synodalia Dioeces. Leodien.* (about 1287), § 11, c. x. Mansi, t. XXIV, 909.

[96] The Council of Angers, of 1365, complains that the people use milk and butter, although they can easily procure oil and fish. *Conc. Andegaven.* (1365), c. xxii. Mansi, t. XXVI, 436.

[97] Cf. this exhortation of Stephen Poncher: "Hortor vos ac moneo Quadragesimam congrue jejunare; et velut censuerunt sacri canones, a carnibus, lacte, caseo, butyro et ovis." *Synod. Eccl. Paris.*, p. 153.

teenth century on, the general indults became more frequent. Germany, Bohemia, and Hungary, then France and Belgium, obtained in turn indults permitting the use of eggs and milk.

In the second half of the nineteenth century the indults were extended almost everywhere. Exemption was first made in the case of butter and milk, not only for the principal meal but also for the collation. A few years ago, this was not allowed on Ash Wednesday and Good Friday; but dispensations have again been extended; and during Lent 1908 the use of milk and butter was, in some dioceses, allowed every day, even on Good Friday.

The use of eggs was a little more restricted at first. For about half a century the Lenten Pastorals remained almost invariable in certain regions; only the first and the last two days of Lent were excepted from the dispensation; some however allowed the use of eggs every day of Lent, with the exception of three days, *viz.* Ash Wednesday, Ember Friday, and Good Friday. Besides, this permission did not extend to the collation of those who were bound to fast. This particular discipline seems therefore to establish in regard to eggs and flesh a certain connexion between the new legislation and the old.

To-day prohibition of meat, milk, and eggs constitutes that kind of abstinence which is called *maigre strict.* It was formerly common, but has suffered many reductions, even in Italy, one of the countries in which it had been best preserved, by the decree of November 7, 1906.

Abstinence from Fish and Cooked Foods.—We have seen that, as late as the ninth century, people in Italy used only raw foods on three days a week during Lent. Still more, of course, did they abstain from fish. Previously fish had appeared on the table of those who fasted most faithfully. The historian Socrates, in the fifth century, bears witness to this fact, and the Council of Toledo, held in 633, also mentions the use of fish as expressly permitted on fast-days.[98] A very marked distinction was therefore made at that time, in point of view of abstinence, between the flesh of fish and the flesh of other animals. The reason of that difference (for a reason had to be found for the divergencies of practice) was of the mystical order. Says St. Isidore of Seville: "The use of flesh and wine was granted to man only after the deluge, and Jesus Christ said, by the mouth of His Apostle: It is good not to eat flesh and not to drink wine, and to be satisfied with vegetables. But since Our Lord Himself used fish after His resurrection, we can eat of it, for neither the Saviour nor the Apostles have subsequently forbidden it."[99]

[98] Cf. *supra,* p. 306.
[99] "Carnes autem et vinum post diluvium hominibus in usum

Thanks to this reasoning the use of fish on fast-days and during Lent was formally permitted. The only point on which doubt continued to exist for some time, was whether fish could be eaten at the collation. The collation being only a mitigation of the fast, an attempt had been made to make it as unlike a regular meal as possible. Could fish, the flesh of which is as nourishing as that of other animals, be allowed at the collation? Would not this food give to the collation the character of a true meal? Under the influence of this consideration the first moralists who permitted the use of fish for the collation, only allowed the use of small fish, whose delicate flesh was considered as less nourishing. However, the distinction was too fine not to succumb to practice; to-day many moralists admit that the flesh of large fish taken at the collation, in small quantities, is no more opposed to the observance of fasting than the same quantity of small-sized fish.

concessa sunt. . . . Sed postquam Christus, qui est **principium** et finis, apparuit, hoc quod in principio suspenderat etiam in temporum fine retraxit loquens per Apostolum suum: Bonum est non manducare carnem, et non bibere vinum. Et iterum: qui infirmus est, olera manducet.—Non igitur quia carnes malae sunt, ideo prohibentur, sed quia eorum epulae carnis luxuriam gignunt, fomes enim ac nutrimentum omnium vitiorum, esca ventri et venter escis, quia scriptum est: *Deus hunc et has destruet.* Piscem sane, quia cum post resurrectionem accepit Dominus, possumus manducare. Hoc enim nec Salvator, nec apostoli vetuerunt." *De Eccles. Offic.*, l. I, c. xlv. Migne, *P. L.*, t. LXXXIII, 777.

However, the use of both flesh-meat and fish at the same meal remains forbidden during Lent, in virtue of a rule imposed by Benedict XIV.[100] The mitigations which the Church grants to the faithful should never exclude penance; she considers it an act of weakness to wish to unite, during this time which should be consecrated to mortification, manifold pleasures and various kinds of foods.

There is no longer in the West any obligation for the faithful to abstain from cooked foods on certain days, though the practice is still observed by pious Christian families on Good Friday as an act of voluntary mortification.

Abstinence from Wine.—Abstinence from wine was a part of the fast in the first centuries, as we have seen from the text of the Apostolic Constitutions. But it was not long maintained as obligatory. At the same period when St. Isidore of Se-

[100] This prohibition, of which no trace is found in the legislation anterior to Benedict XIV, was made explicit by him, especially in the constitution *Libentissime*, where he says that all dispensations from abstinence must mention in express terms the prohibition of eating fish and meat at the same meal during Lent and on other fast-days of the year. It will suffice to cite the two following texts. § 3 "Decrevimus ne ulla in posterum, sive peculiaris, sive generalis pro aliqua civitate vel oppido concedatur facultas adhibendi carnes ad mensam tempore jejunii vel quadragesimae, nisi conditio servandi jejunii . . . interponatur; et illud quoque monitum addatur, nequaquam licere mensam eamdem carne ac piscibus instruere." § 9 "Ne illi quibus licet carnes edere, cum jejunium tempore quadragesimae vel extra quadragesimam fidelibus praescribitur unius comestionis limites excedant, ac ne piscibus simul et carnibus parari sibi mensam patiantur."

ville seems to include wine among the forbidden foods, the fourth Council of Toledo describes abstinence from wine as a supererogatory work of mortification observed only by a few.[101] General conclusions should not be too hastily drawn from this text. At the end of the eighth century, abstinence from wine is mentioned by the Council of Rhispach as of equal obligation, for clerics, with the obligation of abstaining from flesh-meat on Wednesdays and Fridays,[102] and some years later this same abstinence is comprised among the obligations of an extraordinary fast imposed upon the whole Carolingian Empire.[103] Abstinence, not only from wine but from all intoxicating liquors, formed part of the special penance imposed upon homicides.[104]

For the great bulk of the people abstinence from wine was not obligatory to the same degree. Theodulf of Orleans holds that this practice is a mark of great virtue. The general prohibition of wine appears for the last time, but as peculiar to Friday, in the narration which Raoul Glaber has left us of the reforms brought about at the time

[101] "Et a quibusdam etiam nec vinum bibitur." *Loc cit.* BRUNS, t. I, 227.

[102] The text has already been cited above, p. 280.

[103] "Ut omnes a vino et carne his tribus diebus abstineant." *Epist. Caroli ad Ghaerbaldum* (807). BORETIUS, t. I, 245. Cf. *Rihcolfi ad Eginon. epist., ib.,* 249.

[104] Cf. *Capitularia, passim.* BORETIUS, t. II, 189, 244, 245.

of terror about the year one thousand.[105] Wine, pure or diluted with water, was part of the regular fare of the monks, and the scholastic theologians did not forbid it on fast-days even outside of meals. *A fortiori,* they permitted other liquors, syrups and the juice of apples or other fruit, which the Fathers of the fourth and fifth centuries had condemned as delicacies.

If a comparative table were drawn up of the foods permitted on fast-days in the first five centuries and those allowed to-day, the decline which the ecclesiastical discipline has undergone in this matter would cause surprise. The Orientals have shown themselves more faithful to the tradition of the first centuries in the matter of fast and abstinence. Nevertheless, the decline in the Latin Church is not to be condemned, since it has been regulated by the Holy See, and the Westerners on the whole are no less virtuous than their brethren of the East. In the house of our Heavenly Father there are many mansions and all the members of the family have not the same gifts nor the same mission. It is the Holy Ghost who distributes the gifts and determines the mission; by obeying Him in the manner fixed for each one, His glory will be equally procured by all.

The Penalties.—In gradually authorizing mitigations of discipline the Church ceded only inch

[105] See above, p. 284.

by inch. The penalties incurred by those who violated the precept of fasting have been indicated above. Severe punishments were likewise incurred by those who did not keep abstinence. In England, at the end of the seventh century, the Council of Berkhampstead imposed a penalty on all those who ate flesh meat on fast-days.[196]

The Capitularies of Charlemagne are still more severe, and their severity can only be explained by remembering that contempt of abstinence among the Saxons was equivalent to apostasy and that apostasy in this case usually resulted in revolt against the king and in civil war. Contempt of Lent, when it partook of the nature of ridicule of the Christian religion, was punished by death. But the priests conscientiously examined each case and excused those who had disobeyed through compulsion.[107]

No other legislation showed a like severity. The laws of King Canute, like the Council of Berkhampstead, inflicted a fine or stripes.[108] Eccle-

[106] "Si quis servis suis in jejunio carnem det, tam liberis quam servis collistrigium redimat.—Si servus ederit carnem sua sponte, eligat sex solidos, vel cutem suam poenae loco." *Conc. Berghamsted.* (697), c. xv et xvi. Bruns, t. II, 312.

[107] "Si quis sanctum quadragesimale jejunium pro despectu christianitatis contempserit et carnem comederit, morte moriatur; sed tamen consideretur a sacerdote, ne forte causa necessitatis hoc cuilibet proveniat ut carnem comedat." *Capitulatio de Partibus Saxoniae,* c. iv. Boretius, t. I, 68.

[108] "Malum est tempore veri jejunii ante prandium edere, et

siastical laws inflicted purely spiritual penalties, generally excommunication.[109] At other times they punish confessors who had shown excessive leniency in dispensing from abstinence.[110]

The penalties for transgressing the precept of Saturday abstinence, promulgated by the Councils of Avignon, Lucca, Béziers, and Lavaur, have been mentioned above. Other councils tried to render impossible all excessive leniency on the part of priests, confessors, or pastors, by deciding that the bishops alone, or their vicars-general, could grant such dispensations.[111]

At the same time an attempt was made to maintain abstinence from flesh-meat more strictly. Two Spanish councils of the fourteenth century

adhuc pejus seipsum carne defoedare. Si servus hoc fecerit vapulet, vel pretium verberum pro ratione ejus quod factum est [luat]." c. xv. MANSI, t. XIX, 562.

[109] Cf. *Statuta Cenomanensia* (1247): "Sub poena excommunicationis inhibeant sacerdotes, maxime in tempore Quadragesimae praecedenti ne quis in dominica prima quadragesimae carnes manducare praesumat . . ." MANSI, t. XXIII, 750.—The same text is given by the Council of Cognac, about 1260, c. xx, *ib.*, 870. Cfr. *Conc. Terraconen.* (1329), c. lxxx, *ib.*, t. XXV, 875; *Conc. Salmanticen.* (1335), c. vii, *ib.*, 1052; *Conc. Vauren.* (1368), c. lxxxix, *ib.*, t. XXVI, 527.

[110] "Confessores autem religiosi vel saeculares, qui praeterquam in casu necessitatis urgentis licentiam alicui dederint carnes dictis jejuniis comedendi, graviori subjaceant disciplinae." *Conc. Terraconen.* (1329), c. lxx, *ib.*, t. XXV, 875. The Council of Lavaur, 1368, inflicts the same penalty, but makes an exception for the exempt religious, against whom it can do nothing. *Loc. supra cit.*

[111] Cf. the Council of Bourges, of 1584, tit. VIII, c. iv.

blamed the butchers. Venders and buyers alike were excommunicated *ipso facto* if they publicly bought or sold meat on Ember Days or during Lent.[112] For a dispensation the testimonies of two doctors, one of the soul and another of the body are required, in order that the physician of the body, who is generally accused of being too lenient, be not the sole judge in a matter so vitally affecting the soul. Nay more, the bishops demand the power to punish physicians who exceed their faculties in this matter, and even cooks who prepare forbidden dishes on fast-days. As for the sick, meats and other like dishes destined for them could be sold only in private places and to those who presented a written permission from both physician and pastor or at least from the pastor.[113]

If, in spite of these efforts, the Church was not able to keep the observance of abstinence intact, even during Lent, and had to maintain respect for the law by dispensations at a time when the world was still profoundly Christian, there need be no wonder that in our age the bishops ask them-

[112] "Vendentes etiam carnes publice, in supradictis temporibus, eo ipso sententiam excommunicationis incurrant." *Conc. Palentin.* (1322), xvi. MANSI, t. XXV, 711. "Vendentes vero vel ementes publice carnes temporibus supradictis, sint *ipso facto* sententia excommunicationis irretiti." *Conc. Salmanticen.* (1335), c. vii, *ib.*, 1052.

[113] Cf. *Conc. Sanctae Severinae* (1597), *de Jejuniis*. MANSI, t. XXXV, 1049. *Conc. Amalfitan.* (1597), *ib.*, 1095.

selves whether it would not be better to unify the whole discipline of abstinence by reducing its requirements to a minimum. In her indults for Latin America and the negro populations of the New World, the Church went to the extreme of relaxation; but there is reason to believe that she will firmly maintain the law of abstinence as it exists to-day in the Christian countries of the Old World. Never will the Church suffer her maternal love for the people who are confided to her care to degenerate into blind weakness.

CHAPTER IX

THE PRECEPT OF CONTRIBUTING TO THE SUPPORT OF CHURCH AND PASTOR

French catechisms have omitted for the last hundred years one of the commandments of the Church much insisted upon in preceding centuries and which is still enforced, in some form or other, in those countries where the support of the clergy is not entirely insured by the State; at present, French Catholics, too, need again to be reminded of it. We wish to speak of tithes, not however in the sense of a definite tax, as it was understood in former times:

Hors le temps, noces ne feras,
payant les dîmes justement; [1]

or as expressed in French-Canadian catechisms:

Droits et dîmes tu paieras
à l'Église fidèlement; [2]

but in the sense given it, for instance, in the cate-

---

[1] Out of season weddings thou shalt not solemnize,
   Justly paying the tithes.
[2] Dues and tithes thou shalt pay
   To the Church faithfully.

chisms commonly used in the United States: *i.e.*, to contribute to the support of the Church and the ministers of worship.[3] To recall this commandment is by no means an innovation, for there is no commandment on which the Church has insisted more strongly, nor is there any whose existence is proved by more numerous, if not more ancient, testimonies.

The historians of ecclesiastical discipline trace the precept of paying tithes to the very beginning of the Church. Thomassin finds its first application in the act of those early Christians who sold their goods and gave the proceeds to the Apostles for their own support and that of the poor. He says: "One who gives all he has, undoubtedly gives more than first-fruits and tithes."[4] Still the bearing of this example must not be exaggerated. It can hardly be said to be the origin of the tithes with all the characteristics that precept later assumed, in particular the note of obligation. The Christians of Jerusalem, while they gave an admirable example, and performed an eminently meritorious act of charity, were not conscious, nor had they the intention of laying down the foundation of a new law which would indefinitely bind them and their successors.

[3] See in particular the catechisms of Färber and Deharbe.
[4] *Ancienne et Nouvelle Discipline de l'Église*, 3rd part, l. I, c. 1.

The Principle.—The conduct of the primitive Christians nevertheless was very significant. It implied, so to speak, the principle of the tithe; *i.e.* an obligation which the Church accepted and which she afterwards imposed on all. If the faithful wished to be benefited, whenever they deemed it necessary, by the spiritual ministrations of the clergy, they had to supply them with the necessary means of support. The preachers and Apostles could not devote themselves entirely to their mission if they were absorbed by the daily cares of material life. The Christians understood this, and St. Paul more than once took care to recall the fact to those who were tempted to forget it. "If we have sown unto spiritual things, is it a great matter if we reap your carnal things? If others be partakers of this power over you, why not we rather? So also the Lord ordained that they who preach the gospel should live by the gospel. And let him that is instructed in the word communicate to him that instructeth him in all good things."[5]

The name of this new contribution was indicated in the Mosaic Law. The Levites were supported by the tithes paid them by the other tribes; the voluntary offerings of the Christians would be the tithe insuring the necessities of life for the Levites of the New Law. Thus the ministers of the Gos-

[5] I *Cor.* ix; *Galat.* vi, 6.

pel could devote themselves entirely to the salvation of souls and live only for the Holy Sacrifice and the altar. Such was already the teaching of St. Cyprian.[6]

No doubt still other motives induced the leaders of the hierarchy to make the support of the clergy a charge upon the faithful. The example of Paul of Samosata, whose office of procurator added secular to his spiritual cares, and who by reason of his high salary acquired a dangerous independence, must have been a striking lesson.

But these considerations of an inferior order were scarcely needed. Before Paul of Samosata and even before St. Cyprian, Origen had pointed out in Holy Writ the proof of the duties of Christians concerning the tithes. In his eleventh homily on the Book of Numbers he sets forth his theory regarding the first-fruits and tithes. "It is proper and useful to offer the first-fruits to the priests of the Gospel. The Lord has willed that those who preach the Gospel should live by the Gospel, and that those who minister at the altar should receive their share thereof." From the first-fruits he passes to the tithes, and recalls the texts of the Gospel where Jesus Christ, reproaching His bitter enemies, the Pharisees, with vice and

[6] "Sed in honore sportulantium fratrum tanquam decimas ex fructibus accipientes, ab altari et sacrificiis non recedent." ST. CYPRIAN, *Epist*. LXVI. Migne, *P. L.*, t. IV, 398-399.

hypocrisy, pronounces this malediction upon them: "Woe unto you, scribes and hypocrites, Pharisees, who tithe mint and rue and every herb; and pass over all that is more important in the law—justice, mercy and faithfulness!" And where the Master says to His disciples: "Unless your justice abound more than that of the scribes and Pharisees, you shall not enter into the kingdom of Heaven." Origen continues in these terms: "That which Christ exacts of the Pharisees, He exacts all the more of Christians, and that which He does not wish His disciples to do, He does not require of the Pharisees. How, therefore, would our justice be greater than that of the Scribes and Pharisees if, while these enemies of the Saviour dare not touch the fruits of their land until they have offered the first-fruits to the priests and separated the tithes for the Levites, we would not imitate them but use the fruits of the earth without giving a share to the priests or the holy altars."[7]

[7] "Decet enim et utile est etiam sacerdotibus Evangelii offerri primitas. Ita enim et Dominus disposuit, ut qui Evangelium annuntiant, de Evangelio vivant, et qui altari deserviunt, de altari participent. . . . Quod ergo vult fieri a Pharisaeis multo magis et majore cum abundantia vult a discipulis impleri; quod autem fieri a discipulis non vult, nec Pharisaeis imperat faciendum. . . . Quomodo ergo abundat justitia nostra plus quam Scribarum et Pharisaeorum, si illi de fructibus terrae suae gustare non audent priusquam primitias sacerdotibus offerant et levitis decimas seperant; et ego nihil horum faciens fructibus terrae ita abutar ut

During the age of persecution, when the clergy were the first to be persecuted, and the charity of the faithful so unfailingly came to the aid of the confessors, there was no need to recall the obligation of supporting the clergy. But by those very practices the obligation became better accepted, its theoretical side was emphasised, and more and more, to designate this obligation, the term tithe was employed with its full meaning. A "tenth" expressed the minimum, for the laity were in duty bound to supply the clergy with all that is necessary for their maintenance, even should this require more than the tithe. Such is the opinion of St. Jerome, who draws his arguments from both the Old and the New Testament. "If I am," says he, "the portion of the Lord, like the Levites and priests, I have a right to the offerings made to the altar."[8]

We shall not quote the texts which are commonly ascribed to St. Ambrose and St. Augustine, for although they have found a place in Gratian,

sacerdos nesciat, levites ignoret, divinum altare non sentiat." Migne, *P. G.*, t. XII, 640-645.

[8] "Si ego pars Domini sum et funiculus haereditatis ejus, nec accipio partem inter caeteras tribus, sed quasi levita et sacerdos vivo de decimis, et altari serviens altaris oblatione sustentor." *Ad Nepotian. de Vita Clericor.*, no 5. *P. L.*, t. XXII, 531. Cf. *In Malach.*, c. iii.: "Quod de decimis primitiisque diximus, quae olim dabantur a populo sacerdotibus ac levitis, in Ecclesiae quoque populis intelligite." *Ib.*, t. XXV, 1571; *In Matth.*, c. xxii, *Reddite ergo quae sunt Caesaris . . . ib.*, t. XXVI, 163; *In Epist. ad Tit.*, c. lxvii, Caus. XVI, quest. I, in Gratian's Decretum.

their authenticity is doubtful.[9] But as to the obedience of the faithful to these prescriptions, there can be no doubt; and more than one of the ecclesiastical writers of this period might have said what Julian Pomerius said later (about A. D. 500) in his *De Vita Contemplativa:* "We receive with joy the daily offerings and tithes of the faithful."[10] These oblations and tithes were given not only to the clergy, as rightly their due, but to the hermits of the desert as well. At times even the monks thought that they had a right to them and demanded a share in the offerings made to the Church, without awaiting the consent of the bishop or of the administrators appointed by him. So that it was necessary to raise against them protestations like those of the Council of Gangres[11] and the Canons of the Apostles.[12]

This interference shows that the principle of the tithe had been generally accepted. We have another interesting testimony. St. Gregory of Nyssa describes his mother as offering to God as firstfruits and tithe two of her children, the eldest and the tenth.

But these are not juridical texts. They show

[9] See the notes of Friedberg in his edition of the *Corpus Juris,* Cause XVI, quest. I, c. lxvi sqq.; quest. VII, c. iv and viii.

[10] "Lac et lanas ovium Christi, oblationibus quotidianis ac decimis fidelium gaudentes accipimus." Lib. I, c. xxi. Migne, *P. L.,* t. LIX, 437.

[11] Can. vii and viii.

[12] Can. iv.

that the clergy and the monks were supported by the contributions of the faithful, as the priests and Levites of the Ancient Law, but not that there was an express legal obligation for every Christian to give a tenth of his possessions or income to the Church or to the clergy. The word tithe, applied to these contributions, is after all only a metaphor, at least in the East. In Gaul, at the time of St. Caesarius, the term is used seemingly in its strict sense, though it has not yet become the real tithe of a later age; for the duty of paying the tithe is identical with the duty of being charitable; this contribution is described by St. Caesarius as a kind of premium paid to God to insure His protection. The Bishop of Arles addresses his diocesans as follows: "Give the tithes of your harvests each year to the Church and to the poor." He adds that good Christians should not limit themselves to giving the tenth part of their crops, but should give the surplus of the remaining nine-tenths to the poor; and in order to suppress all objections, he repeats: "How dare you refuse the tithe to God who has given you all?" The principal argument he employs is the following: "You wish to use your surplus for your children or for buying precious objects. Very well, these shall be bought, but you will not absolve yourselves from your sins. The tithes, besides, are not your property, they belong to the

Church." [13] "That which you had no desire to give to the priest, you shall one day be obliged to give to a merciless soldier." [14]

This idea of the tithe as a means of obtaining pardon for one's sins and insuring oneself against adversity and temporal loss, crops out repeatedly in this and the following century. Read for instance the following document, a collective letter sent by four bishops of the province of Tours to their people, after the Council held in that metropolis in 567. The prospect was dark and the most dreadful calamities seemed to threaten. In these circumstances the four bishops of Tours, Angers, Nantes, and Le Mans, wrote a collective letter to their people to invite them to do penance and seek forgiveness of their sins. They tell them that the alms they will give will be a guarantee against misfortune: for to spend a portion of their goods

---

[13] "Decimas annis singulis de omni fructu quod colligitis Ecclesiis et pauperibus erogate." *Serm.* 244 inter Opp. S. August. Migne, *P. L.*, t. XXXIX, 2195.—Cf. *Serm.* 276, n° 2: "Ac sic non solum decimas dare debemus, sed etiam de novem partibus, quidquid solutis vel expletis sumptibus nostris remanserit, quasi aliis transmissum fideliter erogare debemus. . . . Et tamen, fratres, non video qua fronte illi non offerimus decimum, a quo accepimus totum." *Ib.*, 2265.—*Serm.* 308, n° 2: "Sed tu forte respondes et dicis: Ex eo quod mihi Deus amplius dederit, quam opus sit, volo filiis et filiabus meis argentum emere, ornamenta pretiosissima comparare. Cui ego respondeo: Ornamenta quidem emis, sed peccata non redimis . . . decimae non sunt nostrae sed Ecclesiae deputatae." *Ib.*, 2336.

[14] "Dabis impio militi quod non vis dare sacerdoti." *Homil.* 16. Migne, *P. L.*, t. LXVII, 1079.

thus, is to insure the safety of the remainder. "Give," say the bishops, "like Abraham, the tithe of what you possess, in order to preserve the rest; not to give is to expose yourselves to the loss of all; give, if necessary, even the tithes of your slaves."[15]

The Law.—We cannot deduce from these texts the existence of a law properly so-called. We do not wish to say that no such law existed prior to the year 567, but merely that it would be difficult to prove.

A really conclusive text is furnished by the Council of Mâcon in 585. It is a text of great importance, both as to contents and manner of expression. In the eyes of the bishops assembled at Mâcon, the tithe is not simply an old custom unhappily fallen into disuse; it is an obligation imposed by divine law, which has been forsaken and which it is the duty of the bishops to recall and enforce. The Council decrees that the ancient custom shall be revived and the tithe paid by all the people under pain of excommunication.[16]

---

[15] "Illud vero instantissime commonemus, ut Abrahae documenta sequentes, decimas ex omni facultate non pigeat Deo pro reliquis quae possidetis, conservandis offerre, ne sibi ipse inopiam generet, qui parva non tribuit, ut plura retentet. Ut etiam unusquisque de suis mancipiis decimas persolvere non recuset." MAASSEN, *Concilia Aevi Merovingici*, p. 137, 138.

[16] Because of its importance I shall give the whole text of that canon: "Omnes igitur reliquas fidei sanctae catholicae causas, quas temporis longitudine cognovimus deterioratas fuisse, oportet

Though the bishops overemphasized the value of ancient texts, they were perfectly within their rights in contending that the paying of tithes was an ancient custom which only the lukewarm had neglected; for zealous Christians had never failed to do their duty on this point. The biographer of St. Radegundis remarks that that pious queen faithfully paid the tithe of all that was given her even before she had received it. Others with less spontaneous fidelity decided to pay the tithe in thanksgiving for favors obtained by the intercession of the saints, especially of St. Martin.

Probably after the Council of Mâcon the "ancient custom" was revived and people paid their dues more generously. The royal power, without precisely confirming by its authority the obliga-

nos ad statum pristinum revocare, ne nos novis simus adversarii, dum ea, quae cognoscimus ad nostri ordines qualitatem pertinere, aut non corregimus aut, quod nefas est, silentio praeterimus. Legis itaque divinae consolentes sacerdotibus ac ministris ecclesiarum pro hereditaria portione omni populum preciperunt decimas fructuum suorum locis praestare, ut nullo labore impediti horis legitimis spiritalibus possint vacare misteriis, quas legis christianorum congeries longis temporibus custodivit intemeratas. Nunc autem paulatim praevaricatores legum peni christiani omnes ostenduntur, dum ea, quae divinitus sancita sunt, adimplere neglegunt. Unde statuimus ac decernimus, ut mos antiquus a fidelibus reparetur et decimas ecclesiasticis famulantibus ceremoniis populos omnis inferat, quas sacerdotes aut in pauperum usibus aut captivorum redemptionem prerogantis suis orationibus populo pacem ac salutem impetrent. Si quis autem contumax nostris statutis saluberrimis fuerit, a membris Ecclesiae omni tempore separetur." MAASSEN, *op. cit.*, 166-167.

SUPPORT OF CHURCH AND PASTOR

tion recalled by the bishops, showed profound sympathy for the Church and granted her valuable immunities, which could not fail to have the force of a good example.[17]

The Carolingian Epoch.—Under the Carolingian régime the tithe attained its full development as a fiscal obligation. If the Council of Mâcon had given it the character of a strict canonical obligation, binding under pain of excommunication, the capitularies from Pepin to Louis le Débonnaire made it an obligation confirmed by civil law. One of the most ancient Carolingian decrees invokes the support of both the ecclesiastical law and civil authority. This decree belongs to a Bavarian council held in 756, whose decrees are prefaced by a short letter to the young Duke Tassilo, whose aid is asked repeatedly, in particular with regard to the tithes. As many sought to avoid this obligation, (which seems at that time well known and firmly established,) under specious pretexts such as the faults of the pastor to whom the tithe must be paid; the Council asks the Duke to confirm the penalty decided upon, which consists in doubling the amount of the tax, and to proceed against those who persist in their disobedience.[18]

[17] See for example the *Praeceptio Clotarii II* (584-628), c. xi. *Capitularia* (Boretius), t. I, 19.

[18] "De decimis Deo reddendis profeta testatur, ut si quis decimam non dederit, ad decimam revertatur. Unde venit (*al.* unde

The protection which the bishops of Bavaria asked from Duke Tassilo was received in a most efficacious way by all the bishops of the Carolingian empire from Charlemagne and his successors. The principle itself, that the State should support the demands of the Church, was one of the first accepted in a general way throughout the empire. A capitulary of 787 said that the tithes should be paid in full by all under pain of a six sous fine.[19] Another regulated the same point especially for those churches which were royal property; the imperial judges were to give example by faithfully paying the tithe to these churches, and by paying it also to other churches that had a long established right to receive it.[20] Others [21] again imposed upon the priest the duty of instructing the faithful in

convenit), ut quicumque aut occasione presbyteri aut avaritiae modo Deo decimas reddere noluerit, ut manus vestrae decretus confirmetur, ut dupliciter ecclesiae censum reddatur et ut vestrae requerillae secundum possibilitatem culpabilis existant." *Conc. Ascheimen.*, c. v. *Monum. German., Concilia*, t. II, p. 57.

[19] "Ut decime pleniter dentur: et a quibus retente sunt, de prima contentu sit culpavilis qui eas retinuit solidos sex, ipsa decima sub juramento." *Capitula de rebus ecclesiasticis*, c. iii. BORETIUS, t. I, p. 186.

[20] "Volumus ut judices nostri decimam ex omni conlaboratu pleniter donent ad ecclesias quae sunt in nostris fiscis, et ad alterius ecclesiam nostra decima data non fiat, nisi ubi antiquitus institutum fuit." *Capitulare de Villis*, c. vi, *ib.*, p. 83.

[21] "Ut unusquisque sacerdos cunctos sibi pertinentes erudiat ut sciant qualiter decimas totius facultatis ecclesiis divinis debite offerant." *Capitula a sacerdotibus proposita*, c. vi, *ib.*, p. 106.

this matter, or mentioned the imperial orders given to the *missi* relative to the tithes.[22]

The most important document of this kind is assuredly that of the general capitulary of Mantua, given by Charlemagne and Pepin about 787. It goes into minute practical details. "If the payment of the tithes is refused in a parish," it says, "it is the duty of the officers of the State to enforce its payment. Four or eight men, or as many as may be necessary, shall be chosen in each parish, and they shall act as witnesses for the priest and the people in order to ascertain who has not paid the tithes. The negligent ones shall be notified by the priests of the church, as many as three times, to pay their contribution, under pain of being excluded; if they do not obey, the officers of the State shall intervene and impose on each of them a fine of five sous in addition to the tithe; if they persist in their disobedience their houses shall be occupied by public authority until the stipulated sum has been paid in full. If this does not suffice and they still refuse, they shall be thrown into prison, until in presence of the Count they consent to a settlement, and pay the tithe and the six sous fine they owe the Church." [23]

[22] Cf. *Capitularia missorum specialia* (802), c. xvii, *ib.*, 101; *Capitulare missorum* (808), c. vii, *ib.*, 140.

[23] I reproduce here the entire text of that important capitulary: "De decimis ut dentur, et dare nolentes secundum quod anno praeterito denuntiatum est a ministris reipublicae exigantur. Id est,

The Church authorities proceeded along the same lines. The bishops, who had the right to inflict fines, invoked arguments of a less material nature, but the chastisements which they threatened to inflict were not always purely spiritual. Experience had shown, they said, that refusal to pay the tithes was punished by God with fearful temporal chastisements. "Whole harvests have been devoured and pillaged by the demons," says a Council of Frankfort (794), and when the harvesters, deceived by the fine appearance of what remained, wished to gather the corn, no one could

eligantur quatuor vel octo homines, vel prout opus fuerit, de singulis plebibus juxta qualitatem, ut ipsi inter sacerdotes et plebem testes existant ubi date vel non date fuerint: hoc ideo, ne ibi juramentum aliquod faciendi necessitas contingat. Non tamen ideo tantos testes mittendos dicimus, ut ipsi semper in dandis decimis praesentes esse pariter necesse sit, sed ut dum pluribus committitur minus graventur; in duobus autem, si affuerint, sufficere credimus. Neglegentes autem ammoneantur a presbyteris ecclesiarum usque ad tertiam vicem ut ipsam decimam dent; quod si contempserint, ab introitu ecclesiae prohibeantur; et si in hoc minime emendaverint, a ministris reipublice districti singuli per caput sex solidos ecclesiae componant et insuper decima dare cogantur. Nam si iterum contemptores extiterint, tunc per publicam auctoritatem domus vel case eorum wiffentur, quousque pro ipsa decima sicut supra dictum satisfaciant. Quod si denuo rebelles vel contradictores esse voluerint, ut super ipsam wiffam suam auctoritatem intrare praesumpserint, tunc a ministris reipublice in custodia mittantur, usque dum ad judicium publicum perducantur, et ibi secundum legem contra comitem vel parte publica componant. Reliqua autem, ut supra dictum est, de decimis et sex solidis contra ecclesiam satisfaciant." *Capitulare Mantuanum secundum generale*, c. viii. *Capitularia* (Boretius), t. I, 197.

eat it, and mocking voices were heard without anyone being seen."[24] The Council of Friuli in the course of a long exhortation mixed threats based on the prophecies of the Old Testament with hopes founded on the goodness of God.[25]

Unfortunately, these efforts do not seem to have achieved very great results. The bishops no doubt attributed their lack of success to the fact that the efforts had not been made simultaneously throughout the whole empire. In 813, a collective effort was made. By order of the Emperor, who wished to give something like a new constitution to his States, the bishops came together in five councils (Arles, Rheims, Mayence, Chalon, and Tours), of which the first three were held at about the same time and presided over by imperial delegates (*missi*). Among the matters treated in these episcopal assemblies that of the tithes was naturally one. Five councils occupied themselves with it, although somewhat differently, according to the special needs of each region and the tendencies of the episcopal body. The Councils of Arles and Rheims were content with simply recalling the known obligation of paying this contribu-

[24] "Ut decimas et nonas sive census omnes generaliter donent, qui debitores sunt ex beneficio et rebus ecclesiarum secundum priorum capitulorum domni regis, et omnis homo ex sua proprietate legitimam decimam ad ecclesiam conferat. Experimento enim didicimus in anno, quo illa valida famis inrepsit, ebullire vacuas anonas a daemonibus devoratas et voces exprobrationis auditas."

tion.[26] But the Council of Mayence threatened the same divine chastisements which the Council of Frankfort had already mentioned, and added another consideration, on which Caesarius of Arles had insisted three centuries before: *viz.:* that the tithe is a sort of insurance premium against the divine wrath.[27] At Tours it seems the situation was still more serious, in fact almost hopeless. Not content with the refusal to pay the ordinary tithe, conscienceless tenants refused to pay even the rent for church lands let to them and the revenues from which were destined exclusively for the maintenance of the clergy and the lighting of the church. The demands made in a plea to the imper-

Concil. Francofurten. (794), c. xxv.—(There is question in this last phrase of a terrible famine which occurred in 793, when mothers devoured their own children: "Famis . . . in tantum excrevit . . . ut homines homines, fratres fratres ac matres filios comedere coegit. Ostensa autem eodem anno in ipso regno per diversa loca verno tempore falsa annona per campos et silvas atque paludes innumera multitudo, quam videre et tangere poterant, sed comedere nullus." *Monum. German. Historica, Concilia Aevi Carolini,* p. 168-169). For the sake of brevity I shall hereafter cite this collection under the initials *M. G., Concilia,* t. II.

[25] *Concil. Forojulien.* (796-797), c. xiv, *ib.,* 195.

[26] "Ut unusquisque de propriis laboribus decimas et primitias Deo offerat, sicut scriptum est: *Decimas et primitias tuas non tardabis offerre Domino Deo tuo* (Exod. xxii, 29)." *Conc. Arelaten.* c. ix. *Ib.* 251. Cf. *Conc. Remen.* c. xxxviii. *Ib.* 257.

[27] "Ammonemus atque praecipimus, ut decima Deo omnino dari non neglegatur, quam Deus ipse sibi dari constituit, quia timendum est, ut quisquis Deo suum debitum abstrahit, ne forte Deus per peccatum suum auferat ei necessaria sua." c. xxxviii. *Ib.* 270.

ial *missi* remained fruitless. Indolence reigned everywhere and the churches were left to fall into ruins.[28]

This dark picture is apt to give us a poor opinion of the faithful of that period. Perhaps, however, they were not the only guilty ones. Bishops and abbots, through a lamentable abuse of power, forbade their tenants to bring their contributions to the pastor of the territory in which their land was located. The Council of Chalon had to recall the rule that the tithes should be paid to the parochial clergy. Others committed still graver excesses, and together with the Counts, accepted bribes from those who refused to pay the tithe.[29]

The efforts of the five councils mentioned undoubtedly brought results, for the first capitularies of Louis the Pious insist rather on certain specifications than on the principle of the tithe, which appears to be generally accepted. Many thought that the tithe was only due on the fruits of the earth, and that the product of personal labor and the increase from animals were exempt. At other times the bishops preferred to receive the tithe in money rather than in kind. The emperor

---

[28] *Conc. Turon.* c. xlvi. *Ib.* 292.

[29] "Dictum est nobis, quod in quibusdam locis, episcopi et comites . . . ab his qui decimas non dant, wadios accipiant . . . quod paenitus abolendum decrevimus . . . et constituimus, ut . . . qui decimas post crebras admonitiones et praedicationes sacerdotum dare neglexerint excommunicentur." c. xviii.—"Questi sunt prae-

decided that these contributions were to be assessed not only on the harvests, wine, pastures, and fields, but also on the products of personal labor and on the increase from animals, and that the bishop could exact the tithe in money.[30]

But soon new complaints were heard. The capitulary of Worms (829) speaks of people who have altogether or partly neglected to pay the tithes and double-tithes [31] for many years, and decides that the imperial *missi* shall compel them to pay first the tithe and, besides, the imperial *bannus*. Should they refuse or continue to be negligent, the income on which the tithe was due shall be taken from them.[32]

These threats had no more effect than the previous measures. A few years after the Council of Worms the situation became more deplorable still. It even seems that the special tithe, due for the use of ecclesiastical goods, is the most neglected of all,

terea quidam fratres, quod essent aliqui episcopi et abbates, qui decimas non sinerent dare ad ecclesias, ubi illi coloni missas audiunt. Proinde decrevit sacer iste conventus, ut episcopi et abbates de agris et vineis, quae ad suum vel fratrum stipendium habent, decimas ad ecclesias deferri faciant; familiae vero ibi dent decimas suas, ubi infantes eorum baptizantur, et ubi per totum anni circulum missas audiunt." c. xix. *Ib.* 277.

[30] Cf., in particular, *Capitula per sex scribenda*, c. v. *Monum. Germ., Capitularia*, t. I, 287, and *Admonitio ad omnes regni ordines* (823-825) c. xxiii, *Ib.* 307.

[31] Those who occupied lands belonging to the Church owed a special tithe in addition to the regular tithe.

[32] *Capitulare Wormatiense*, c. v. *M. G., Capitularia*, t. II, 13.

for the most severe penalties are enforced against those who refuse to pay it. The Council of Meaux complains that, because of such negligence, the clergy are starving, church buildings are falling into ruins, and the bondmen of the Church are persecuted. The guilty ones are threatened with excommunication until they mend their ways, and if they refuse, the royal authority shall force them, even after excommunication, to surrender those benefices on which they did not pay tithes.[33]

Let it be remembered, on behalf of the poor payers, that the circumstances were anything but propitious. The continuous wars of Louis the Pious with his sons, and of his sons among themselves, the invasions of the Britons in the western part of the empire, and the depredations they committed, weighed heavily on the people. As for those in power, they disregarded the purely spiritual threat of ecclesiastical penalties, and if the

[33] "Hi vero, qui ex rebus ecclesiasticis nonas et decimas persolvere et sarta tecta ecclesiae secundum antiquam auctoritatem et consuetudinem restaurare debent et hoc non solum neglegunt, verum et per contemptum dimittunt atque clericos fame ac penuria obprimunt, ecclesiastica quoque aedificia dissolutione adnullari permittunt, tamdiu ab ecclesiastica communione separentur, usque dum diligentia emendare studeant, quod socordia neglexerunt. Quod si iterum iteraverint, post excommunicationis satisfactionem regia potestate compulsi juxta legale et antiquum dictum 'qui neglegit censum, perdat agrum.' Servi autem ecclesiarum quibuscumque potestatibus subditi, unde melior consuetudo vel devotior commendatio ex tempore et jussione domni Hludowici vel certe domni Karoli seu etiam Pipini absque molestia servire sinantur." *Concil. Melden.* (845), c. lxiii. *Ibid.* 413.

imperial magistrates tried to inflict upon them the civil penalties indicated by the law, they simply exposed themselves to cruel vengeance calculated to discourage any further attempt. It was useless for the capitularies to recommend these officers to place the fear of God and the love of justice above everything else, when the power of the State did not protect them against the attacks of men.[34]

We shall merely mention in a foot-note the texts which confirm the discipline and renew the threat of excommunication against the refractory ones, or recall the thought of divine chastisements.[35] There is a curious decree of the capitulary of Kiersy (877) which discriminates between Jewish and Christian merchants and decides that the former shall pay a tenth and the latter only an eleventh.[36]

[34] "De decimis, . . . quicumque neglexerit, canonico judicio corrigatur; et qui in hoc aliquid contrasteterit, sciat se nostra imperiali auctoritate emendandum. Judices namque commoneantur Dei timorem ante oculos habere, et pro nulla persona justitiam immutare audeant, sed quod verum est, justissime perquirant et veraciter judicent." *Hludowici II Capitulare* (850), c. iii. *Ib.* 84.

[35] *Conc. Valentin. III* (855), c. x. MANSI, t. XV, 9; *Conc. Ticinen.* (876), c. xix. MANSI, t. XVII, 328; *Conc. Moguntin.* (888), c. xvii et xxii. (This speaks of the Christians who defrauded in regard to the quantity in the proportion of five to one.) *Ib.* t. XVIII, 68-70; *Conc. Triburien.* (895), c. xiv et xv. *Mon. Germ., Capitularia,* t. II, 221, 222; *Conc. Calchuten.* (787), c. xvii. MANSI, t. XII, 946.

[36] "Et de cappis (See the note in the *Monumenta Germaniae* which explains this word as meaning *circumcised*) et aliis negotia-

As if the attachment of each individual to his own possessions did not offer a sufficient obstacle to the payment of that onerous assessment, new ones arose in the rivalries of the priests and the avarice of the lords. The former went outside their circumscribed limits to demand the tithe which was not due to them and thereby deprived the legitimate beneficiaries of it, or even went so far as to steal it without heeding in the least the excommunication which threatened them;[37] others were satisfied with claiming a part of the tithe received by the pastor.[38] And in many other ways did the rich and the poor endeavor to cut down the tithes they owed to the churches, robbing some clerics to enrich others![39]

As we have seen, neither the Church nor the imperial power had been able to compel the full payment of these contributions. There is even reason to believe that the threatened excommunication was never enforced. The ground of this belief is a text in the *Examen Confessarii* of Burchard's Penitential, which Msgr. Schmitz and Ballerini call "the Penitential of the German churches." Neglect to pay the tithes is visited

toribus, videlicet ut Judaei dent decimam et negotiatores christiani undecimam." *Capitulare Carisiacense*, c. xxxi. Mon. German., Capitular., t. II, 361.

[37] *Concil. Ravennen.* (877), c. xviii. MANSI, t. XVII, 340.
[38] *Concil. Meten.* (888), c. ii. MANSI, t. XVIII, 78.
[39] *Conc. Confluentin.* (922), c. viii. *Ib.* 346.

with a twofold punishment, *viz.* a payment four times larger than that originally due and twenty days' penance on bread and water.[40]

The gathering of the tithes was therefore the occasion of incessant conflicts between the Christian populace and its priests. Undoubtedly all did not refuse to pay that sacred tax whose *raison d'être*, usefulness, and even absolute necessity they understood; but the resistance of nominal Christians, the successful encroachments of those in power, and the fraudulent practices of a large number constituted a deplorable example for the great bulk of the lukewarm. Still the privation of legitimate revenues was sometimes a lesser evil than the troubles caused by too exacting demands. Peaceful bishops, like Herard of Tours, understood this and exhorted their clergy to be satisfied with warning and urging and to avoid quarrels and lawsuits.[41]

During all this time, while the obligation of pay-

[40] "Neglexisti decimam tuam Deo dare, quam Deus ipse sibi dari constituit, id est non dedisti ei decimam de cunctis fructibus tuis, quos tu ad tuos usus collegere desiderasti, vel collegisti, et de cunctis tuis animalibus, et decimum animal quod Deo debueras dare, et quod suum erat, illud pejori commutasti? Si fecisti vel consensisti, Deo quod suum erat in quadruplum restitue, et viginti dies in pane et aqua debes poenitere." *Poenitentiale Ecclesiarum Germaniae*, n. 141, in SCHMITZ, *Die Bussbücher und die Bussdisciplin*, t. II, 440.

[41] "Nullus sacerdotum decimas cum lite et jurgio suscipiat, sed praedicatione et admonitione." HERARDI *Turonensis Capitul.* c. cxxxii. Migne, *P. L.*, t. CXXI, 773.

ing the tithe was strengthened in principle and determined in extent, the clergy were also instructed how it was to be employed and to whom it should go.

From the very beginning the oblations, the firstfruits, and all goods given to the Church were divided by the bishop between the clergy and the poor. Caesarius of Arles in the sixth century recommends this simpler method for the distribution of the tithes, though Pope Gelasius some years previously had recommended distribution of the revenues and offerings of the faithful into four parts; but neither of these methods appears to have been uniformly adopted in the distribution of the tithes. The first of the two capitularies of Mantua, the one purely ecclesiastical, specifies that of the tithes paid by the faithful to parochial or baptismal churches nothing is to be given to the principal or bishop's church.[42] Other texts show a division into four parts [43] (as when appeal was made to the decision of Gelasius), others

[42] "De decimis vero quae a populo in plebibus vel baptismalibus aecclesiis offeruntur nulla exinde pars majori aecclesiae vel episcopo inferatur." *Capitulare Mantuanum primum, mere ecclesiasticum*, c. xi. *Monum. Germun., Capitular.*, t. I, 195.

[43] "Ut decimae populi dividantur in quattuor partes, id est una pars episcopo, alia clericis, tertia pauperibus, quarta in ecclesiae fabricis applicetur, sicut in decretis pape Gelasii continetur." c. xxvii. (See the text of this decree in Gratian, c. XII, q. II, c. xxvii.) *Concil. Rispacen.* (800), c. xiii. *Mon. Germ., Concilia*, t. II, 209. Cf. *Arnonis Instructio pastoralis*, c. x. *Ib.* 200.

344 THE COMMANDMENTS OF THE CHURCH

into three,[44] and again others into two parts.[45]

We have spent much time, perhaps too much, on the Carolingian period. The reason is that the knowledge of this period is of the greatest importance for our question. Nearly the whole of the discipline of the tithe was definitively determined in the eighth and ninth centuries. The collectors of ecclesiastical canons, Regino and Burchard, inserted into their collections the texts of the Carolingian laws, and, except for modifications of comparatively little importance, it was under that form that the tithe was thereafter imposed, even outside the empire. This then was considered as certain: there were two kinds of tithes; the *real* tithe which was due on all the goods enumerated by the Council of Trosly: lands, vineyards, slaves, flocks (*pecuniis*), situated in the territory of the parish; and the *personal* tithe on all the profits of personal activity, booty of war, commerce, trade, profit accruing from wool-shearing and on all other gains.[46] This tithe was collected by the pastor,

[44] "Ut ipsi sacerdotes populi suscipiant decimas. . . . Et ad ornamentum aecclesiae primam elegant partem, secundam autem ad usum pauperum atque peregrinorum per eorum manus misericorditer cum omni humilitate dispensent, tertiam vero partem semetipsis solis sacerdotes reservent." *Capitula a sacerdotibus proposita* (802), c. vii. *Monum. German., Capitular.*, t. I, 106.

[45] *Concil. Turon.* (813), c. xvi. *M. German., Concilia*, t. II, 288.

[46] "Ea quae parochiis in terris, vineis, mancipiis atque pecuniis, et de militia, de negotio, de artificio, de lanarum tonsione et de caeteris quibuscumque sibi a Deo largitis commerciis." *Conc. Troslejan.* (909), c. vi. MANSI, t. XXIII, 283.

who had the duty of instructing the faithful on this as on other points, of recording the names of those who had paid him and making the prescribed distribution in the presence of witnesses.[47] The priest owed no tax whatever on the product of these taxes,[48] but those who possessed ecclesiastical goods, whether by royal or imperial grant, owed a tithe and a double tithe. Lastly we have noted the existence of a proportionate rate of assessment imposed upon the Jewish merchants and upon Christians.

Outside the Carolingian Empire.—The great name of Charlemagne, the power wielded by his successors, even when weakened by their dissensions, the marked personality of some bishops of the empire, all tended to impart special weight to the Carolingian decisions. We have already mentioned in the citations given above, an English council (*Calchutense*) which adopted the Carolingian regulations in regard to the tithe. Another, in the first third of the tenth century, promulgated an order by King Athelstane demanding the payment of the tithe on all possessions, commencing with his own, before the feast of the Beheading of St. John the Baptist.[49] Later on, to make mat-

[47] *Capitula a sacerdotibus proposita,* c. vii. *Mon. Germ., Capitul.,* t. I, 106.

[48] Cf. *Capitula singillatim tradita,* c. iv. *Ib.* 333. *Capitulare ecclesiasticum* c. x. *Ib.* 277.

[49] *Concil. Gratelean.* (about 930), c. i. MANSI, t. XVIII, 351.

ters easier, it was decided that payment was to be made at three different periods: the tithe on cultivation fifteen days after Easter; that on the increase of animals, calves and lambs, about Pentecost; that on the spontaneous fruits of the earth, around All Saints' Day.[50]

It is hardly necessary to add that the tithe was obligatory in the whole Church, in Rome, in Italy, in Dalmatia, in Austria, in Germany, as well as in England, Scotland and Ireland.[51] But while there is unanimity on this main point, the diverse temperament of these nations manifested itself in details. The Roman Council of 1059, for instance, decides that the tithes shall be at the disposal of the bishop; that of Seligenstadt (1022) ordains that if a slave abandon his master in order to escape paying the tithe, no one shall receive him and the master shall take possession of

[50] "Decimationes frugum et vitulorum, et agnorum, necnon et aratrales eleemosynae, ecclesiasticaque munera, domino per singulos annos temporibus rependantur congruis: eleemosynae videlicet aratrales quindecim diebus post Pascha peractis, vituli quoque et agniculi decimales erga Pentecosten; frugum vero terrae decimationes circa Omnium sanctorum ecclesiis persolvantur opportunis." *Conc. Ænhamen.* (1009), c. x. MANSI, t. XIX, 307.

[51] Cf. *Conc. Roman.* (1059), c. v. MANSI, *ib.* 898; *Conc. Cassilien.* (1172), c. iii, *ib.* t. XXII, 134; *Conc. London.* (1175 c. xiii et 1200 c. ix), *ib.* 150 et 718; *Conc. Saligunstadien.* c. xxii, *ib.* t. XIX, 399; *Conc. Scotticum* (1225), c. xxi et lxix, t. XXII, 1228 et 1242; *Conc. Viennen.* (1267), c. vii, *ib.* t. XXIII, 1172; *Constitution. Aquilejen.* (1339), *ib.* t. XXV, 1116; *Conc. Frisingen.* (1440), c. xi, *ib.* t. XXXII, 9; *Conc. Colonien.* (1536), pars VIII, c. vi, *ib.* 1270, etc., etc.

the goods which he has entrusted to him;[52] in England the tithe was so decidedly parochial that the constitutions of St. Edmund of Canterbury gave the pastor power to excommunicate and refuse Easter communion to those who did not pay it;[53] while in Austria, the usurpers were denied admission to the church.

After the Twelfth Century.—About the middle of the twelfth century, there appeared a collection of canons whose influence on the unification of discipline was destined to be considerable, *viz.* the *Concordia Discordantium Canonum* of Gratian, better known as *Decretum Gratiani*. This collection contains some twenty texts on our subject, of which, however, not all are authentic.[54] Although Gratian did not study the question from our point of view, but in its bearing on the controversy between monasteries and parishes, or with the in-

[52] "Quod omnes slavi decimas dent sicut ceteri christiani et ad hoc banno constringantur. Si vero propter hujusmodi constrictum dominum suum deseruerit aliquis, nemo illum suscipiat, immo omnium bonorum suorum prior dominus potestatem habeat." *Conc. Saligunstad.*, c. xx.

[53] "Concedimus etiam quod quilibet sacerdos parochialis detentores decimarum in sua parochia potestatem coercendi habeat: et si contumaces fuerint, et commoniti se non correxerint, excommunicandi. . . . Et sic nota quod quilibet sacerdos potest excommunicare pro decimis debitis non solutis. Et cum sit crimen decimas notorie debitas retinere: videtur quod notorie detinenti debitas vel alia jura debita ecclesiis possit in Paschate licite denegari corpus Christi." *Const. provinciales S. Edmundi*, c. xl. MANSI, t. XXIII, 428.

[54] Especially in Causa XVI, quaest. I and VII.

tention of showing that the laity had no right to the tithes, his compilation is none the less instructive and exercised an important influence on later discipline. Through the commentaries of later canonists, the discipline of the tithe and its penalties was rendered more uniform, until it became practically identical everywhere. Besides, the ancient texts which were cited gave a firmer basis to more recent diocesan ordinances or customs, and some bishops even cherished the hope that henceforth the obligation of paying the tithe, being better affirmed, would be more conscientiously fulfilled.

Those bishops were soon disillusioned. It is a far cry from the knowledge of a troublesome duty to its fulfillment. The complaints of negligence or ill-will on the part of the faithful did not diminish. Each succeeding century devised a new method of enforcing the tithe and each in turn has left us ample evidence that the new means proved inefficacious. The two methods practiced most were warning in the confessional and imposing upon all preachers, especially the Mendicant Friars, the obligation of exhorting their hearers to pay the tithe.

One of the most ancient texts which recommends the warning to penitents, is a decree of a council of Riez. After denouncing those who withhold the tithe, as thieves who are to be sequestered from the faithful parishioners, it adds: "They should be informed in confession that they cannot be absolved, that the other sins they confess cannot be forgiven, and that if they should succeed in obtaining absolution, it would be null and void."[55]

Much more reliance was placed upon the other mode, *viz.* insisting that all preachers, especially the Mendicant Friars, should recall the obligation of paying the tithe. The very insistence used and the expressions employed lead us to believe that the monks were suspected of having other tendencies. Some of them had gone so far in their misdirected zeal as to dissuade the faithful from paying their tithes to the churches. That was no doubt the fault of but a few; however it was so detrimental to the common welfare that the popes deemed it necessary to punish such conduct. In a decree of the Council of Vienne, Clement V recalled, confirmed, and completed an ordinance issued by Gregory X on this subject, which later

[55] "Et in confessionibus significetur eisdem quod absolvi non possunt, et peccatis confessatis seu oblitis non solvantur in futurum. . . . Et quod si contingat eos absolvi, de futuro prodesse non poterit ad salutem." *Conc. Regien.* (1286), c. xx. MANSI, t. XXIV, 584.—The Constitutions of Aquileja oblige priests, under pain of excommunication, to ask their penitents if they have fulfilled the duty of the tithe, and the ordinance even names the Dominicans, Franciscans, Hermits, and other religious "cujuscumque sint ordinis." Mansi, t. XXV, 1116. Cf. *Conc. Rothomag.* (1445) c. xxxii. *Ib.*, t. XXXII, 31.

became the chapter *Cupientes, de Poenis* (*in Clementinis*). The decree can be summed up thus: (1) excommunication *ipso facto* is pronounced against monks who, from the pulpit or elsewhere, dissuade their listeners from paying the tithes; (2) he obligation is imposed on all monks, under threat of the judgment of God and eternal damnation, when they preach on the first, fourth, and last Sunday of Lent, on the feasts of the Ascension, Pentecost, the Nativity of St. John the Baptist, the Assumption and Nativity of the Blessed Virgin, to instruct the faithful in their duty concerning the tithe, if the pastor or the curate ask them to speak on it. (The same is to be done in the confessional.) Should any monk knowingly omit this duty, he shall be punished by his superiors. Lastly, those who omit reminding the faithful in confession of their duty, are to be *ipso facto* suspended from all preaching until they have repaired their negligence; and to be excommunicated *ipso facto* if they dare to continue preaching without having repaired their omission.[56]

It can be easily realized that the bishops willingly recalled this decree or at least the discipline which it enforced. Clement V had warned all monks; the bishops addressed themselves above all to the Mendicants, and added a new pen-

[56] We do not give the text, which is very long; it can be found in the *Corpus Juris, loc. cit.*

alty: a monk who omitted his duty in preaching, should be deprived of the faculties to absolve in cases reserved to the bishop, and above all in the case of those who retained the tithes, which was specially reserved.[57]

In spite of all these precautions and all this preaching, difficulties were still encountered in securing the payment of the tithe. Some did not hesitate to claim that the tithe should be a voluntary offering.[58] The consequence was that the clergy and the churches suffered. The threat of excommunication renewed by the Council of Trent,[59] and the threat of denouncing the culprits to the secular judge,[60] did not obtain the desired effect and added nothing to the popularity of the assessment.

What the Tithe Really Was.—What was this tax the payment of which could not be secured by ex-

[57] "Mendicantes, curati, et alii proponentes Verbum Dei populum moneant, exhortentur, informent et inducant ad decimas persolvendas. . . . Et licet dicti Mendicantes, in suis sermonibus de jure hoc facere teneantur: volumus tamen, quod quotiescumque praedicare contigerit, hoc faciant sine fraude: alias non habeant potestatem absolvendi a peccatis in casibus episcopis reservatis, et maxime non habeant potestatem absolvendi dictas decimas retinentes: sed eamdem potestatem singulis dioecesanis specialiter reservamus." *Conc. Noviomen.* (1344), c. ix. MANSI, t. XXVI, 9. Cf. *Conc. Senonen.* (1460), art. IV, c. iii. *Ib.* t. XXXII, 428.

[58] "Jam aliqui dicant et asserant, decimalia jura non nisi ad voluntatem fore solvenda." *Conc. Senonen., loc. cit.*

[59] Sess. XXV, c. xii, *De Reform.*

[60] *Conc. Bituricen.* (1584), tit. XXXV, c. xi. Mansi, t. XXXIV, 916.

hortations and threats of ecclesiastical or civil penalties?

The tithe notably diminished in the course of centuries. Whilst in the Carolingian epoch there were two kinds, the personal and the real, the former had almost disappeared in the seventeenth century.[61]

Even the real tithe was diminished: it was not collected any more on civil incomes,[62] but only on natural fruits, both the spontaneous fruits of the earth and those produced in part by human industry.

Besides, says Fleury, the tithe is not always exactly the tenth part of the fruits; in the majority of cases it is less; *e.g.*, one sheaf of twelve or fifteen, and in some places the twentieth or thirtieth part only. There were two kinds of tithes: large and small. Large tithes are those of wheat and other grains, of wine and other liquors, of hay and all the large fruits, according to the quality of the land.[63] The small or green tithes are

[61] "The personal tithe is no longer paid in the majority of dioceses." Fleury, *Institution au Droit Ecclésiastique*, 2e partie, chap. xiii.

[62] "The real tithe is not taken on civil incomes, such as the rent of houses and the arrears of incomes." (*Ib.*)

[63] "There are some countries where certain fruits are considered large fruits and as such are tithable for those who pay the large tithes, though in other places they do not come under the name of large tithes; thus wine, which is not commonly counted among the large fruits, is considered to be such in a

those from vegetables or herbs. There were also tithes of *charnage,* like calves, lambs, small pigs; these were regulated by the custom of the country. There are again ancient and new tithes. The ancient are the usual tithes; the new ones are the tithes from newly reclaimed lands, or lands which are newly planted in fruits subject to tithe.

How was it that a tax which was so moderate, became so odious? Many reasons could be given, among them the following:

The first was the method of taxation and collection. It was a common thing in canon law, at least as regards a certain class of tithes, that they were to be paid before deducting the expenses.[64] Therefore they were levied in kind upon the field, in the very place where the fruits had been gathered, before anything had been taken away, and for this reason, the proprietors were held to give notice of the day on which they intended to bring in their harvest. This burdensome obligation irritated those who were affected by it.[65] Let us add that rigorous canonists pressed the logic of their deductions so relentlessly as to exact from the

wine-making country, and such also is the case with several other fruits when they are the principal product of the soil." Fleury's footnote.

[64] *Non est in potestate* (Celestine III), xxii, X, *De Decimis,* and the Gloss *in h. loc.* Cf. *Constit. Provinc. S. Edmundi,* c. xi. Mansi, t. XXXIII, 428.

[65] Still, in certain places, the tithe was paid in money.

poor the tithe of the alms they received.[66] Undoubtedly this was never translated from theory to practice, but the simple laying down of such a principle must have caused dreadful exasperation.

The second reason was that the tithe was a part of a detested system. It was the last of a series of irritating and burdensome taxes. Tocqueville describes in a striking manner the long list of those feudal taxes which weighed so heavily on the peasantry. The lords everywhere drew an income which now had no longer any *raison d'être*. "Should the peasant wish to defend his seeded fields against their game, the same [lords] prevent him; they wait for him at the bridge to make him pay toll. He finds them at the market, where they sell him the right to sell his own goods; and after returning home, when he wants to use the rest of his wheat, that wheat which has grown under his eyes and at the cost of his own labor, he can do so only after having had it ground in the mill and baked in the oven of the lords. It is in supplying their incomes that a part of the revenue of his little domain goes, and these incomes can not be prescribed and are unredeemable. Whatever he may do, everywhere he comes across these troublesome neighbors, who disturb his pleasures, impede his work, and eat up his products; and when he is through with these, oth-

[66] Fleury, *op. cit.*, chap. xi.

ers, dressed in black, come and ask him for the best part of his harvest." [67]

We have mentioned above in what measure it is true that the tithe took from the peasant "the best of his harvest," but coming as the last in a long series of dues, it appeared the most burdensome of all.

Will the tithe ever be reëstablished as a pro rata income tax? Not likely. It does not exist under that form in any Christian country to-day. In France the laws of the Revolution, beginning with that of September 21, 1789, suppressed it at the same time with the old feudal rights.

In the countries where it is still preserved as a true tax of legal obligation, when one gives what he can, no more is demanded. Appeal is made to the generosity of the faithful, but their goods are no longer taxed. The personal tithe, which was the first to disappear, was the only one to be revived, at least in spirit, and but recently Pope Pius X intimated very clearly to the bishops of France how much he disliked the idea of imposing upon the faithful, under penalty, a contribution in the nature of a tax.[68]

As early as the sixteenth century, in the diocese of Cologne, the faithful were invited to supple-

[67] Tocqueville, *l'Ancien Régime et la Révolution*, II, c. i.
[68] Letter of Cardinal Merry del Val, October 8, 1907, to the bishops of France.

ment the insufficient income of the clergy by a quarterly offering (at Christmas, Easter, Pentecost, and the Assumption) of two *deniers*.[69] It is under an analogous form that the collection called *denier du culte* is now taken up in France. In the United States the faithful, as a rule, provide generously for the wants of Church and clergy, and perhaps the only reminder of the olden tithe is to be found in those comparatively few parishes where the representatives of the people, in consultation with the pastor, assess each family according to its reputed income in order to raise the amount necessary for the support of church, school, and clergy.

[69] *Conc. Colonien.* (1536), pars VIII, c. vi. Mansi, t. XXXII, 1270.

THE END

INDEX

INDEX

Abbas, 286, 298
Abraham, 329
Abstinence, The law of, 277 sqq., 301 sqq.; Penalties for transgressing that law, 316 sqq.
Adalard, 159
Adrian I, 281, 294
Advent, Fast of, 273 sqq.
Agde, Council of, 33, 35, 38, 122, 194, 197, 199, 202, 203, 258, 293
Age, At which confession becomes obligatory, 170 sqq.; At which Easter communion becomes obligatory, 213 sqq.; At which fasting becomes obligatory, 266 sqq.
Aix, Council of, 98
Aix-la-Chapelle, Council of, 128
Alanus of Lille, 165 sq.
Albi, Council of, 141, 168, 170, 207
Albigenses, 44 sq.
Alexander II, 47
Alexander III, 88, 94
Alexander of Hales, 263, 267
Alfred the Great, 131
Alleluia, Significance of the, 244
All Saints, Feast of, 131, 139, 143, 247, 346
Alms, Tithe of, 354
Alphonsus, St., 100, 219
Amalarius of Metz, 199
Ambrose, St., 281, 288, 290, 325
Ancyra, Council of, 301
Andrew, St., 126, 127

Annual confession, 152 sqq.
Annus discretionis, 213 sqq.
Anse, Council of, 279, 295
Ansegise, 196
Antoninus, St., 12, 57, 173, 215, 217 sq.
Apostles, 23 sqq., 112, 124, 132, 227, 247, 292, 321, 322
Apostolic Constitutions, 29, 67, 117, 124, 239, 262, 287, 302, 306, 313
Apt, Council of, 140
Arcadius, 65, 116
Arles, Council of, 177, 335
Ascension, Feast of the, 117, 118, 124, 126, 127, 130, 132, 143, 146, 249
Ash Wednesday, 159, 161, 162, 262, 310
Assizes, 86
Assumption, Feast of the, 126, 127, 143, 146, 247, 356
Athanasius, St., 256
Athelstane, 345
Atto of Verceil, 195
Auger, Edmund, S.J., 3 sq.
Augustine, St., 85, 91, 118, 120, 131, 132, 153, 193, 281, 289, 291, 325
Augustine, St. (of Canterbury), 230
Autun, Council of, 195
Auxerre, Council of, 241, 242
Avignon, Council of, 171, 208, 210, 211, 212, 214
Avranches, Council of, 275
Avitus, St., 248

INDEX

Ayton of Basle, 177
Azor, 54, 95, 172, 173, 174, 182

Bailly, 101
Ballerini, 341
Baptism, 156, 236, 237, 238
Baronius, 224
Basil, St., 191, 261
Basilides, 255
Bayeux, Council of, 253
Bede, St., 274, 307
Beghards and Beguins, 179, 212
Beleth, John, 246, 285
Benedict XIV, 144, 145, 276, 313
Benevento, Council of, 216
Berardi, 17, 102
Berkhamstead, Council of, 106, 316
Béziers, Council of, 171, 299
Billuart, 60, 253
Bination, 47 sq.
Binsfeld, 96, 97
Blood for food, 303
Bonacina, 220
Bondmen, 37 sq., 106, 125, 131, 132, 268
Boniface, St., 126, 242
"Book of Jesus," 6, 13, 16
Bourges, Council of, 84, 87, 183, 205, 211
Bouvier, 101
Buda, Council of, 51, 53
Burchard, 41, 80, 82, 84, 196, 201, 232, 252, 341, 344
Burial, Refusal of ecclesiastical, 182 sqq., 216
Busembaum, 56, 99 sq., 102, 268, 271
Butchers, 318

Caesarius, St., 31 sqq., 38, 68, 89, 123, 125, 194, 195, 201, 272, 327, 336, 343
Calchutense, 345

Callixtus, Pope, 224, 229
Canisius, 4
Canons of the Apostles, 287, 301, 326
Canterbury, Council of, 168
Canute, 132, 316
Carletti, see Clavasio
Cassian, 293
Casulanus, 290, 292
Catéchisme de l'Empire Français, 17
Chalon, Council of, 78, 335, 337
Charlemagne, 46, 84, 231, 263, 303, 316, 332, 333, 345
Charles Borromeo, St., 98, 236
Charnage, 353
Cheese, Abstinence from, 306, 307, 308
Chichester, Council of, 168
Childebert, 73
Children, At what age they must go to confession, 170 sqq.
Christmas, 115, 116, 117, 122, 124, 126, 127, 130, 131, 132, 143, 146, 164, 194, 200, 201, 202, 204, 207, 246, 273, 356
Chrodegang, Rule of, 159, 164, 167, 177
Chrysostom, St., 153, 193, 262
Church in which Easter Communion had to be received, 210 sqq.
Church, Support of, 320 sqq.
Cibi quadragesimales, 306 sq.
Circumcision, Feast of the, 126, 127, 132, 143
Clavasio, Angelo de, 9, 12, 57, 215, 218, 268, 269, 271
Clement V, 349, 350
Clement VIII, 55
Clerics obliged to frequent communion, 203
Clermont, Council of, 175

INDEX

Cloveshow, Council of, 39, 131, 197
Cohabitation, Marital on Sunday, 85 sq.
Collation, 266, 312
Cologne, Council of, 211
Communion, Precept of annual, 189 sqq., 200 sqq.; *ad minus in pascha*, 205 sqq.
Compiègne, Council of, 80, 243
Compost ou Kalendrier des Bergers, 22
Concordat, French, 146
Conférences d'Angers, 59
Confession, 151 sqq., 162 sqq.
Constantine, 30, 64, 79
Cooked foods, Abstinence from, 311 sqq.
Corporal punishment for missing Mass, 44
Corpus Christi, Feast of, 143
Court sessions forbidden on Sunday, 78 sqq., 91 sq.
Coutances, Council of, 205, 253
Coyac, Council of, 283
Cyprian, St., 113 sq., 116, 119, 190, 323
Cyril of Jerusalem, St., 302

Dagobert I, 74
Daily Communion, 193
De Angelis, 222
Decentius of Eugubium, 292, 294
Deharbe, 21
De Lugo, 220
Denier du culte, 356
De Sacramentis, 203
Diana, 20, 97
Didache, 27, 236, 278, 280
Didascalia, 255, 257, 261, 262, 263, 280, 302, 306
Dionysius of Corinth, 27
Dionysius of Alexandria, 255

Dioscorus of Alexandria, 47
Dispensations, From Sunday labor, 87 sqq.; From fasting, 270 sqq.; From abstinence, 305 sq., 309 sq.
Duchesne, 25 sq., 225, 226
Durand of Mende, 246, 252, 260, 273, 275
Durand, Stephen, 246

Easter, 111 sqq., 116, 117, 118, 122, 124, 125, 127, 129, 130, 132, 139, 143, 153, 164, 174, 176, 179, 189 sqq., 194, 197, 200, 201, 202, 206, 207, 211, 212, 218, 236, 237 sq., 246, 247, 255, 346, 356
Easter Communion, 189 sqq., 267, 270, 347
Ebionites, 28
Edmund of Canterbury, 207, 347
Egbert of York, 195, 230
Eggs, Abstinence from, 306 sqq.
Electuaria, 265 sq.
Elpidius, 64
Elvira, Council of, 28 sq., 36, 288
Ember days, Fast of the, 224 sqq., 318
Eneas of Paris, 307
Enham, Council of, 132, 230, 283, 296
Epiphanius, St., 262, 303
Epiphany, 116, 117, 118, 122, 124, 126, 127, 128, 132, 133, 143, 193, 273
Escobar, 97, 102
Estinnes, Council of, 231, 242
Etheria, 242
Eucharist, 113, 189 sqq., 240
Eucherius, 121
Eudes de Sully, 283, 297
Eugene IV, 219, 269
Excommunication, 184 sq., 191,

196, 212, 216, 219, 317, 329, 341, 350, 351

Fabian, Pope, 196
Fagnani, 57, 253, 279, 286, 298
Färber, 21
Fast, Of the Ember days, 224 sqq.; Of the Vigils, 235 sqq.; Of Lent, 254 sqq.
Feasts, First Christian, 112 sqq.; Obligation of the faithful to celebrate, 116 sqq.; Reduction of, 142 sqq.; Feasts with vigils, 246 sq.
Feasts of devotion, 121
Ferraris, 146, 253, 276
Feudalism, 45, 61 sq., 210
Fifth Commandment, 224 sqq.
First Commandment, 23 sqq.
First-fruits, 321, 323, 324
Fish, Abstinence from, 311 sqq.
Flesh-meat, Abstinence from, 303 sqq.
Fleury, 352
Fourth Commandment, 189 sqq.
Frankfort, Council of, 334, 336.
Frequent Communion, 197
Friars, Mendicant, 50 sqq., 177 sqq., 348, 349, 350
Friday abstinence, 280
Friuli, Council of, 335
Frustulum, 266

Gandolf, 286
Gangres, Council of, 326
Gatian of Tours, St., 160
Gelasius, Pope, 343
Gentiles, 25
Geoffrey of Vendôme, 235
Gerson, 269
Good Friday, 132, 138, 197, 201, 254, 255, 267, 310, 313
Gousset, 17, 101
Graffiis, J. de, 92, 94 sq.
Gran, Council of, 203

Gratian, Decree of, 196, 262 sq., 282, 285, 325, 347
Grease as a prohibited food, 303 sq.
Gregory II, 259
Gregory VII, 234, 235
Gregory X, 349
Gregory XIII, 181
Gregory of Nazianzus, St., 118
Gregory of Nyssa, St., 326
Gregory of Tours, 48, 72
Gregory the Great, St., 131, 230, 260
Guido de Baysio, 298

Henry VIII, 143
Henry of Susa, see Hostiensis
Herard of Tours, 40, 232, 342
Hildebert of Lavadin, 235
Hippolytus, 192
Holy Saturday, 197, 239, 254, 255, 287, 305
Holy Thursday, 158, 197, 201, 202, 260
Holy Week, 257, 262, 306
Homicides, 314
Honorius of Autun, 245
Hostiensis, 51, 86, 91, 93, 171, 180
Huguccio, 286
Humbert, Cardinal, 296

Idiotae, 61
Ignatius of Antioch, St., 27
Indults, Lenten, 310 sq.
In Encoeniis, Synod, 191
Innocent I, 278, 281, 292, 293, 295, 298
Innocent III, 47, 247, 275, 297, 298, 304
Innocent IV, 286
Irenæus, St., 28, 254
Isidore, St., 259, 281, 293, 294, 306, 311, 313 sq.

INDEX

Januarius, 290
Jerome, St., 192, 259, 281, 289, 294, 325
Jewish feasts, 111 sq.
Jews, 24 sqq., 63 sq., 66, 68, 87, 111, 114, 141, 237, 292, 340
John the Baptist, St., 126, 127, 133, 143, 246, 247, 296, 345
Jonas of Orleans, 200, 307
Julian, Emperor, 118
Julian Pomerius, 326
Justin, St., 27, 190, 238

Kiersy, Capitulary of, 340

Labor, permitted on Sunday, 94 sqq.; Exempts from fasting, 267 sq.
Lacroix, 100
La Fontaine, 139
Laodicea, Council of, 66, 304, 306
Lateran Council, Fourth, 152, 167 sqq., 176, 203 sqq., 213, 216
Lavaur, Council of, 299
Lawrence, St., 120, 133, 143, 247
Law-suits forbidden on Sunday, 79
Laymann, 98, 106
Lehmkuhl, 61, 102
Lent, 117, 154, 155 sqq., 175 sqq., 193, 197, 203, 229, 237, 249, 254 sqq., 303 sqq., 316, 318
"Lent of St. Martin," 274
Leo the Great, St., 31, 47, 125, 227, 228, 229, 259
Leo IV, 279
Leo X, 53, 55
Levites, 322, 324, 325
Lex Bajuvariorum, 83
Liber Pontificalis, 224, 229, 259

Liège, Council of, 175, 214, 309
Liquids do not break the fast, 265
Liquor, Intoxicating, 314
Litanies, 248 sqq.
Litany of St. Mark, 128, 233, 248 sqq.
Liturgical celebration of feasts, 116 sq.
London, Council of, 138
Louis le Débonnaire, 331
Louis the Pious, 337, 339
Lucca, Council of, 171, 214, 298
Lucinus, 289
Lyons, Council of, 249

Mâcon, Council of, 36, 70, 79, 125, 274, 278, 329, 331
Maigre strict, 310 sq.
Mamertus, St., 248
Mansi, 159, 194
Mantua, Capitularies of, 333, 343
Marc, 60
Margaret, St., 202, 203
Mark, St., 128, 248, 250, 251
Markets forbidden on Sunday, 78 sqq., 91 sq., 93
Martène, 160
Martin, St., 127, 133, 247, 274, 330
Martyrs, 113 sqq., 237
Mary, B. V., 115, 131, 132, 136, 299
Mass, Assistance at, 23 sqq., 117 sqq., 144 sq.
Maximus of Turin, 121
Mayence, Council of, 80, 127, 231, 251, 284, 335, 336
Meat, see Flesh-meat
Meaux, Council of, 129, 339
Melchiades, Pope, 259
Melito of Sardis, 27
Michael, St., 127
Milan, Council of, 98

INDEX

Milk, Abstinence from, 306 sqq.
Missa pro populo, 146 sq.
Monica, St., 290
Montanists, 255
Montazet, 59, 101
Montfort, Count de, 87
Morin, 225, 226, 229

Nantes, Council of, 45
Napoleon, 101
Narbonne, Council of, 73, 171, 214
Natalis, Alexander, 58, 98 sq., 99, 101
Nativity of the B. V. M., Feast of the, 126, 143
Navarrus, 57
Nestorians, 66
Nicæa, Council of, 256
Nicholas I, 40, 81, 130, 198, 245, 274, 279, 282, 295
Nicholas II, 84
Nîmes, Council of, 205
Number of the Commandments, 1 sqq.

Oaths not to be taken on Sunday, 92
Obligation to celebrate feasts, 116 sqq.
Old age exempts from fasting, 268
"*Omnis utriusque sexus*," Canon, 152, 167 sqq., 170 sq., 176, 177, 182, 184 sq., 204 sq., 207, 210
Ordinations, 244
Origen, 323, 324
Origin of the Commandments, 2 sqq.
Orleans, Council of, 35, 69, 78, 248, 258, 293

Osius, Bishop, 29
Otto of Bamberg, 164, 201, 284, 308
Oxford, Council of, 48, 132, 133, 235

Pachomius, St., 278
Palencia, Council of, 206
Palm Sunday, 175, 212
Paris, Council of, 39, 87
Parish priests, 50 sqq.
Parochial Mass, 45 sqq., 50 sqq.
Parvi, William, 5 sq.
Pastor, Confession to be made to one's own, 176 sqq.; Confessions of, 180 sq.; Suzerainty of the, 210 sqq.; Duty of supporting the, 320 sqq.
Patrick, St., 31, 194
Patron Saint, 143
Paul of Samosata, 323
Paul, St., 24, 67, 116, 119, 126, 127, 131, 132, 136, 143, 247, 263, 302, 306, 322
Paul III, 181
Penance, 206, 313
Penitential Books, 78, 85, 155, 159, 243, 278, 295, 341
Pentecost, 111 sqq., 117, 122, 124, 127, 130, 132, 139, 143, 164, 194, 200, 201, 202, 204, 207, 246, 247, 309, 346, 356
Pepin, 331, 333
Period of the Easter Communion, 212 sq.
Perpetuus, St., 247, 274
Peter Chrysologus, 121
Peter Damian, St., 296
Peter de Honestis, 296, 308
Peter of Ancharano, 173
Peter, St., 67, 116, 119, 126, 127, 131, 132, 143, 228, 247, 273, 293

INDEX

Peter the Venerable, 279, 285, 297
Pharisees, 323 sq.
Philastrius of Brescia, 239
Pius IV, 181
Pius V, 3, 5, 181
Pius IX, 147, 305
Pius X, 14, 20, 355
Plaisance, Council of, 235
Pliny, 63, 236
Poenitentiale Vallicellanum III, 155, 158
Polycarp, St., 113
Pomeranians, 164
Poncher, Stephen, 300
Pontas, 56, 60
Pont-Audemer, Council of, 205
Pontificale Romanum, 157
Prague, Council of, 140
Procession of St. Mark, 251
Proprius Sacerdos, 211 sq.
Public penance, 155, 157 sq., 163
Pulleyn, Robert, 203, 285, 308
Purification, Feast of the, 126, 127

Quarantine, 256 sqq., 272
Quartodecimans, 237
Quasimodo, 212 sq.
Quedlinburg, Council of, 235, 308

Radegundis, St., 330
Raoul Glaber, 284, 314
Ratherius of Verona, 200, 233, 263
Ratramnus of Corbie, 282, 284, 295
Recared, 73
Reduction of feast days, 142 sqq.
Regino, 41, 82, 84, 177, 196, 232, 279, 282, 285, 295, 344

Regular clergy, 50 sqq., 179 sqq., 326
Religious instruction, 38 sqq.
Remi, St., 127
Rest, Weekly, 104; On feast days, 131 sqq.
Restoration in France, 101, 104
Revolution, French, 101, 102, 355
Rhabanus Maurus, 274
Rheims, Council of, 80, 154, 335
Rhispach, Council of, 281, 294 sq., 314
Richard of Sarum, 168, 205, 206
Richelieu, 14
Riez, Council of, 348
Right to distribute paschal communion, 211 sq.
Robigalia, 250
Rodulf of Bourges, 40, 82, 160, 198, 267
Rodulphus Glaber, 296
Rogation days, 233, 248 sqq.
Roman Catchism, 2 sq.
Rome, Council of, 296, 346
Rouen, Council of, 37, 46, 87, 98, 168, 234
Rubrics, Conformity of the Mass with, 56 sqq.
Rufinus, 282

Sabbath, 25 sq., 32, 63, 68, 112, 124, 236, 288
Salamanca, Council of, 205
Sanchez, 271
Saracens, 85, 141
Saragossa, Council of, 273
Sardica, Council of, 29
Saturday fast and abstinence, 287 sqq.
Schmitz, 341
Season of the year for annual confession, 174 sqq.

INDEX

Second Commandment, 110 sqq.
Seligenstadt, Council of, 47, 233, 346
Sens, Council of, 168, 205
Septuagesima, 175, 206
Servile work, Abstention from on Sunday, 63 sqq.; Defined by St. Thomas, 90; Works permitted on Sunday, 91; Abstention from, on feast days, 124 sqq.
Sick, The, exempt from fasting, 268, 318
Sidonius, Appolinaris, 248
Silvestre, 57
Simon the Magician, 293
Sixth Commandment, 277 sqq.
Sixtus IV, 53, 181
Socrates (church historian), 262, 303, 311
Solemn first communion, 216
Sommes le Roi, 8
Sonnatius, 176
Soto, 57
Stations, 251
Stephen, St., 43, 77, 117, 124, 133
Stipends, 147 sq.
Strigony, Council of, 164
Sunday, 26 sqq., 63 sqq., 124, 238
Sunday rest, At what hour did it begin? 106 sq.
Support of church and pastor, 320 sqq.
Sylvester, Pope, 294

Tarragona, Council of, 171, 205
Tassilo, 331 sq.
Telesphorus, Pope, 259
Temporal punishments, For missing Mass, 42 sqq.; For performing servile labor on Sunday, 72 sqq.
Tertullian, 64, 113, 190, 238, 254
Theatres, 31, 121
Theodore of Canterbury, 196
Theodosius, 65, 79, 116
Theodulf of Orleans, 40, 159, 197, 199, 262, 306, 307, 314
Third Commandment, 151 sqq.
Thomassin, 299, 321
Thomas, St., 89 sq., 94, 215, 263, 265, 267, 269, 271, 285
Tithes, 320 sqq.
Tocqueville, 354
Toledo, Council of, 202, 209, 216, 266, 270, 306, 311, 314
Toulouse, Council of, 45, 168, 169, 207
Tours, Council of, 98, 195, 249, 276, 328, 335, 336
Trent, Council of, 55, 99, 141, 181, 351
Treves, Council of, 205, 208
Trinity, Feast of the, 143
Trosly, Council of, 344
Trullo, Council in, 294, 306

Ulric, St., 201
United States, 300, 321, 356
"Universa," Bull, 142
Urban II, 235
Urban V, 276
Urban VIII, 141 sqq., 144, 147
Urbicus, 290, 291

Valentinian, 65, 79, 116
Vallicellanum I, 295
Vespers, 41, 42, 49, 58 sqq.
Victor, Pope, 254
Vienne, Council of, 349
Vigilantius, 240
Vigils, 121, 236 sqq.

INDEX

Wednesday abstinence, 278 sqq.
Wine, Abstinence from, 313 sqq.
Worcester, Council of, 134, 168

Workingmen exempt from fasting, 268 sq.
Worms, Capitulary of, 338

Yves of Chartres, 196